For Reference

Not to be taken from t

D0174920

San Diego Christian College
Library
Santee, CA

"*Duriez is a leading scholar in both Lewis and Tolkien studies, so it is no surprise he has packed so much useful information about Lewis between two covers.* The A–Z of C.S. Lewis *serves well as a thorough and concise reference source. But it is more than that, as Duriez also offers insightful and substantive interpretive remarks about Lewis's recurring ideas, and the core concepts of his most enduring books. A valuable addition to the bookshelf for both casual readers of Lewis and more serious students of his life and legacy.*"
DAVID C. DOWNING, AUTHOR OF *THE MOST RELUCTANT CONVERT* AND OTHER KEY BOOKS ON C.S. LEWIS.

"*With* The A– Z of C.S. Lewis, *Colin Duriez provides both novice readers and experienced scholars with a rich and ready resource for expanding their knowledge of the formidable Professor Lewis. There is an art to creating a compelling encyclopedia that demands both relevant and accurate information; we are indeed indebted to Duriez for his keen mastery of the Lewis canon that guides his judicious choices for inclusion and annotation. With this volume, he adds once more to his estimable catalogue of works that illuminate the life, works, and relationships of Lewis.*"
BRUCE L. EDWARDS, SCHOLAR AND AUTHOR OF MANY BOOKS ON C.S. LEWIS, AND EDITOR AND WEBMASTER, *THE C.S. LEWIS REVIEW*: WWW.CSLEWISREVIEW.ORG

"*It's good to see Colin Duriez's ever-useful* A–Z of C.S. Lewis *back in print in a new expanded and updated version. It's a very helpful reference work for scholars and fans alike but it's also a great pleasure simply to dip into and read. It's full of helpful, pithy summaries that combine scholarship, clarity, and brevity. I like the attention Duriez pays to Lewis as a critic and scholar as well as to the more famous Narnia books. Many of the entries show clearly how Lewis was engaged with the intellectual life of his own day and especially how relevant he is to issues being discussed today.*"
MALCOLM GUITE, GIRTON COLLEGE, CAMBRIDGE

"Among the many books that claim to introduce readers to the life, thought, and works of C.S. Lewis, this one stands out. It is a lively encyclopedia of everything and everybody related to Lewis. In an engaging style, Duriez presents valuable entries on people, places, characters, books, and ideas in Lewis's life and writings. The A–Z of C.S. Lewis is remarkably comprehensive and thoroughly cross-referenced, with the added advantage of enough suggested reading to satiate voracious readers of many kinds. Because of its scope and clarity, it should be in the collection of every Lewis fan and scholar."
SØRINA HIGGINS, REVIEW EDITOR OF SEHNSUCHT:
THE C.S. LEWIS JOURNAL

"This is one of the most useful books I know. I look for excuses to read it."
WALTER HOOPER, LITERARY ADVISOR TO THE C.S. LEWIS ESTATE

"The A–Z of C.S. Lewis delivers what the title promises. In this rich, encyclopedic overview, Lewis scholar Colin Duriez serves as an expert and engaging guide to the essentials of Lewis's life, thought, and writings. I highly recommend this volume to all who enjoy Lewis's books and would like to better understand the 'Christian world of C.S. Lewis.'"
MARJORIE LAMP MEAD, ASSOCIATE DIRECTOR, THE MARION E.
WADE CENTER, WHEATON COLLEGE, ILLINOIS, USA

"An invaluable work of reference and a fascinating volume in which to dip and browse, this is the perfect companion for every Lewis reader by an acknowledged expert on the life, thoughts, works, and worlds of one of the great imaginative writers of the twentieth century."
BRIAN SIBLEY, AUTHOR OF SHADOWLANDS, BBC RADIO ADAPTATIONS
OF THE CHRONICLES OF NARNIA, AND MUCH MORE

"Covering the whole range of Lewis's life and work, this encyclopedia is thorough, accurate, and well balanced. I highly recommend it."
MICHAEL WARD, AUTHOR OF PLANET NARNIA

R
823
L673C
D962a

THE
A–Z
OF
C.S. LEWIS

*An encyclopedia of his life,
thought, and writings*

COLIN DURIEZ

LION

Text copyright © 1990, 2000, 2002, 2013 Colin Duriez
This edition copyright © 2013 Lion Hudson

The right of Colin Duriez to be identified as the author of this work has
been asserted by him in accordance with the Copyright, Designs and
Patents Act 1988.

All rights reserved. No part of this publication may be reproduced or
transmitted in any form or by any means, electronic or mechanical,
including photocopy, recording, or any information storage and retrieval
system, without permission in writing from the publisher.

Published by Lion Books
an imprint of
Lion Hudson plc
Wilkinson House, Jordan Hill Road,
Oxford OX2 8DR, England
www.lionhudson.com/lion

ISBN 978 0 7459 5586 5
e-ISBN 978 0 7459 5789 0

Original 2000 edition published in the USA by Crossway Books, a
division of Good News Publishers, Wheaton, Illinois 60187, USA. First
British edition published in 1990 by Monarch Publications Ltd.

Acknowledgments
pp. 54, 143, 168: Extracts taken from *Brothers and Friends: The Diaries of
Major Warren Hamilton Lewis* copyright © The Marion E. Wade Center,
Wheaton College, Wheaton Illinois.

p. 308: Extract from *The Encyclopedia of Fantasy*
by John Clute and Paul Barnett copyright © John Clute and Paul
Barnett, 1997. Reprinted by permission of Little Brown.

Extracts by C.S. Lewis copyright © C.S. Lewis Pte. Ltd. Extracts
reprinted by permission.

A catalogue record for this book is available from the British Library

Printed and bound in the UK, September 2013, LH26

Contents

*In memory of
my father,
Charles Duriez
1915–2002*

Preface

C.S. Lewis's *The Chronicles of Narnia* are consistently among the bestselling children's books, firmly established as classics along with *Alice in Wonderland*, *The Hobbit*, and *The Wind in the Willows*. Lewis, who for many years was an atheist, is also unmatched as a popularizer of the Christian faith in recent times, and is certainly one of the most widely read believers in the history of the church. In specialist circles, his books of literary criticism – introducing writers such as John Milton or the period of the Middle Ages – are still in print, half a century after his death.

Yet how well is C.S. Lewis actually known? I suspect that many of us have only read one kind of his wide range of writings – his science fiction, perhaps, or his children's stories, or his popular theology (especially *The Screwtape Letters* and *Mere Christianity*), or his literary criticism. Some will undoubtedly have discovered his work and life through seeing the play or film versions of *Shadowlands*, or have come to know him through television or film adaptations of some of the Narnia stories.

The A–Z of C.S. Lewis has been written to help an exploration and discovery (or rediscovery!) of his world. The rich variety of Lewis's writings is part of an integrated whole. He combined reasoning and imagination in a unified and bright vision of reality – and of the God he discovered, whom he came to see as the giver of reality.

C.S. Lewis is an enigmatic figure. Different people seek to understand him in their image as they warm to him. In the Richard Attenborough version of *Shadowlands*, for instance, Lewis is a retiring bachelor don, quarantined from women and children, brought into the real world by his love for the abrasive dying

American, Joy Davidman Gresham. After her death from cancer, he grieves in a temporary agnosticism. To his close friends in the Inklings club, however, Lewis was the jovial life and soul of the party, puffing on his pipe, swilling his theology down with the best bitter or cider, delighting in a good joke or pun. For an enormous number, Lewis has been the defender of the faith, and, for very many, the media evangelist who led them to faith, particularly through the published BBC radio talks, *Mere Christianity.*

For people who met Lewis, but weren't in his close circle of friends, he could seem reserved. They couldn't get close to him. Some students he tutored at Oxford found him formidable; some considered him bullying in argument. Others responded to his intellectual challenges, and became his friends, such as George Sayer, John Wain, and Harry Blamires. Some of his friends were not intellectual at all. Much of this reserve, of course, was the typical product of his background, the shaping of his early twentieth-century upper-middle-class environment in Ulster. Also, he was fundamentally secretive, having a rich inner life that he guarded, and shared mainly in his writings. Psychologically, much might be explained by the death of his mother in childhood, poignantly reflected in his Narnian Chronicle *The Magician's Nephew.*

Lewis also felt himself part of an older world – what he called the Old West – seeing himself as a relic, a dinosaur. His roots and orientation lay back in time before the modern world existed. He was in fact fervently anti-modernist, surrounding himself to an extent with those who shared his antipathy, such as J.R.R. Tolkien. Yet his writings have been received around our modern world by a rich variety of people. The same is true of the films made of his stories of Narnia.

For convenience of use, I have used asterisks within articles to show other references. This is to allow my readers to follow through themes and subjects that capture their interest. If this omits a significant cross-reference, I give it at the article's end. Where appropriate I have added further reading. There are a number of general articles, providing some overviews to aid exploration and discovery. At the end of the book is a list of C.S. Lewis's works (most of which are described within the A–Z). A modest book like this dare only claim the range of a comprehensive A–Z because its subject was truly encyclopedic in his constantly fascinating interests, friendships, reading, concerns, and writings, which are facets of him I have tried to capture.

The range of this book helps it to include different aspects of C.S. Lewis's thinking and imagination. My hope is that it extends Lewis's own aims in the breadth of his writings. At the same time I have tried to do justice to the subtlety and depths of Lewis's thought by avoiding oversimplifying and by suggesting links to the deeper intellectual and literary currents of his day for those who wish to explore further. Behind all the exploration that my guide hopes to encourage is the quest for an answer to the puzzle of Lewis's continuing and growing relevance to today's world, where there is place both for wild hope and a distressing sense of the dangers that we face.

A passage in one of his letters encourages me to think that C.S. Lewis may not have been totally out of sympathy with my book, and the enjoyment that went into its writing, and, hopefully, will mark its reading.

> To enjoy a book… I find I have to treat it as a sort of hobby and set about it seriously. I begin by making a map on one of the end leafs: then I put in a genealogical tree or two. Then I put a running headline at the top of each page: finally I index at the end all the passages I have for some reason underlined…. One is *making* something all the time and a book so read acquires the charm of a toy without losing that of a book. (C.S. Lewis, 1932; from *They Stand Together: The Letters of C.S. Lewis to Arthur Greeves (1914–1963).*)

It is over two decades since the appearance of *The C.S. Lewis Handbook*, and over a decade since the original *Encyclopedia* built upon it. What you are now holding is a substantially updated version of that encyclopedia. This takes into account new insights into Lewis's work, such as Michael Ward's *Planet Narnia*, which has led to a much greater appreciation of Lewis's sublime skill in creating *The Chronicles of Narnia*. Readers, of course, have continued in new generations to appreciate these stories, with sales worldwide of around 85 million in 29 different languages for *The Lion, the Witch and the Wardrobe*, and huge additional sales for the other books in the Narnia series. People have flocked to see the film versions from Walden Media.

The original *Encyclopedia* benefited by being read through by Douglas Gresham and Walter Hooper. Some entries are drawn from articles written and talks given over the years. Feedback from these, and books I've published that feature him directly or are related to him, concerning his friends J.R.R. Tolkien and the Inklings, have helped in the development of this book. A list of others to whom I'm indebted in various ways over the more than twenty years since the original *The C.S. Lewis Handbook* would be far too long to place here. I must limit myself to mentioning Tony Collins at Monarch, Christopher Catherwood, Andrew Walker, Elizabeth Fraser, Marjorie Mead and her colleagues at The Marion E. Wade Center, Wheaton College, Illinois, USA, Leland and Mary Ryken, Mary Bechtel, Cindy Bunch, Marta Garcia de la Puerta, Margarita Carretero González, John Gillespie, Lila Bishop at Crossway, Alison Barr at SPCK, Bruce L. Edwards, Brian Sibley, David C. Downing, Michael Ward, and at Lion Hudson: my editor Ali Hull, Jessica Tinker, Kirsten Etheridge, Jude May, Leisa Nugent, Rhoda Hardie, and others of their supportive colleagues. Any errors are of course my own.

Colin Duriez
Keswick, January 2013

A

Abhalljin See: **Aphallin**

Abingdon A small town not far from Oxford* at whose nearby
RAF base C.S. Lewis gave his very first talk on Christianity to
wartime personnel of Bomber Command. He considered the
experience an abject failure. Working at communicating more
successfully in such talks helped him when the BBC* invited
him to give national radio broadcasts, which were published and
eventually collected into the bestselling *Mere Christianity**.

The Abolition of Man **(1943)** C.S. Lewis considered this one
of his most important books, a view that was shared by Owen
Barfield*, who commented that it is "his most trenchant and
valuable philosophic statement" and contains "much of his
best and hardest hitting thought". The small book is concerned
with the education* of children, and in it Lewis developed
his argument against what he saw as an alarming tendency in
modern thinking. In a letter in 1955 he ruefully commented that
The Abolition of Man "is almost my favourite among my books but
in general has been almost totally ignored by the public".

This powerful tract defends the objectivity of values like
goodness and beauty against the already by then modern view
that they are merely in the mind of the beholder, reflecting
the social attitudes of a culture. Lewis argues that "until quite
modern times all teachers and even all men believed the universe
to be such that certain emotional reactions on our part could be
either congruous or incongruous to it – believed, in fact, that
objects did not merely receive, but could *merit*, our approval or
disapproval, our reverence, or our contempt".

13

If values are objective, argued Lewis, one person may be right and another wrong in describing qualities. If one says that a waterfall is beautiful, and another says that it is not, that "beautiful" does not merely describe emotions within the beholder. Only one of them is right; their opinions are not equally valid. A similar situation exists over the goodness or badness of an action. Judging goodness or badness is not simply a matter of opinion. Lewis argued indeed that there is a universal acknowledgment of good and bad over matters like theft, murder, rape, and adultery, a sense of what Lewis called the Way, or Tao*. "The human mind has no more power of inventing a new value than of imagining a new primary colour, or, indeed, of creating a new sun and a new sky for it to move in."

Abandonment of the Tao spells total disaster for the human race, argued Lewis. Specifically human values like freedom and dignity become meaningless, he felt; the human being is then merely part of nature*. Nature, including humanity, is to be conquered by the technical appliance of science. Technology, with no limits or moral checks upon it, becomes totalitarian. An elite plans the future generations, and the present generation is cut off from the past. Such an elite is conceivably the most demonic example of what Lewis called the "inner ring"*, a theme he explored in an essay written in the war years and in his science fiction story *That Hideous Strength**. It is a social and cultural embodiment of what, in an individual, would be deemed self-absorption and egoism.

Lewis elsewhere sums up the urgency of the point he makes in *The Abolition of Man*:

> At the outset, the universe appears packed with will,
> intelligence, life and positive qualities; every tree is
> a nymph and every planet a god... The advance of
> knowledge gradually empties this rich and genial
> universe: first of its gods, then of its colours, smells,

sounds and tastes, finally of solidity itself as solidity was originally imagined. As these items are taken from the world, they are transferred to the subjective side of the account: classified as our sensations, thoughts, images or emotions… We, who have personified all other things, turn out to be ourselves mere personifications. ("The Empty Universe" in *Present Concerns*, 1986)

In such thinking, the human being has become nothing. An objective morality, he concludes, is an essential property of our very humanity. See also: **subjectivism**

Adam and Eve in Narnia In the Bible*, Adam and Eve are the first humans, with all people in every part of the world descending from them. Narnia* is a land of talking beasts*, but humans are there from the beginning, having come from our world. The original humans who witness the creation of Narnia in *The Magician's Nephew** are Digory Kirke*; Polly Plummer*; Digory's uncle, Andrew Ketterley*; and a London hansom cab driver, Frank*. Jadis*, late of Charn*, is also with them; it is through her that evil is introduced into Narnia at its very beginning. Frank is chosen to be the first king of Narnia by Aslan*. Aslan decrees that all kings or queens of Narnia have to be human ("Sons of Adam or Daughters of Eve"*), reflecting a hierarchy by which Narnia is ordered. Frank's wife, Helen, is the first human to be drawn into Narnia by Aslan's call. From Frank and Helen many humans, including future kings and queens, are descended, but other humans, the Telmarines*, stumble into Narnia through a portal, in this case a cave in a South Sea island.

Adonis In Greek mythology, a beautiful youth dear to the love goddess Aphrodite, mother of Cupid*. He is killed while boar hunting, but is allowed to return from the underworld for six months every year to rejoin her. The anemone springs from his blood. Adonis was worshipped as a god of vegetation, and known as Tammuz in Babylonia, Assyria, and Phoenicia. He seems also to have been identified with Osiris, the Egyptian god of the underworld.

Lewis was interested in Adonis, partly because of his respect for pre-Christian paganism*, and because the myth embodied the idea of death and rebirth explored in *Miracles**. See also: **myth became fact**

The Aeneid **of Virgil** This classical epic poem was considered by Lewis one of the books that most influenced his vocational attitude and philosophy of life, and he partly translated it (see: **reading of C.S. Lewis**). Written between 29–19 BC, it embodies Roman imperial values in its Trojan hero, Aeneas. He is destined to found a new city in Italy. After the fall of Troy, the home-seeking Aeneas roams the Mediterranean with his companions. Making land in North Africa, he falls in love with Dido, Queen of Carthage. He later abandons her and establishes the Trojans in Latium, where the king offers him his daughter, Lavinia, in marriage. Turnus, a rival suitor, opposes him until killed in singlehanded combat. The poem builds upon a rich tradition of classical epics, including Homer's *Odyssey* and *Iliad*.

Lewis read from his never-completed translation of *The Aeneid* to the Inklings*. The readings must have had a powerful effect, as the translation seems designed to be read aloud. What has survived, which was only recently discovered, has now been published, edited, with commentary, by A.T. Reyes. It includes all of Book 1, most of Book 2, much of Book 6, and fragments from the other Books of Virgil's poem.

Further reading
A.T. Reyes, *C.S. Lewis's Lost Aeneid: Arms and the Exile* (2011)

Aesthetica A southern region of the world in *The Pilgrim's Regress*, charted on the *Mappa Mundi**. In it lies the city of Thrill.

A

---

affection See: *The Four Loves*

"After Ten Years" An unfinished piece published in *The Dark
Tower and Other Stories**. Lewis abandoned it after the death of Joy
Davidman Lewis*. It concerns Menelaus (called "Yellowhead"
in the story) and his wife Helen of Troy, after the Trojan War.
The intended novel appears to reflect themes of love deepened
by Lewis's friendship with Charles Williams*, particularly the
impact of Williams's *Descent into Hell** (1937). It would have
carried on the exploration of paganism* most realized in Lewis's
*Till We Have Faces**. Menelaus, it appears, would have had to
choose between true love and an idealized image of Helen, as
Scudamour has to choose between two Camillas in the flawed
but powerful fragment "The Dark Tower".

agape See: **charity**

Ahoshta An elderly Tarkaan and Grand Vizier in the Narnian*
Chronicle *The Horse and His Boy**. He is due to marry Aravis* in
an arranged marriage. Baseborn, he works his way up the social
hierarchy by intrigue and flattery. His appearance has little to
attract the reluctant Aravis: he is short and wizened with age,
and has a humped back.

Alambil One of the Narnian planets whose name means "Lady
of Peace" in *The Chronicles of Narnia**. When in conjunction with
the planet Tarva* it spells good fortune for Narnia. See also:
Narnia: geography

albatross In *The Voyage of the "Dawn Treader"**, this large
seabird leads the *Dawn Treader** out of the terrifying blackness
surrounding the Dark Island*, after Lucy Pevensie* calls in
desperation to Aslan* for help. It is one of many signs of Aslan's
providence in Narnia*. There is a long maritime tradition of the

albatross as guide and harbinger of good fortune (featured in Samuel Taylor Coleridge's "The Rime of the Ancient Mariner").

Alcasan, Francois A distinguished radiologist in *That Hideous Strength**. An Arab, Alcasan cut short an otherwise brilliant career in France by poisoning his wife. His severed head is rescued by the N.I.C.E.* after his execution on the guillotine and kept alive, perched on a metal bracket in a laboratory at Belbury*. He is (in Lewis's grim joke) the head of the Institute, embodying its belief that the human body is now an unclean irrelevance in mankind's evolutionary development, and revealing that physical immortality is a possibility. It is, in fact, uncertain that Alcasan himself has survived, because the macrobes, the bent eldila*, speak through his head, needing human agents for their devilish activities. He parallels the dehumanization of the Un-man* of Perelandra*, illustrating Lewis's belief in the gradual abolition of humanity in modern scientific society.

Alcasan's bearded head wears coloured glasses, making it impossible to see his tormented eyes. His skin is rather yellow, and he has a hooked nose. The top part of his skull has been removed, allowing the brain to swell out and expand. From its collar protrude the tubes and bulbs necessary to keep it alive. The mouth has to be artificially moistened, and air pumped through in puffs to allow its laboured speech.

Mark Studdock* is introduced to the head as a sign of his deeper initiation into the N.I.C.E. Dr Dimble* speculates that its consciousness is one of agony and hatred. See also: ***The Abolition of Man***

Aldwinckle, Elia Estelle "Stella" (1907–1990) While reading theology at Oxford* University, South African-born Stella Aldwinckle came under the influence of Lewis's friend Austin Farrer*. In 1941, she became a member of the Oxford Pastorate, devoted to serving Oxford undergraduates. Later that year she founded the Oxford University Socratic Club*, choosing Lewis as its first president.

Alexander, Samuel (1859–1938) A realist philosopher who was important in the development of C.S. Lewis's thought. Alexander was Professor of Philosophy at Manchester University, England, 1893–1924. He sought to develop a comprehensive system of ontological metaphysics, leading to a theory of emergent evolution. He proposed that the space–time matrix gestated matter; matter nurtured life; life evolved mind; and finally God* emerged from mind. His books include his Gifford lectures published as *Space, Time and Deity* in 1920. He later worked on aesthetic theory and wrote *Beauty and Other Forms of Value* (1933). See also: **idealism, C.S. Lewis and; enjoyment and contemplation**

Alimash A Captain of the Chariots in Calormen* in the Narnian* Chronicle, *The Horse and His Boy**, and the cousin of Aravis*. The horse Bree* remembers him as a worthy nobleman who, after an important battle, the capture of Teebeth, filled his nosebag with sugar.

allegory An extended metaphor, or sustained personification. In literature, it is a figurative narrative or description that conveys a hidden meaning, often moral. Key examples in English literature are John Bunyan's *The Pilgrim's Progress* and Edmund Spenser's *The Faerie Queene*. Tolkien's* short story *Leaf by Niggle* is an allegory, as is Lewis's *The Pilgrim's Regress**. The biblical parables have allegorical elements – allegory is a type of instruction. Lewis gives his own definition in a letter written 29 December 1958: "a composition… in which immaterial realities are represented by feigned physical objects".

When Tolkien's *The Lord of the Rings* first appeared, some interpreted the One Ring as meaning the atomic bomb. In his foreword to a new edition, he corrected them: "I much prefer history, true or feigned, with its varied applicability to the thought and experience of readers. I think that many confuse 'applicability' with 'allegory'; but the one resides in the freedom of the reader, and the other in the purposed domination of the author." Contrasting myth* and allegory, Lewis similarly wrote: "[A myth is] a story out of which ever varying meanings will grow" whereas allegory suggests one meaning (letter, 22 September 1956).

Lewis discusses allegorical interpretations of the psalms in his *Reflections on the Psalms** (chapter 12). Allegorical interpretation of the Bible* was common in the Middle Ages, when allegory was popular.

Lewis's fondness for allegory was part of his eclecticism. He was at home in the vast range of the premodern imagination, from the ancient Greeks through the entire medieval and Renaissance periods. See also: **Imagination; Aslan;** *The Allegory of Love*

The Allegory of Love: A Study in Medieval Tradition (1936)
This erudite book is among the outstanding works of literary criticism* of the last century. "To mediaeval studies in this country Lewis's logical and philosophical cast of mind gave a wholly new dimension," commented Professor J.A.W. Bennett*. This interest in ideas is shown in his concern with the philosophical and semantic development of the terms *phusis, natura,* and *kind*. Lewis traced these concepts from the beginnings of allegory* through Chaucer and Spenser, turning to them again near the end of his life in his book *Studies in Words**.

Lewis began work on *The Allegory of Love* in 1928, and it spanned the period of his conversion to theism and then to Christianity. He also wrote *The Pilgrim's Regress**, influenced by both his discoveries about the allegorical tradition and his conversion. Material he gathered while writing the study of love in allegory eventually led to his key book on the history of ideas, *The Discarded Image**. In a letter written in 1934, as *The Allegory of Love* neared completion, he suggested that the secret to understanding the Middle Ages, including its concern with allegory and courtly love, was to get to know thoroughly Dante's *The Divine Comedy*, *The Romance of the Rose*, the Classics, and the Bible* (including the apocryphal books of the New Testament). The Middle Ages provide the key and the background to both Lewis's thought and fiction.

Once it was completed and while he was looking for a publisher, he summarized the book to the Oxford University Press: "The book as a whole has two themes: 1. The birth of allegory and its growth from what it is in Prudentius [a fourth-century Christian poet] to what it is in Spenser [author of *The Faerie Queen*]. 2. The birth of the romantic conception of love and the long struggle between its earlier form (the romance of adultery) and its later form (the romance of marriage)." The OUP accepted the book for publication.

Something of the intellectual excitement of the book can be conveyed by a few statements from it: "We shall understand our present, and perhaps even our future, the better if we can succeed, by an effort of the historical imagination, in reconstructing that long-lost state of mind for which the allegorical love poem was a natural mode of expression" ; "'Love', in our sense of the word, is as absent from the literature of the Dark Ages as from that of classical antiquity"; "Men's gaze was turned inward… The development of allegory [was] to supply the subjective element in literature, to paint the inner world".

The Allegory of Love demonstrates Lewis's characteristic interest in the Christianization of paganism* (in this case, romantic love), an interest deeply shared by Tolkien*. Harry Blamires* points out that Lewis "revived the genre of historical criticism by his work on medieval and Renaissance literature in *The Allegory of Love* (1936) and *English Literature in the Sixteenth*

Century (1954)". His revival of this genre is perhaps even more significant than these works themselves. Notably, while Lewis's conclusions in the books are by no means always accepted, the books as historical scholarship are universally admired.

***All My Road Before Me: The Diary of C.S. Lewis 1922–1927* (1991)** Edited and abridged by Walter Hooper*, these handwritten diaries* record some of the days in Lewis's life between 1922 and 1927. The title is a quotation from *Dymer**, a poem that Lewis was writing at this time. The choice of events and contents concentrates on Mrs Janie Moore*, with whom Lewis shared a home, and to whom he read most of the entries as they were written. Therefore, as Owen Barfield* discovered upon reading them, there is sadly no record of the "Great War"* of ideas between him and Lewis. The diaries vividly render the daily domestic life that Lewis shared, as well as walks, weather, books, writing, and uncertainties over employment.

Andrew, Uncle Andrew Ketterley, the Victorian uncle of Digory Kirke* in the Narnian* Chronicle *The Magician's Nephew**. He is the uncle to which the title alludes, an amateur magician who forces Digory and his friend Polly Plummer* into the Wood Between the Worlds* by means of magic rings*. He is tall, very thin, with a long clean-shaven face and a sharply pointed nose, extremely bright eyes, and a great tousled mop of grey hair. When he smiles he shows all his teeth, and the children cannot help noticing his long white fingers. Like his counterpart, Jadis*, he considers himself superior to all rules and that animals are his mere tools. He is manipulative, playing on Digory's concern for his dying mother (Andrew's sister), and unscrupulous, sending Polly into unknown dangers. Uncle Andrew represents the bad scientist, more concerned with power than with truth.

angels As an orthodox Christian, Lewis believed in the literal
existence of angels. He considered them real beings in the actual
universe (letter 29 December 1958), appearing historically, he
was convinced, in the Gospels, at the Annunciation of Christ. In
parts of *The Discarded Image** Lewis summarizes medieval beliefs
about angels.

For Lewis angels are supernatural* beings (*Miracles**,
Appendix A). For imaginative* force and freshness, Lewis avoids
the term "angel". In his science-fiction trilogy* (for which he
acknowledged that the book of Ezekiel was an important source
for angels) he employs the terms "Oyarsa" and "eldila"* (see:
Out of the Silent Planet).

It is interesting that Lewis does not have much of an
intermediary role for angelic beings. God* directly and
personally communicates (as in Aslan*, the creator–lion of
Narnia*) as well as uses messengers and angelic interpreters.
His most important imaginative use of angels is in his science-
fiction trilogy, where he draws upon a medieval imaginative
picture of reality, admirably documented elsewhere in his *The
Discarded Image**.

Lewis's most well-known depiction of angels is in *The
Screwtape Letters**, which concerns the machinations of fallen
angels, or demons*, in trying to ensure the damnation of a young
man, who is entrusted to the bungling demon, Wormwood*.

Famous forerunners of Lewis on angels include John Milton
(*Paradise Lost*), William Blake (many works), and Dante (*The
Divine Comedy*). They also include the unjustly neglected John
Macgowan*, and his *Dialogues of Devils*. Angels accompany Mr
Weston (representing God) in T.F. Powys's *Mr Weston's Good Wine*
(1927). Angels appear prominently, though disguised, in the
events of the three Ages of Middle-earth depicted in Tolkien's*
The Silmarillion, *The Hobbit*, and *The Lord of the Rings*.

Anglican Church See: **The church**

Annie, Aunt Anne Sargent Hamilton (1886–1930) was married to "Gussie" (Augustus), the brother of Lewis's mother, Flora Lewis*. Both Jack and his brother, Warren Lewis*, were very fond of her, especially after the loss of their own mother.

Anradin A Tarkaan of Calormen* in *The Horse and His Boy**, and crimson-bearded master of Bree*, the stolen talking horse of Narnia*. He treats Bree badly and tries to buy Shasta*. Later he supports Rabadash* in the Battle of Anvard*.

Anscombe, G.E.M. (1919–2001) Between 1970 and 1986, Irish-born Elizabeth Anscombe was Professor of Philosophy at Cambridge University. A Roman Catholic, she was a member of the Oxford University Socratic Club*. She was a translator and editor of works of the eminent philosopher Ludwig Wittgenstein (1889–1951), under whom she studied while a research student at Cambridge. After the war she took on a research fellowship at Somerville College, Oxford* University, and was a fellow there from 1964 to 1970.

Elizabeth Anscombe's debate with Lewis at the Socratic Club, where she challenged one of his central arguments propounded in his book *Miracles**, has entered the Lewis mythology (a number of elements of which have been perpetrated by Lewis's biographer A.N. Wilson). According to this mythology, which has a surprisingly wide acceptance, Lewis was so discouraged by the encounter that he abandoned theoretical Christian apologetics and turned to the writing of fantasy for children – that is, *The Chronicles of Narnia**. This is simply not true. The writing of the Chronicles, in fact, is part of a development in Lewis's popular imaginative* apologetics that began with *Out of the Silent Planet**.

Elizabeth Anscombe's critique was powerful, and intended to be constructive. She felt that Lewis responded to it in an honest and serious way, evidenced by the fact that he substantially revised the third chapter of *Miracles* (appearing in the new 1960 paperback edition). The questions debated concern some of the deepest issues of human thinking.

The philosopher Basil Mitchell recalls that in the 1960s the Anscombe–Lewis debate was rerun, with Elizabeth Anscombe again participating, and the philosopher John Lucas presenting Lewis's case. In Mitchell's view, Lucas was able to sustain Lewis's side of the argument. Lewis's thesis, he concluded, was a robust philosophical one (interview with Basil Mitchell, in Andrew Walker and James Patrick (eds), *A Christian for All Christians* (Hodder & Stoughton, 1990)). See also: **naturalism and supernaturalism**

Further reading

G.E.M. Anscombe, *An Introduction to Wittgenstein's Tractatus* (1959); G.E.M. Anscombe, *Collected Philosophical Papers: Ethics, Religion and Politics* (1981); G.E.M. Anscombe, *Collected Philosophical Papers: Metaphysics and the Philosophy of Mind* (1981 – containing her original paper challenging Lewis); Cora Diamond and Jenny Teichman (eds), *Intention and Intentionality: Essays in Honour of G.E.M. Anscombe* (1979).

Ansit, Lady In *Till We Have Faces**, Bardia*, the captain of the king's guard in Glome*, marries her for love, and she bears him many children. After Bardia's death, Ansit tells Queen Orual*, who was also in love with Bardia, how much her possessiveness stole him from his wife and family.

Anthroposophia A region of the world in *The Pilgrim's Regress**, situated to the south of the Main Road*, referring to the ideas of anthroposophy*. See also: ***Mappa Mundi***

anthroposophy A modern "spiritual science" founded by Rudolf Steiner (1861–1925) and followed and promoted by Owen Barfield*. It explores and aims to promote the evolution of human consciousness, so that people can return to an original participation with the natural world, but enriched by our historical and cultural development over history. The original participation of humanity has been ruptured by materialism*. Christianity has a central place in the evolution of human consciousness, but is understood in the light of this evolution. Anthroposophy contains Eastern and Western philosophical elements. Both Steiner and Barfield consider this gnostic movement compatible with Christian teaching, even though it is far from orthodox. Anthroposophists recognize that the being they call Christ is to be acknowledged as the centre of life on earth. Steiner's claim was no less than that "the Christian religion is the ultimate religion for the earth's whole future".

Rudolf Steiner advocated a new perception of Christianity that is really also a new perception of reality itself. He drew an analogy with Copernicus, whose ideas altered the very way we look at nature*, rather than reshaped its order: "Nature stayed as it was, but people learned to think about nature in a way that accorded with the new view of the world." Like natural science, Steiner argued, Christianity is rooted in reality; it is "mystical fact". Barfield believed that this central point of Steiner's anticipated the discovery Lewis made at his conversion to Christianity, where Tolkien* persuaded him that the Gospel narratives have all the qualities of a good story, yet also actually happened in history; in Lewis's terms, "myth became fact"*. Yet although there does at first sight seem to be a strong parallel here between Steiner and Lewis, it is only based on the ambiguity of the term "fact", a notoriously difficult term. For both Lewis and Tolkien, the factual nature of the Gospel narratives was understood in terms of normal historical documents, whereas Steiner allowed himself to be free and easy in his interpretation of the four Gospels according to the esoteric "spiritual" and "scientific" discipline of anthroposophical meditation.

Barfield drew inspiration from anthroposophy and Rudolf Steiner for his many writings. His adherence to this view formed the basis for the "Great War"* between Lewis and him. Barfield's influence on Lewis and Tolkien was mainly through his early work *Poetic Diction**, and concerned the nature of poetic language. Even though Barfield influenced Lewis through this "Great War" of ideas in the 1920s, that helped to prepare Lewis for accepting orthodox Christianity, rather than any anthroposophist ideas. Significant differences remained between the close friends until the end of Lewis's life.

Further reading
Rudolf Steiner, *Anthroposophy and Christianity* (English translation, 1985).

Anvard The capital of Archenland*, the seat of King Lune* in *The Horse and His Boy**. Anvard is a small, many-towered castle at the foot of the northern mountains. It is protected from the north wind by a wooded ridge. The ancient castle is built of a warm, reddish brown stone. Pleasant green lawns extend to the front of the entrance gate, but it has no moat. See also: **Narnia: geography; The Battle of Anvard**

***Anya,* Joy Davidman (1940)** A novel by Joy Davidman, who later married C.S. Lewis (see: **Lewis, Helen Joy Davidman**). It was completed in 1938 and published in 1940, by which time Joy, then an atheist, was a convinced Marxist and member of the Communist Party. She was twenty-five.

That first novel received good reviews. It narrates the life of a Ukrainian Jewish woman from her youth to middle age. The events and characters are based upon real people and incidents that were part of the living memory of Joy's mother. However, the themes and concerns of the novel sprang from Joy's developing view of the world. Like Joy, Anya is a free spirit. She is determined not to be overpowered by the dominant forces of a society in radical change. The original dust jacket proclaimed: "Like its heroine, this novel is glowing, sensuous, alive. It is written in a vein suggesting D.H. Lawrence, with poetic artistry and with all five senses awake to the warmth, color, and feel of things."

Aphallin Also called Abhalljin. A distant island beyond the seas of Lur in *Perelandra**, the Third Heaven. It is a cup-shaped land that contains the House of Kings, in which sits King Arthur, taken there by God* to remain in bodily form until the end of time, along with the Old Testament characters Enoch, Elijah, Moses, and Melchizedek – the king of mysterious origin and character.

Aravir In *Prince Caspian**, the morning star* of Narnia*, which gleams like a little moon. See also: **Narnia: geography**

Aravis Only daughter of Kidrash* Tarkaan, lord of the Calormen* province of Calavar*, and descended, she is taught, from the god Tash*. She is important in *The Horse and His Boy**, along with Shasta* and the Narnian* talking horses, Bree* and Hwin*. Aravis runs away from home when her mother arranges a marriage to Ahoshta* – sixty years old, with a face like an ape. She meets up with and eventually marries Shasta (Cor*) and becomes queen of Archenland* at the end of the story. Aravis, despite her faults, displays the qualities of the virtuous pagan*, qualities also found later (in *The Last Battle**) in Emeth*. She is as true as steel and would never abandon a companion. She is also attracted to Aslan*, though the only hint of his existence at first comes to her through Bree's frequent expression "By the Lion's Mane". Aravis discovers that Aslan has guided her, and also wounded her with the same welts her unfortunate maidservant received because of her mistress's escape. This awakens her from her indifference. When she meets Queen Lucy*, they become instant friends.

Archenland Found in Lewis's Narnian Chronicles*. To Narnia's* south, and connected by a high mountain pass, Archenland is ruled over by King Lune* from Anvard* during the time of the co-regency of Peter and Edmund, Susan and Lucy Pevensie*, in *The Lion, the Witch and the Wardrobe** and *The Horse and His Boy**. Leading to the high mountains are pine-covered slopes and narrow valleys. The highest peaks are Stormness Head* and Mount Pire*. In Archenlandian mythology, the twin-peaked Mount Pire was once a two-headed giant* turned to stone. Archenland's southern boundary is marked by Winding Arrow River*. Beyond this lies a vast desert that separates Archenland and the troublesome Calormen*. Travellers en route to Archenland from Calormen could use the conspicuous double peak of Mount Pire as a landmark. Archenland's wine is highly regarded, and is so potent that water has to be mixed with it before drinking. See also: **Narnia: geography**; **Narnia: history**

Archon See: **eldila**

Argan Prince of Phars* in *Till We Have Faces**, and troublesome to neighbouring Glome*. Eventually he is defeated in single combat by Queen Orual*, allowing a peaceful alliance between the kingdoms. He has straw-coloured hair and beard, and is thin yet somehow bloated, with pouting lips.

Argoz One of the Seven Lords* of Narnia* sought by Caspian* X in *The Voyage of the "Dawn Treader"**. He is eventually discovered slumbering a deep sleep of years at World's End Island*.

Arlian In the Narnian* Chronicle *Prince Caspian**, one of the Telmarine* lords of Caspian* IX, executed for treason by the usurper, Miraz*.

Arnom In *Till We Have Faces**, the progressive new priest of Ungit*, whose "new theology" takes in ideas from Greek rationalism. He is a dark man the same age as Queen Orual*, and "smooth-cheeked as a eunuch".

Arsheesh An unpleasant Calormene* fisherman who raises the apparently orphaned Shasta* in *The Horse and His Boy**. Near his cottage is a narrow estuary with mud banks. Beside the cottage are a single tree and a donkey's stable.

Arthurian Torso: Containing the Posthumous Fragment of the Figure of Arthur by Charles Williams and A Commentary on the Arthurian Poems of Charles Williams **(1948)** This book contains an unfinished prose work by Charles Williams* on the Figure of Arthur, and a commentary by C.S. Lewis on his friend's unfinished cycle of Arthurian poems, *Taliessin Through Logres* and *The Region of the Summer Stars*. The title refers to the geographical image of the female human body that Williams employs in the poems. Lewis intended his commentary to be complementary to Williams's prose work in helping the reader to appreciate the difficult poetry. He also suggests an order for reading the poems that establishes a narrative continuity.

Lewis robustly defends his friend's poems, arguing that their obscurity is valid. He points out their biblical orthodoxy, and expounds their implicit Christian themes of incarnation and love. Lewis also shows Williams's belief that even when great empires collapse, a faithful remnant survives.

Charles Williams's thought and poetry had a deep and lasting influence on Lewis's thinking and a number of his post-war writings. It was because of Lewis's popularity in the United States, and Williams's association with him, that, in 1974, William Eerdmans were able to publish, in one volume, *Arthurian Torso* and Williams's Arthurian poems.

Askins, Dr John Hawkins (1877–1923) Known as "Doc" to Lewis, Askins was the younger brother of Mrs Janie Moore*, Lewis's adopted mother. Deeply affected and disturbed by his war service in the Royal Army Medical Corps, Askins studied the new practice of psychoanalysis and dabbled in the occult. He and his family moved near to his sister in 1922, settling in Iffley, near Oxford*. Lewis was shocked by his ravings and eventual death in 1923. Prior to that the two had had many conversations in which the subject of immortality figured. It is likely that these experiences influenced what has been dubbed "The Easley Fragment"*, Lewis's fragment of an unfinished Ulster novel.

Aslan Lewis's invented world of Narnia* contains many talking lions, the kings of beasts, but Aslan (Turkish for "lion") is not only this but also the creator and ultimate sovereign of the land. His father is the Emperor-over-sea*, dwelling beyond the Eastern Ocean*, past Aslan's Country* and World's End*. Aslan is a central presence in the Chronicles*, his character and significance becoming clearer as the stories unfold.

Lucy Pevensie's* response to Aslan, such as hugging him, is one of the secrets of the lion's success as an imaginative creation. C.S. Lewis fashions a figure of authority, the creator and true sovereign of Narnia, who is eminently approachable by the innocent and good. Those who also, like Edmund* and later Eustace Scrubb*, approach him in fear and repentance find a friend like no other.

Aslan is intended to be a symbol* of Christ in Christian teaching: Christ not as he appeared and will appear in our world (as a real man), but as he appears in Narnia (as a "real" Narnian talking lion). The symbol of the lion (a traditional image of authority) perhaps owes something to Lewis's friend Charles Williams's* novel *The Place of the Lion*. In his *The Problem of Pain** Lewis writes: "I think the lion, when he has ceased to be dangerous, will still be awful."

All seven of *The Chronicles of Narnia** teem with orthodox Christian meanings found also in Lewis's other writings, such as the true character of God*, mankind, nature*, heaven*, hell, and joy*. The key to these meanings lies in the fact that Aslan is a figure of Christ, out of many possible figures of him. If readers are unaware of this, they can still enjoy the stories in their own right; if they are aware, the meaning of Christian truths often comes strangely alive. For instance, many readers who are so familiar with the Gospel narratives as to be unmoved by the accounts of Christ's death are moved to tears at the death of Aslan.

As a child Lewis attended St Mark's* (Anglican) Church in Dundela, on the outskirts of Belfast*. The traditional symbol of St Mark is the lion, a fact reinforced by the name of the church's magazine, *The Lion*. See also: **allegory**

Aslan's Country This sacred place lies high up and beyond Narnia's* Eastern Ocean*. It features in Lewis's *The Voyage of the "Dawn Treader"**. Also Jill Pole* and Eustace Scrubb* arrive there when they are drawn out of our world in *The Silver Chair**. Seen from World's End*, Aslan's Country appears to be made up of mountains of enormous height, yet forever free of snow, clothed in grass and forests as far as the eye can glimpse. The highest peak is known as the Mountain of Aslan. Viewed from its summit, clouds above the Eastern Ocean look like small sheep. The distinctive water of Aslan's Country quenches hunger and thirst. Approaching visitors find a deepening and splendid brightness that confers increasing youthfulness to those long exposed to it. Its brightness is like that experienced by Elwin Ransom* in Deep Heaven in Lewis's science-fiction trilogy*. The quality of light in Deep Heaven and Aslan's Country reminds the reader that Lewis was very much inspired by the medieval imagination, with its marked response to brightness, rather than the modern imagination, with its awe* at the vastness of deep space or large quantities.

A

In *The Voyage of the "Dawn Treader"*, as the ship nears his country, Aslan* appears to the children, Edmund and Lucy Pevensie* and Eustace, first as a lamb* and then as the familiar great lion. Because his country is a borderland of worlds, including the children's England, he partly reveals his identity in our world by appearing as a lamb.

Aslan's How In *Prince Caspian*, a huge mound that during the course of ages has been built over the Stone Table* where Aslan*, the great talking lion, was sacrificed. It is located in the Great Woods* of Narnia*, but in open space, and has hollowed galleries and caves. From its top the traveller can see the forests of Narnia and, to the east, the great ocean. A "how" is the old name (still used in some parts of Britain) for a hill, mound, or cairn, and indeed the how has the character of a Celtic shrine. It is one of many reminders of the sweep of Narnia's history. Caspian* bases himself here with his loyal fighters during the threat from the forces of his Uncle Miraz*.

Aslan's Table The travellers in *The Voyage of the "Dawn Treader"** come across this table on World's End Island*, laden with uneaten food. Sprawled over it are three sleepers*, missing lords of the Seven* sought by King Caspian*. The table runs the length of a clearing, with open sky above. A crimson cloth covering the table highlights the stone knife* lying on it, once used to slay Aslan*. The food on it is replenished magically each sunset.

astronomy of Narnia The astronomy of Narnia reflects a medieval model, particularly of the sixteenth century, which Lewis loved. Narnia itself is located on a flat world (or, at least, its inhabitants perceived it as flat). The planets and stars* are living beings. One of them, Ramandu*, a retired star, is encountered on his island in *The Voyage of the "Dawn Treader"**.

That there is some scientific study of the night sky is suggested by the instruments found in the house of the magician* in *The Voyage of the "Dawn Treader"*. Doctor Cornelius* is well-versed in astronomy in *Prince Caspian*, tutoring Caspian* in the subject. As in the late medieval and Renaissance period, astronomy and astrology coexist in Narnia, with astrological portents being given significance. Centaurs* are skilled in rendering the meaning of such omens. Lucy* is well versed in Narnian astronomy; in *Prince Caspian* she notices several summer constellations: the Ship, the Hammer, and the Leopard* (a favourite with her). See also: **Narnia; The planets**

Atlantis Atlantis is a splendid city with palaces, temples, and scholars, even in the dawn of time, according to Uncle Andrew* in *The Magician's Nephew*. In *That Hideous Strength*, it is a lost world and the origin of Logres, the spiritual and true England established during the time of King Arthur and Merlin*. Merlin is a member of the Atlantian Circle and retains an instinctive feel for the powers of nature*, lost to modern science. The wizard's magical art is a last survival of the older and different realm of Atlantis*, or Numinor, as it is sometimes called, which existed in the pre-glacial period before primitive Druidism. It was brought to Western Europe after the Fall of Atlantis, and differs greatly from the Renaissance magic that is more familiar to readers today. *The Chronicles of Narnia** preserve the idea of a spiritual or essential England in *The Last Battle**, and a corresponding real Narnia*, which is made visible at the end of the world.

The Atlantian heritage in *That Hideous Strength* retains something of Eden, mankind's unfallen state, captured mythically in Lewis's planetary world of Perelandra*. This heritage is passed on through the succession of the Pendragon of Logres to Elwin Ransom*. It is also preserved in the language of Old Solar*, spoken before the fall of mankind and beyond

A

the moon's orbit. The N.I.C.E.* wish to utilize this heritage of magical power through reviving the sleeping body of Merlin, preserved through the ages by a spell, for its own satanic ends.

In *The Magician's Nephew*, the magical rings* that allow Polly Plummer* and Digory Kirke* to travel to other worlds, including the space that becomes Narnia, and Charn*, are made from Atlantian dust, passed on to Uncle Andrew by his godmother. They are linked to the Deep Magic* that has existed in Narnia from its dawn. Atlantis also features prominently in *The Silmarillion*, familiar to Lewis through his friendship with Tolkien*, as Númenor, a name Lewis borrowed. Lewis employs the image of Atlantis's overwhelming by flood to describe the impact of his mother's death in his autobiography *Surprised by Joy*.

Further reading
J.R.R. Tolkien, *The Silmarillion* (1977); J.R.R. Tolkien, "The Notion Club Papers", Christopher Tolkien (ed.), *Sauron Defeated* (1992); Charles Williams, *Taliessin Through Logres* (1938); Charles Williams, *The Region of the Summer Stars* (1944); Stephen Lawhead, *Taliesin* (1987); Plato, *Critias*; Plato, *Timaeus*; Pierre Benoît, *L'Atlantide* (1919); Sir Arthur Conan Doyle, *The Maracot Deep* (1929).

Augray In *Out of the Silent Planet*, a sorn* whom Elwin Ransom* meets on his way across the high harandra* to Meldilorn*. Augray gives him oxygen, for the atmosphere on Malacandra* is thin, and shelters him in his cave. Later Augray carries Ransom on his high shoulders to his destination.

Avra A sparsely inhabited island in *The Voyage of the "Dawn Treader"*, the third of a group known as the Lone Islands*, and the location of the estates of Lord Bern*. Avra has a medieval-like economy and social structure, and its pleasant slopes reach down to the shoreline. Lord Bern's people are all free, working happily in the fields, resulting in a prosperous and contented fief. See also: **Narnia: geography**

awe An emotion that Lewis considered close to fear, but implying no consideration of danger. It was caused by the presence of the numinous*. In *The Problem of Pain*, Lewis expresses his belief that awe was a direct experience of the supernatural*.

Axartha Tarkaan In *The Horse and His Boy*, he is Grand Vizier of Calormen* before Ahoshta*.

Azaroth A minor Calormene* deity.

Azim Balda In the Narnian Chronicles*, a town at the junction of many roads to the south of Tashbaan*, the capital of Calormen*. It is an important centre of communications and the core of the country's postal system, by which mounted messengers of the House of Imperial Posts carry letters throughout the vast country. See also: **Narnia: geography;** ***The Horse and His Boy***

Azrooh A Calormene* warrior in *The Horse and His Boy* supporting Rabadash* in the Battle of Anvard*, killed by King Lune*.

B

Bacchus The classical god of wine (Roman, *Bacchus*; Greek, *Dionysus*), who makes an emphatic but fleeting appearance in Narnia* (*The Lion, the Witch and the Wardrobe*, *Prince Caspian*), representing the wild and pagan* side to nature*, which Aslan* rules firmly but doesn't suppress. Bacchus is accompanied usually by Silenus* and the Maenads*, with whom he dances in joyful and exuberant celebration of the fullness of nature, a dance and feast revolving around Aslan.

Baker, Leo Kingsley (1898–1986) A contemporary and friend of Lewis, Leo Baker was a fighter pilot with the RFC (RAF) during the First World War. He was awarded the Distinguished Flying Cross after being severely wounded in August 1918. The following year he returned to Oxford* as an undergraduate, and introduced Owen Barfield* to Lewis. Leo Baker was a frequent visitor to the Lewis–Mrs Moore* household, as recorded in Lewis's diary, *All My Road Before Me*.

After graduation he became an actor, a profession he eventually had to give up because of his war wounds. He and his wife set up a weaving business in Chipping Campden, Gloucestershire. During the Second World War he taught in a Rudolf Steiner School in Gloucester (see: **anthroposophy**). After this he became drama advisor for his regional authority in various senior roles.

Balder In Scandinavian mythology, Balder (or Baldur) is the god of light and joy. He is son of Odin and Frigg, king and queen of the gods. In a dream Frigg is warned that Balder's life is threatened.

She makes all the forces and beings in nature swear that they will not harm Balder. There is one exception that she overlooked, however – the mistletoe. When the gods hurl darts and stones at Balder, Loki places mistletoe in the hands of Balder's twin brother, Hoder, the blind god of darkness. Balder is killed. Odin sends Hermod, another of Balder's brothers, to the underworld to plead for his return. If everything in the world weeps for him, he can return from death. Everything does so but for one ancient giantess (said to be the mischievous Loki in disguise). Balder is not able therefore to return to life.

In *Surprised by Joy**, Lewis records the impact this story had upon him even in its barest form. He was lifted up into vast northern skies. The desire he felt then had an intensity almost impossible to put into words. Lewis confesses that he loved Balder before he loved Christ. He came to believe however that Christ's incarnation in history made abstract reality tangible to human beings much more successfully than mere myth (see: **myth became fact**). See also: **paganism**

Balfour, Arthur James (1848–1930) British prime minister between 1902 and 1905. His Conservative policies were important for Unionists in what eventually became Northern Ireland. As a boy Lewis would have heard Balfour's name on the lips of his father Albert Lewis* and his father's friends, for whom politics was a dominant theme of conversation. Among his works are *Essays and Addresses* (1893), *The Foundations of Belief* (1895), *Theism and Humanism** (1915), and *Theism and Thought* (1923). *Theism and Humanism* was one of Lewis's chosen list of ten books that had a particularly formative influence on him (see: **reading of C.S. Lewis**).

In his paper "Is Theology Poetry?" (1944), Lewis speaks of *Theism and Humanism* as "a book too little read". Balfour's book was a significant influence on Lewis's seminal *Miracles**, particularly on his treatment of naturalism*. Like Lewis,

B

Balfour thought of himself as a plain man, with a plain man's common sense. Lewis was keen to employ a plain style in his theological writings.

Further reading

Arthur James Balfour, *Chapters of Autobiography* (1930); Blanche E.C. Dugdale, *Arthur James Balfour V2: First Earl of Balfour 1906–1930* (2007); Max Egremont, *Balfour: A Life of Arthur James Balfour* (1980); Ruddock F. Mackay, *Balfour: Intellectual Statesman* (1985).

Bar The chancellor of jolly King Lune* in *The Horse and His Boy**. He turns traitor and kidnaps the infant Prince Cor* (named Shasta* by those who found him in Calormen*) when he heard that Cor would save Archenland*. Later Lord Bar is killed in battle.

Barfield, Owen (1898–1997) A close friend of Lewis's and a fellow Inkling*, Owen Barfield was a child of "more or less agnostic" parents, one a London solicitor, the other a suffragette. They retained a deep respect for Christianity, however. He was born in London, and attended Highgate School. He had two sisters and a brother. His mother was musical, and also taught him to read. At school he was keen on gymnastics. In the spring of 1917 he was called up to the army; he was then eighteen.

Barfield served with the Royal Engineers, and joined the Signal Service. In the Wireless Department he studied theory of electricity. He had already learned Morse code from his elder brother. While he was still training the armistice was signed, so he had no combat experience at all, though he was sent to Belgium. There he had very little to do, as pigeons were still used for communications. He had already won a scholarship to Oxford* University. He did not get up to the university until October 1919, studying at Wadham College, reading English, and attempting some of his own writing. At this time he formed a lifelong friendship with Lewis, and also later became an advocate of anthroposophy*, the religious school of thought developed by Rudolf Steiner. Barfield and Lewis would walk together or ask each other to lunch, but did not really see a lot of each other until after graduation, when the "Great War"* started between them.

While an undergraduate Owen Barfield experienced what has aptly been described as an "intellectual epiphany" (*New York Times* obituary, 19 December 1997) while studying the Romantic poets. As with Tolkien*, his main intellectual stimulus came from language. Owen Barfield recalled in 1966: "What impressed me particularly was the power with which not so much whole poems as particular combinations of words worked on my mind. It seemed there was some magic in it; and a magic which not only gave me pleasure but also reacted on and expanded the meanings of the individual words concerned" (*New York Times* obituary). Language, he believed, had the power to transform human consciousness and to embody historic changes in this consciousness.

He married Maud Douie (1888–1980), some years his senior, in 1923. Like him, she danced, and he met her at the English Folk Dance Society. She was looking for a male dancer for a concert party around Cornish villages. For several years he was a freelance writer, doing various odd jobs to supplement his income. He had started writing poetry while at school.

After graduation he also began a BLitt, the thesis of which became his book *Poetic Diction** (1928). In 1925 he published a children's book, *The Silver Trumpet*, which later was a success in the Tolkien household. In 1926 his study *History in English Words* appeared. *Poetic Diction* deeply influenced Lewis and Tolkien.

In 1929 Barfield moved back to London, to train in his father's firm of solicitors. He infrequently attended Inklings meetings. He would visit Oxford once a term, he recalled, and this sometimes coincided with "an Inklings". In about 1930 he finished his "metaphysical argument" with Lewis, the "Great

War". This roughly coincided with the process of Lewis's conversion to Christianity. After the "war" he had jokingly said to Lewis that while Lewis had taught him to think, he had taught Lewis what to think. Lewis undoubtedly forced him to think systematically and accurately, passing on hard-won skills he had acquired from his tutelage under W.T. Kirkpatrick*. Barfield in his turn helped Lewis to think more imaginatively; to combine his imagination* with his formidable intellect. This was a "slow business", remembered Barfield.

Maud Barfield, his wife, was an Anglican, and antipathetic to Steiner and anthroposophy. She gradually modified her resistance, and he in turn became an Anglican in 1950, but was embarrassed by Lewis's "fundamentalism". Christianity for him meant the increasing involvement of the divine within human life and destiny. Like Rudolf Steiner, he became convinced that the incarnation, life, and death of Christ was at the centre of the "evolution of consciousness". Also like Steiner, he believed in reincarnation. Owen Barfield had no children of his own, but he and Maud adopted two children, and fostered a third. The daughter, Lucy (to whom *The Lion, the Witch and the Wardrobe** is dedicated), developed multiple sclerosis.

During his early years as a solicitor – 1929 to 1934 – he contributed essays, poems, and reviews, mostly to anthroposophical journals. There was then a quiet period until a collection of essays, *Romanticism Comes of Age*, was published in 1944. His poetic drama *Orpheus* was performed at the Little Theatre, Sheffield, in 1948. An autobiographical novel appeared in 1950, entitled *This Ever Diverse Pair*, under the pseudonym G.A.L. Burgeon. Owen Barfield continued to write essays. A major statement of his philosophy, perhaps as significant as *Poetic Diction*, came out in 1957, called *Saving the Appearances: A Study in Idolatry*, concerned with the implications of a scientific perception of reality upon ordinary human consciousness.

Two years later Owen Barfield retired from his legal profession and his writing output significantly increased, including *Worlds Apart: A Dialogue of the 1960s* (1963), *Unancestral Voice* (1965), *Speaker's Meaning* (1967), *What Coleridge Thought* (1971), *The Rediscovery of Meaning and Other Essays* (1977), *History, Guilt and Habit* (1979), and *Owen Barfield on C.S. Lewis* (1989). In 1993 *A Barfield Sampler* was published. His reputation steadily grew in the American academic world, and he gave a number of lectures there. He was for many years Lewis's literary executor, soon joined by Walter Hooper*. When he originally started advising Lewis legally, Lewis faced a major catastrophe over his income tax, an episode captured in a chapter in *This Ever Diverse Pair*.

Lewis's debt to Owen Barfield was enormous. He paid tribute to him in *Surprised by Joy* * and earlier in *The Allegory of Love* * ("the wisest and best of my unofficial teachers"). Tolkien too was shaken to his roots by Barfield's insights in *Poetic Diction*. Owen Barfield has been appreciated as a leading twentieth-century thinker by figures as diverse as novelist and Nobel Prize winner Saul Bellow, historian and cultural analyist Theodore Roszak, literary scholar G.B. Tennyson, and classicist and philosopher Norman O. Brown. He outlived Lewis by thirty-four years and Tolkien by twenty-four, dying on 14 December 1997, in Forest Row, East Sussex.

Further reading

G.B. Tennyson (ed.), *Owen Barfield on C.S. Lewis* (1989); Lionel Adey, *C.S. Lewis's "Great War" with Owen Barfield* (1978); C.S. Lewis, *Surprised by Joy* (1955) Simon Blaxland de Lange, *Owen Barfield, Romanticism Come of Age: A Biography* (2006).

Batta The big-boned and fair-haired foreigner from the north in *Till We Have Faces**, who is the nurse of Orual* and Redival*. Because of her troublemaking, Orual has Batta hanged when she becomes queen, as part of her reforms.

The Battle of Anvard The unsuccessful attack by Rabadash* the Calormene* in *The Horse and His Boy*, using 200 horsemen, attempting to secure Anvard*, as part of a plan to conquer Narnia*. See also: **Anvard**

Battles of Beruna Two battles are recorded in *The Chronicles of Narnia*. In the first, the White Witch* is defeated, in *The Lion, the Witch and the Wardrobe*, at the Fords of Beruna*. These fords are later bridged, and a second battle near Beruna occurs in *Prince Caspian*. This takes place during the War of Deliverance*. The Telmarines* surrender after finding that the bridge has disappeared. See also: **Beruna**

Baynes, Pauline Diana (1922–2008) Lewis chose Pauline Baynes to illustrate his Narnia* books after seeing her illustrations for a story by Tolkien*, *Farmer Giles of Ham* (1949). Commenting on her work for *The Silver Chair*, Lewis observed: "There is, as always, exquisite delicacy." As George MacDonald* had done with the artist Arthur Hughes, Lewis found an illustrator whose imagination* complemented his own.

Pauline Baynes played an important part in visualizing the world of Narnia, working from a basic sketch map by Lewis – she drew a Narnia map for the end papers of the original hardback books, a popular poster map (1968), and a map of the voyage of the *Dawn Treader*. As well as *Farmer Giles of Ham*, Pauline Baynes illustrated other books by Tolkien.

Further reading
http://www.paulinebaynes.com/

BBC (British Broadcasting Corporation) As well as recording several series of wartime radio talks in 1941, 1942, and 1944 that became *Mere Christianity*, Lewis occasionally recorded other radio talks for the BBC. He read the text of his "*De Descriptione Temporum*"* for instance over the air. Most of the wartime recordings seem to have been deleted by the BBC but several of the other talks are available on audio tape from the Episcopal Radio-TV Foundation.

Beaver, Mr and Mrs Loyal Narnian* talking beavers who lead Peter*, Lucy*, and Susan* to the meeting point with Aslan* in *The Lion, the Witch and the Wardrobe*, after feeding them and the traitor Edmund* in their home at Beaversdam*. Mr Beaver is a hard-working, warm-hearted, and direct creature who tells the children some of the history of Narnia. Mrs Beaver is the archetypal homemaker, busy with her sewing machine, domestic and hospitable. She delays their escape from Maugrim* and his police as she packs carefully for the journey, much to the others' frustration. See also: **talking animals**

Beaversdam Built by Mr Beaver* in *The Lion, the Witch and the Wardrobe*, the original dam spans the upper reaches of the Great River* in a steep narrow valley. It becomes the site of a historic settlement bordered to its north by fertile grasslands. The town has an important marketplace. Two Telmarine* lords, called the Brothers of Beaversdam, rule there during the reign of Caspian* IX.

Beaver's house In *The Lion, the Witch and the Wardrobe* this is an odd little house perched on the top of the dam built by Mr Beaver* (see: **Beaversdam**). It resembles an enormous beehive, and smoke from its fire emerges from a hole in its roof. The snug house has one room, in the corner of which Mrs Beaver* habitually works her sewing machine. There is a meal table, covered with a clean, rough cloth, and nearby an oven built into a range that accommodates the kettle and cooking pots. Instead of beds, the room has bunks built into the wall. Hams and strings of onions hang from the curved roof. Against the walls are clustered Mr Beaver's paraphernalia: gumboots, oilskins, hatchets, shears, spades, fishing rods, nets, and the like.

Behmenheim Region depicted in the *Mappa Mundi** of *The Pilgrim's Regress**, after Jakob Boehme, or Behmen (1575–1624). He is a German mystic whose influence spread to Germany, Holland, and England. He published a treatise, *Aurora*, in 1612. He sees the origin of evil as a necessary opposition to good, and posits that God's eternal nature contains a principle to reconcile good and evil.

Belbury In *That Hideous Strength**, "a florid Edwardian mansion… built for a millionaire who admired Versailles". It is acquired by the N.I.C.E.* for their headquarters, and contrasts directly with the household community run by Elwin Ransom* at St Anne's*.

Belfast Birthplace of C.S. Lewis in 1892. The second largest city of the island of Ireland, and later the capital of Northern Ireland. In his essay "Christian Reunion", Lewis speaks of the religious situation that presided over his early life, and differences and affinities between Protestants and Roman Catholics.

Belisar A great Telmarine* lord who with Uvilas is murdered at Miraz's* instigation during a hunting party, in the reign of Caspian* IX. The event, recorded in *Prince Caspian**, is made to seem like an accident with arrows.

The bell and the hammer *The Magician's Nephew** tells how, in Charn*, Digory Kirke* and Polly Plummer* come across a little golden arch on a stone pillar from which hangs a small bell made of gold. A hammer lies beside the arch. An enchanted verse is cut into the stone, the words of which tempt Digory to strike the bell, awaking Queen Jadis* and all her evil.

"Belsen" Wynyard School, Watford, Hertfordshire, was so named after the Nazi concentration camp by Lewis in his autobiography, *Surprised by Joy** because of the abuse suffered there by pupils (see chapters 2 and 3). The young Lewis brothers attended it. The brutal head teacher, Revd Robert Capron (1851–1911), was later certified insane.

Bennett, J.A.W. (1911–1981) A New Zealander, Inkling*, and colleague of Lewis's at Magdalen College, Oxford* University, from 1947. In 1964 he took on Lewis's post as Professor of Medieval and Renaissance Literature at Cambridge University. His inaugural lecture was devoted to the subject of Lewis and entitled "The Humane Medievalist" (1965).

Bern Also spelled Berne. One of the Seven Lords* of Caspian* IX in *The Voyage of the "Dawn Treader"**. The voyagers find that he lives on Avra*, one of the Lone Islands*. His estate is called Bernstead*. After the removal of Gumpas*, Caspian* X makes him a duke.

Bernagh The home of Lewis's friend Arthur Greeves*, near Little Lea*, at the time they first became acquainted. *The Pilgrim's Regress** was written here during a two-week holiday with Greeves. The building became for a period a private nursing home (called "Red Hall") and has since been demolished.

Bernstead The estate on Avra* Island, governed by Lord Bern*. His people here are free within a climate of slavery* on the Lone Islands*, and enjoy prosperity and happiness.

Beruna A small and snug red-roofed town half a day's march from Aslan's How*. Established by Telmarines*, it is walled and gated, with an important marketplace. It is near the meeting of the Great River* and its tributary, the River Rush*. The few Old

Narnians* living there are delighted when Aslan* delivers the town as Caspian's* forces grapple with Miraz's* army.

Beruna Bridge A bridge built over the original ford by Beruna (see: **Beruna, Fords of**) in Miraz's* modernizing regime. It is destroyed in *Prince Caspian** by Aslan*, freeing the river-god*. A more appropriate bridge is allowed later in Narnia*.

Beruna, Fords of Fords over the River of Narnia*, later bridged, near the Stone Table* (Aslan's How*). During the night of Aslan's* terrible death, as recorded in *The Lion, the Witch and the Wardrobe**, his loyal forces encamp here. At the time of the events recorded in *Prince Caspian**, the town of Beruna* is situated here.

Betjeman, Sir John (1906–1984) Lewis was Betjeman's tutor in English language and literature, a period in which antipathy grew between the two, expressed at times in the latter's poetry. Lewis was impatient over Betjeman's reluctance to work, while the poet blamed Lewis for his leaving Oxford* University without a degree. Many years later the two were reconciled to some extent. Sir John was chosen as Poet Laureate 1972.

Further reading
John Betjeman, *Collected Poems* (1958).

The Bible The debate about the authority and infallibility of the Bible is a complex one. Generally, Lewis may be taken as orthodox in his high view of Scripture, but he offered some tentative views, partly as a response to questions, on inspiration and the Word of God. For Michael J. Christensen, in *C.S. Lewis on Scripture* (1979), Lewis stands between the position of theological liberalism (which lessens biblical authority in favour of religious experience or rationalism) and evangelicalism (for which the Bible is the final authority on all of life).

Christensen usefully observes:

> To get… to his fundamental assumptions regarding
> the nature of Scripture, we must give thoughtful
> analysis to (1) his provocative theological persuasions
> and speculative sentiments, which suggest his view of
> Scripture, (2) his theory of the function of literature and
> the role of literary criticism, which largely determine his
> approach to biblical literature, and (3) his appreciation
> of myth (properly defined) and understanding of
> revelation, which apply directly to the Bible.

Though Christensen's book contains many valuable insights, it is flawed in drawing Lewis into a debate he never addressed. Two evangelicals who were in correspondence with Lewis, Clyde S. Kilby and Kathryn Lindskoog, have commented insightfully on Lewis's view of Scripture in relation to evangelicalism. It is clear that while Lewis sharply attacked theological liberalism, he had little critical to say about evangelicalism. Writing to Clyde Kilby, he offered a series of detailed difficulties that he had with an evangelical view of inspiration. These were offered in a spirit of helpfulness, in the expectation that anyone grappling with the authority of Scripture must give honest answers to such questions. None of the questions is incapable of solution. Lewis however treated theological liberalism as the antithesis of all that he stood for as a supernaturalist* and a "mere Christian".

For evangelicals and other orthodox groups sharing common ground, such as Roman Catholics, Lewis offers a great deal that is useful. As a literary critic*, Lewis's insights are valuable in approaching the Bible as a literary text (though Lewis was sceptical of a simple "the Bible as literature" approach). His book *Reflections on the Psalms** provides a useful model in this. Lewis's observation about inspiration, that truth is scattered in many myths around the world, and not only in the Bible, deserves attention. It bears similarity with the Reformer John Calvin's view that truth is to be welcomed where it is to be found in non-Christian thinking. Lewis's *Miracles** provides fascinating insights into the wider implications of the doctrine of incarnation, which Christians believe is God's* supreme revelation of himself. For them, language, story, and myth* can, in God's grace, be incarnations of truth; for C.S. Lewis, following J.R.R. Tolkien*, they are able to anticipate or echo the incarnation of truth itself. One essay of Lewis's in particular, "Transposition" (see: **transposition**), attempts to show the logic of incarnation, as the richer level of meaning* is transposed or translated into a lower, poorer level. This logic is found in the Gospel records, where, for Lewis, true history and the greatest of all stories are one; myth becomes fact*.

Lewis (deeply influenced by Owen Barfield*) suggests that comparatively recently we have lost an ancient unity between the poetic and the prosaic, the symbolic and the literal. In the Bible, to give an example, "spirit" is equally "spirit" and "breath" and "wind". In a similar way, for Lewis the term Word (*logos**) of John's Gospel is a profound unity integrating many meanings that we today have to separate out. The same would be true of early Genesis; the common dichotomy of facticity and poetry in reading these chapters is misleading. For this reason Lewis advocated a diet of old books, that is books belonging to the period he called the Old West*.

Lewis saw the symbolic appeal of the Bible most focused in the Gospels. These, in form and in substance, have for Lewis an extraordinary imaginative draw. Indeed, the poet W.H. Auden points out, in *Secondary Worlds*, that they subverted classical ideas about the imagination*. Lewis (persuaded by Tolkien and Hugo Dyson*) became convinced that the events documented in the Gospels, located in the real world of first-century Palestine, nevertheless retain the quality of myth – that is, they are the

epitome of human storytelling. But, for him, just as they retain the quality of myth, they equally are true history. Though this combination was alien to a Graeco-Roman mentality, it was fully consistent with the logic and imagination of a theology steeped in the Bible. See also: **myth became fact; symbolism**
Further reading
W. H. Auden, *Secondary Worlds* (1968); Michael J. Christensen, *C.S. Lewis on Scripture* (1980); Colin Duriez, "The Theology of Fantasy in Lewis and Tolkien" in *Themelios*, Vol. 23, No. 2 (1998).

Bide, Revd Peter (1912–2003) An Anglican clergyman of the Chichester Diocese and friend of C.S. Lewis who performed the Christian marriage between Lewis and Joy Davidman*, after praying for her healing from cancer at Lewis's request. Prior to this, Peter Bide had discussed the efficacy of prayer* for healing with Lewis, as in some cases he had experienced healing after praying for people. Lewis regarded his wife's recovery as miraculous, and indeed, after it first appeared that she was dying, she had over three years of remission.

In performing the wedding ceremony at Lewis's desperate request, Bide chose to ignore the reluctant refusal of the Bishop of Oxford* to give Lewis and his wife a Christian ceremony, a refusal on the grounds that Joy was a divorcee, even though she was the innocent party in the event.

Bird and Baby See: **The Eagle and Child**

birds of morning These large white birds appear each morning on World's End Island* in *The Voyage of the "Dawn Treader"**. They bring fire-berries* that renew Ramandu*, then they pick clean what food is left on Aslan's Table*. This is an implicit allusion to Isaiah 6, in the Bible*, where one of the seraphim attending God's heavenly throne brings a live coal to purify Isaiah's mouth.

Bism An underground world deep below Narnia*, not to be confused with the Green Witch's* perverted Underland*, which lies above Bism. The word comes from the Greek for "bottom," hence abyss, "bottomless". The children in *The Silver Chair** catch a glimpse of Bism through a chasm in the earth. Here the bright gems of all colours are alive, and it is the home of gnomes*. Through Bism runs a river of fire inhabited by salamanders*. See also: **Narnia: geography**

black dwarves One of three types of dwarf in Narnia*, with hard, thick horselike hair. They include Nikabrik*, Griffle*, Diggle*, and the driver of the White Witch's* sleigh. They tend to be obstinate and cynical. See: **dwarves; five black dwarves**

The Black Woods In *Prince Caspian**, woods near the ruins of Cair Paravel* and the sea. It is rumoured by the Telmarines* that the woods are full of ghosts. Telmarines fear the sea and they let the woods grow to protect them from it.

Blamires, Harry (b. 1916) A former pupil of Lewis's, Harry Blamires is a literary critic, historian, and author, among other fiction, of a kind of Divine Comedy in the genre of *The Screwtape Letters**. His trilogy is *The Devil's Hunting Grounds* (1954), *Cold War in Hell* (1955), and *Highway to Heaven* (1955). He is also well known for popular theology, including *The Christian Mind* (1963).

Bodleian Library, Oxford See: **reading of C.S. Lewis**

Boggles These are summoned in *The Lion, the Witch and the Wardrobe** by the Witch Witch* to the execution of Aslan* on the Stone Table*. They are evil spirits, and the term covers a variety of demonic frighteners from folk tales that people would boggle at in horror, such as spectres, bogeymen, and hobgoblins.

Boxen An imaginary kingdom created by C.S. Lewis as a young child, in collusion with his brother, Warnie Lewis*. The stories have been collected and edited by Walter Hooper* into a book of the same name (1985). In his autobiography, *Surprised by Joy**, Lewis describes the origin of Boxen. The first stories were written, and illustrated, to bring together his paramount pleasures from reading, which were clothed animals and knights-in-armour. As a result, he created stories about courteous mice and rabbits in full armour who set out to vanquish cats rather than giants. In creating an environment for the tales, a medieval "Animal-land" was born. In order to include Warnie in its creation and shaping, features of the modern world like trains and steamships had to be included. Thus a history had to be created, and so on.

Bracton College In *That Hideous Strength** by Lewis, this is one of several university colleges at Edgestow*. It owns Bragdon Wood*, later acquired by the N.I.C.E.* for sinister purposes. Edgestow and its colleges are roughly modelled on Durham, though Lewis disclaimed any definite connection. In his preface to the book he tells us that he selected his own profession as the setting for his tale because he naturally knew it best. It is not because he thought fellows of colleges more likely to be corrupted than anyone else! The other colleges are St Elizabeth's College, a nineteenth-century women's college beyond the railway, Northumberland, standing below Bracton on the River Wynd, and Duke's, opposite the Abbey. Jane Studdock* had studied at St Elizabeth's, and is now a postgraduate at the university.

Bragdon Wood Owned by Bracton College*, in Lewis's *That Hideous Strength**, the wood is enclosed by a high wall with only one entry, a gate by Inigo Jones within the college. The wood is perhaps quarter of a mile broad and a mile from east to west, with the River Wynd flowing by it. In the centre of the wood is a well with worn steps going down to it and the remains of an ancient pavement around it, built in the time of King Arthur. "Merlin's Well" is situated by Merlin's* subterranean tomb, where, unknown to the college, he lies in suspended animation.

Bramandin A city of the ancient dead world of Charn* in *The Magician's Nephew**.

Bree Bree is a talking Narnian* horse in *The Horse and His Boy**, one of the most sustained talking animal characters in the Chronicles*. A dappled horse, he disguises his true nature after being stolen and becoming the horse of Anradin* Tarkaan in Calormen*. He runs away with Shasta*, and the two come across Aravis* and Hwin* (another Narnian talking horse). Bree is haughty and sceptical about Aslan's* reality, though he constantly swears "by the Lion's Mane". He is also concerned about his dignity when his tail has to be cropped (paralleling Reepicheep's* humiliation in losing his tail). His redeeming feature, however, is his love of rolling in the grass. Bree believes that all the talk of Aslan being a talking beast and a lion is merely metaphorical language – it only means he is as fierce or as strong as a lion. He is undeceived (see: **undeception and recognition**) when Aslan appears in all his reality. See also: **talking animals**

Brenn In Narnia*, the second of the Seven Isles*, with its main town being Redhaven*.

Bricklethumb A red dwarf* in *The Horse and His Boy**, who, with his brother Duffle*, feeds Shasta* (Cor*) when he first comes into Narnia*.

Bright People Inhabitants of heaven* who travel to the outer lands to meet shades from hell who are allowed a visit, in *The*

Great Divorce*. Lewis imagines himself one of the visitors, meeting the solid figure of his mentor George MacDonald*.

Broad, Mr An allegorical* figure in *The Pilgrim's Regress** representing a modernizing religion that "is friends with the World and goes on no pilgrimage".

Brothers and Friends: The Diaries of Major Warren Hamilton Lewis **(1982)** Clyde S. Kilby and Marjorie Lamp Mead edited these diary extracts from over a million words filling twenty-three journals. The result is a fascinating and indispensable portrait of Warren Hamilton "Warnie" Lewis* that also vividly pictures the day-to-day life of C.S. Lewis and his household at The Kilns*. Warnie's own biography of his brother was never published, and exists in typescript at The Marion E. Wade Center at Wheaton College. As Warnie reread his journals up to 1949 on 6 September 1967, nearly four years after "Jack's" death, he records: "One thing that stands out from these books is that the great pleasures of my life have been J[ack]'s society, books and scenery in that order… One thing I now bitterly regret about these diaries is that I preserved hardly any of my innumerable conversations with J. If only I had known that he was to leave me to end my life in loneliness, with what jealous care I would have Boswellised him."

The diaries* are also notable for the rare records of meetings of the Inklings*, and of Lewis's friendship with and marriage to Joy Davidman Lewis*, a person Warnie wholly and unjealously admired. See also: **letters of C.S. Lewis**

Buffin A much-respected clan of giants* of Narnia*. This ancient family makes up for its lack of brains with its rich traditions.

Bulgy Bears Three sleepy bears in *Prince Caspian**, who are among the loyal Old Narnians*. They offer Caspian* honey. See also: **talking animals**

Bultitude, Mr A bear in *That Hideous Strength** who, along with a jackdaw and other animals, makes up the household of Elwin Ransom* at St Anne's*, into which he is welcomed after escaping from a provincial zoo after a fire. Lewis seems particularly fond of this character, basing him upon a bear at Whipsnade Zoo that his brother Warnie* and he knew as "Mr Bultitude". Lewis had, according to Warnie's diary, dreamed of adding a bear to their private "menagerie" at The Kilns*.

In the story Jane Studdock* encounters Mr Bultitude unexpectedly occupying most of her bathroom, "a great, snuffly, wheezy, beady-eyed, loose-skinned, gor-bellied brown bear". Later he was captured by the N.I.C.E.* and narrowly escaped vivisection.

Lewis takes the name from a character, Paul Bultitude, in the humourous *Vice Versa* (1882), by F. Anstey, the pseudonym of Thomas Anstey Guthrie (1856–1934). Lewis read this in childhood. In 1948 the story was made into a film, directed by Peter Ustinov, starring Petula Clark and James Robertson Justice. Anstey writes: "Mr Bultitude was a tall and portly person, of a somewhat pompous and overbearing demeanour." As a widower, who found the company of his son "an abominable nuisance", he may have reminded Lewis of his father. Like Lewis Senior, Mr Bultitude was baffled by his son's request to leave his miserable boarding school. The relation between father and son is dramatically altered when the two swop bodies through the power of an Eastern talisman, and the father is forced to attend his son's school.

Bulverism A common phenomenon in argument, where an opponent's case is reduced to causes and therefore dismissed, as in "You only say that because you are a woman." Psychological interpretations are particularly prone to this fallacy – for instance, the view that belief in God is wish fulfilment. Naturalism*, discussed in *Miracles**, reduces all thinking and thus beliefs to causes, and in the process eliminates the validity of its own truth claims.

"Bulverism" is Lewis's name for this widespread view, a view that typically explains why a person is wrong before demonstrating that a person is wrong. This view marks the death of reason. Lewis points out, "Either we can know nothing *or* thought has reasons only, and no causes." Much of *Miracles* consists of a sophisticated rebuttal of this attitude. His essay "Bulverism: or The Foundation of Twentieth Century Thought" can be found in *Undeceptions**, and *First and Second Things* (1985).

Burnt Island A low, green island in *The Voyage of the "Dawn Treader"**, within sight of Dragon Island*. Here the only living creatures the travellers discover are rabbits and goats. Ruins of stone huts, several bones, and broken weapons between the fire-blackened areas suggest that it had been inhabited fairly recently. A small coracle found there is given to Reepicheep*, befitting his diminutive size. See also: **Narnia: geography**

C

cabby Name given to the London hansom horse and cab driver in the late Victorian period in which *The Magician's Nephew** is set. See: **Frank, King**

Cair Paravel Capital of Narnia*, the beautiful castle stands on the estuary of the Great River*. In *The Lion, the Witch and the Wardrobe**, it is the seat of High King Peter* and the other ruling kings and queens. Originally it is situated between two streams, but erosion turns its location into a small island. When the Pevensie children* return to Narnia ages later (as told in *Prince Caspian**), the castle is in ruins. Caspian* X rebuilds it to its former splendour. In their subsequent visit, recounted in *The Silver Chair**, Eustace Scrubb* and Jill Pole* hear told the ancient tale of *The Horse and His Boy**.

Cair Paravel is noted for its splendid Great Hall, restored by Caspian, its ivory roof, floor paved in many colours, and walls covered in tapestry. The west door of this banqueting hall is hung with peacock feathers and the east door opens in the direction of Aslan's Country* over the ocean. Cair Paravel is like the Court of Arthur, with a round table, and embodies the ideal of equal rule. Lewis may have been inspired by the description of the Arthurian court at the beginning of the medieval poem *Sir Gawain and the Green Knight*. *Caer*, from which "Cair" derives, is Welsh for "castle". In *The Lion, the Witch and the Wardrobe*, Peter saw it at sunset from a distant vantage point, resting like a great star on the seashore. See also: **Narnia: geography**

Calabria, Giovanni (1873–1954) Founder of a Roman Catholic order, the Poor Servants of Divine Providence, Don Giovanni began a correspondence with Lewis in Latin, after reading *The Screwtape Letters**. The letters have been collected and translated into English by Martin Moynihan, a former student of Lewis's, under the title *Letters: C.S. Lewis and Don Giovanni Calabria: A Study in Friendship* (see: **letters of C.S. Lewis**).

Calavar The only named province of Calormen* in *The Horse and His Boy**, which is ruled by Kidrash* Tarkaan, Aravis's* father.

Caldron Pool In *The Last Battle**, a large pool under the cliffs at the western end of Narnia*. It owes its name to the bubbling and dancing movement of its churning water. See also: **Narnia: geography**

Calormen A huge, hot land to the far south of Narnia*, (the Latin word *calor* means "hot"), Calormen is ruled by a dark and sometimes cruel people, with a rich civilization. Its capital is Tashbaan*, and it has many provinces, each ruled by a Tarkaan, or lord. Calormen is the setting for *The Horse and His Boy**. To its north lies Archenland*, from which it is isolated by a large desert.

Unlike democratic Narnia and Archenland to its north, Calormen has a strictly hierarchical, caste-like society. The dark-skinned peasant majority have little or no rights and slavery* is common. It is basically an agricultural society, though fishing, crafts, and trade have an important place. A troublesome country, Calormen historically has coveted the northern lands of its peaceable neighbours, and particularly becomes a threat in the period described in *The Last Battle**. Calormen originated in the Narnian year 204, when outlaws fled south from Archenland. See also: **Narnia: history**

C

Calormene Inhabitant of Calormen*. Calormenes have dark faces, and the men have long beards and wear flowing robes and orange-coloured turbans. As a people, they express mixed qualities of wisdom, prosperity, courtesy, and cruelty. Their speech is full of elaborate expressions, such as "May fountains of prosperity water the gardens of virtue and prudence." The narrator tries hard to overcome some prejudices he feels toward Calormenes but just occasionally succumbs, as when he speaks of their breath smelling of garlic and onions. The noblest of Calormenes are represented in the Chronicles* in the persons of Aravis* and Emeth*.

Camillo A talking hare who in *Prince Caspian* * attends the Great Council*.

Campbell College A public (that is, private) school near Lewis's childhood home of Little Lea*, on the outskirts of Belfast*, Northern Ireland. Lewis attended the institution briefly after the closure of "Belsen"*, his former school. The institute has a fine reputation, and Lewis's life-long friend Jane McNeill* was the daughter of a former head teacher there. The College's War Memorial lists pupils who served in the First World War, including Lewis.

Canyon, the An important region in *The Pilgrim's Regress* * that John* the pilgrim must cross in order to fulfil his quest* and be saved.

Caphad A kingdom south of Glome* in *Till We Have Faces* *, from which King Trom* obtained his short-lived and delicate second wife, mother of Psyche*.

Carter A bullying pupil at Experiment House* in *The Silver Chair* *, who particularly seems to enjoy torturing animals.

Caspian The name of the first ten of the Telmarine* kings. In the book *Prince Caspian**, the Caspian of the title is the one who becomes Caspian X, after defeating the usurper, Miraz*. He appears also as a central figure in *The Voyage of the "Dawn Treader"**, and, in old age, in *The Silver Chair**. Caspian X marries the daughter of Ramandu*, later murdered by the Green Witch* of the line of Jadis*. He is succeeded by his son, Rilian*, who is for many years the prisoner of the witch.

The first of the kings of Telmar*, Caspian I, conquers Narnia* and silences the talking animals*, its proper inhabitants. Caspian IX is murdered by his brother Miraz. See also: **Narnia: history**

The castle of the White Witch In *The Lion, Witch and the Wardrobe*, Edmund* finds the castle on a tributary of the Great River*. It is a stone building with high walls, a courtyard, and many towers. The courtyard is cluttered with unfortunate Narnians* turned to stone by the witch. The castle is a police stronghold, controlled by Maugrim*, complete with dungeons and smelling of fear. The castle is entered by high iron gates. Aslan* however leaps over the walls to unpetrify the statues.

Cecil, Lord Edward Christian David Gascoyne (1902–1986) David Cecil taught English literature and modern history as a fellow at Wadham College, Oxford* University, until 1930, when he gave up his post to write. He returned to teaching eight years later to become a fellow of English at New College. He married a member of the Bloomsbury group. From 1948 to 1970 he was Goldsmith's Professor of English Literature, remaining a fellow of New College. He was a valued member of the Inklings*. He was author of many books, some of them reaching a wide readership, including *Poets and Storytellers* (1949), *Visionary and Dreamer: Two Poetic Painters: Samuel Palmer and Edward Burne-Jones* (1969), and his most popular study, *A*

Portrait of Jane Austen (1978). His first biography was *Striken Deer* (1929), a portrait of the poet William Cowper, which later won the Hawthornden Prize. His anthology *The Oxford Book of Christian* Verse (1940) included Charles Williams's* "At the 'Ye who do truly'" and he became warm friends with him through the Inklings meetings. The philosopher, historian, and theorist Sir Isaiah Berlin spoke of him as "one of the most intelligent, irresistable, attractive, gifted, life-enhancing, shrewd and brilliant man of letters of his time". His portrait was painted in oils by Augustus John (1935, Tate collection).

Further reading
Clyde S. Kilby and Marjorie Lamp Mead (eds), *Brothers and Friends: The Diaries of Major Warren Hamilton Lewis* (1982); Rachel Trickett, "Lord David Cecil", *Dictionary of National Biography* (2004–13); Hannah Cranborne (ed.), *David Cecil: A Portrait by his Friends* (1991).

centaur This half-human–half equine creature of classical mythology appears in Lewis's Narnian Chronicles*. The upper half of a centaur's body is human; the remainder is composed of the body and legs of a horse. Centaurs have a prophetic role, as with the stargazer Glenstorm*. Other named centaurs are Cloudbirth* and Roonwit*. They are knowledgable about the properties of roots and herbs, Narnian astronomy*, and astrology. In the Chronicles the centaurs of classical mythology have been softened and made gentler. Lewis saw the centaur as an appealing illustration of how nature* might one day be harmonized with Spirit (*Miracles**, chapter 14).

charity Agape, or gift-love. See: *The Four Loves*

Charn A dead world that is the domain of Jadis*, later known as the White Witch*, in *The Magician's Nephew**. Charn was once the city of the King of Kings, and wonder of all worlds. It is a gloomy world, dominated by a giant red dying sun. As far as the eye can see ruins extend. A great river had once flowed through Charn, but now only a wide ditch of grey dust remains. In Charn, Digory Kirke* awakes Jadis and all her evil by striking a forbidden bell. Through him, she is drawn first into our world and then into Narnia*.

The blight of Charn represents evil before Eden, as in John Milton's epic poem *Paradise Lost* and in early English poetry such as *Genesis* and *Christ and Satan*. In the Wood Between the Worlds*, the drying up of the pool that leads to Charn signifies its complete annihilation, a terrible lesson of the contingency of worlds. The term Charn alludes to a charnel house, where corpses or bones were piled.

"Chartres" Lewis's name for Cherbourg School, Malvern, in his autobiography, *Surprised by Joy**. Presumably he named it thus after the elegant medieval cathedral, to hide its identity, but retaining a French allusion. He attended the school from January 1911 to June 1913 after briefly attending Campbell College*, Belfast*. The school moved to the town of Evesham in 1925, but the school building can still be found on Abbey Road, Malvern, now named "Ellerslie". See also: **Malvern College**

Chervy the Stag He informs King Edmund*, Queen Susan*, and Prince Corin* of the Calormene* attack on Anvard* in *The Horse and His Boy**.

chest The seat of balance in the mature human being, according to Lewis (drawing on ancient thought). The chest harmonizes our cerebral and visceral aspects. For Lewis, modern people increasingly lack chests – a process he warned would eventually lead to the abolition of humanity (see: ***The Abolition of Man***). Lewis pictures the human soul, with its "North"* and "South"* regions of head and heart, in the *Mappa Mundi** of his *The Pilgrim's Regress**.

Chesterton, Gilbert Keith (1874–1936) A celebrated convert to Christianity who influenced C.S. Lewis's thinking. Lewis says in *Surprised by Joy** that he found Chesterton attractive because of his characteristic goodness. Chesterton wrote, like Lewis, in defence of Christian faith and fantasy*. An essayist, critic, novelist, and poet, his best known writings include *The Everlasting Man** (1925), *Orthodoxy* (1908), the Father Brown stories, *The Man Who Was Thursday* (1908), *The Napoleon of Notting Hill* (1904), and biographies of Robe rt Browning and others. Typical of his astuteness as a critic is his comment on George MacDonald* in his *The Victorian Age in Literature*: "... a Scot of genius as genuine as Carlyle's; he could write fairy tales that made all experience a fairy tale. He could give the real sense that every one had the end of an elfin thread that must at last lead them into Paradise. It was a sort of optimist Calvinism."

Chesterton's *The Everlasting Man* was listed by Lewis as one of the ten most influential books that shaped his thinking and vocational attitude (see: **reading of C.S. Lewis**).

Chief Voice The leader of the Dufflepuds* who tells Lucy Pevensie* their history in *The Voyage of the "Dawn Treader"**. All the other Dufflepuds repeat what he says, which is usually inane, with approval.

Chippingford A market town in *The Last Battle**, down the river from Caldron Pool*, where Shift* the Ape sends Puzzle* the Donkey to buy food.

Chlamash A Tarkaan or lord of Rabadash's* who supports him in the Battle of Anvard* in *The Horse and His Boy**, and is forced to surrender to King Edmund*.

Cholmondeley Major A member of the bullying gang of pupils at Experiment House* in *The Silver Chair** who causes misery for Eustace Scrubb* and Jill Pole*.

choriambuses In *The Voyage of the "Dawn Treader"**, instruments of the magician Coriakin* for measuring a choriambus – a metrical foot made up of two short syllables between two long. This and the other instruments of the magician are a joke on Lewis's part at the idea of a mechanical instrument for such tasks.

"Christianity and Literature" (1939) An essay that first appeared in *Rehabilitations and Other Essays**. It represents C.S. Lewis's early thinking on the subject. For his fully developed views on the place of literature in human life, see his book *An Experiment in Criticism** (1961).

C.S. Lewis begins his essay by pointing out that Christian literature as such has no literary qualities peculiar to itself – it depends on the basic qualities of structure, suspense, variety, diction, and the like. By these norms a work is good or poor literature. Furthermore, the poorness of poor Christian writing, for example, a bad hymn, will consist to some degree in confused or erroneous thought and unworthy sentiment. It is not so much these structural norms about which he is concerned. Rather, he disagrees strongly with the circle of ideas used in modern literary criticism. This conflict is more of attitudes than of clearly defined concepts. He asks what the keywords of modern criticism are. They are words such as creative (as opposed to derivative), spontaneity (as opposed to convention), and freedom (as opposed to rules). Great authors are innovators, pioneers, explorers. Bad authors bunch in schools and follow models.

In contrast, while the New Testament says nothing explicitly about literature, it does reveal quite a different emphasis. For

Lewis, this emphasis is tellingly suggested in the apostle Paul's passage about the woman being the glory of a man, as a man is the glory of God. The idea is that man is derived from God in Adam, and woman derived from man in Eve. Man imitates God, and woman imitates man. There is a hierarchy here of imitation.

Lewis says that in pointing out this theme of imitation, he is not building a theological system. As a layman, not a theologian, he has no intention of doing this. He does feel, however, that he can suggest that the stages of this hierarchy (Father over Son in the Trinity, angels* over human beings, a husband over his wife) are connected by imitation, reflection, and assimilation. This is why Christians are commanded to imitate, or put on, Christ – that is, to model themselves upon him. Thus, his followers are told in Galatians 4:19, Christ is to be formed or portrayed inside each believer. Furthermore, Christ on earth seemed to speak of copying or modelling himself upon what he sees the Father doing.

In the New Testament, the art of life is the art of imitation. The mentality this generates, Lewis argues, rules out the dominant values of modern criticism, such as originality. "'Originality', in the New Testament," he writes, "is quite plainly the prerogative of God." Lewis continues: "Our whole destiny seems to lie in the opposite direction, in being as little as possible ourselves, in acquiring a fragrance that is not our own but borrowed, in becoming clean mirrors filled with the image of a face that is not ours... the highest good of a creature must be creaturely – that is, derivative or reflective – good."

Lewis couches this idea of reflection or imitation in terms of a very general literary theory. Authors should never see themselves as creating beauty or wisdom that is totally new. Rather, they are capturing within their artistic work some mirroring of beauty and wisdom that has always existed. Such a theory would rule out the notion of genius, as it is commonly held, and also oppose the view that literature is an expression of the author's self. See also: **literary critic, C.S. Lewis as a; meaning and imagination;** *The Personal Heresy*

Christian Reflections **(1967)** Published after C.S. Lewis's death, this collection of essays represents the breadth of his popular theology. One essay, "Christianity and Literature"*, had previously appeared in *Rehabilitations and Other Essays** (1939).

The contents are as follows.

"Christianity and Literature". An early attempt by C.S. Lewis to relate his faith to literature.

"Christianity and Culture". In this, the value or otherwise of culture is considered, against those who try to make culture into a religion. Lewis is considering high culture, not culture more generally (that is, all human formative activity, including society and politics, as well as the sciences and humanities). However, he affirms the value of all human employments, when offered to God. "The work of a charwoman and the work of a poet become spiritual in the same way and on the same condition."

"Religion: Reality or Substitute?" Lewis considers the question of whether the Christian faith is a substitute for some real well-being believers have failed to achieve on earth.

"On Ethics". As in *The Abolition of Man**, C.S. Lewis argues for the objectivity of moral values. Mankind cannot create a new system of values, only obey or disobey values that all human beings acknowledge. "Those who urge us to adopt new moralities are only offering us the mutilated or expurgated text of a book which we already possess in the original manuscript." A so-called new morality would deprive us of our full humanity.

"*De Futilitate*". Lewis examines the modern sense that life is futile and meaningless.

"The Poison of Subjectivism". Similar in theme to *The Abolition of Man*. (See: **subjectivism**.)

C

"The Funeral of a Great Myth". An attack on popular ideas of evolution and progress, as distinct from evolution as a biological theory of change.

"On Church Music". C.S. Lewis asks if church* music has any particular religious relevance.

"Historicism"*. A key essay on the belief that people can, by the use of their natural powers, discover an inner meaning and pattern in the historical process, a view Lewis repudiates.

"The Psalms". Contains ideas filled out in his book *Reflections on the Psalms**, including reflections on the theme of judgment.

"The Language of Religion". Religious language has been a central debate in the philosophy of religion. C.S. Lewis's conclusion is that there is no specifically religious language. In the process, he rejects the notion that poetic language is merely an expression, or a stimulant of emotion. Rather, he argues that it is a real medium of information, though with necessary limitations. Religious language is not a special language, but ranges between ordinary and poetic talk.

"Petitionary Prayer: A Problem Without an Answer". Prayer is a theme that constantly preoccupied C.S. Lewis, and he returns to it in *Letters to Malcolm: Chiefly on Prayer**.

"Modern Theology and Biblical Criticism". This is a paper Lewis read at a Cambridge theological college in 1959, giving his criticisms of modern, liberal theology.

"The Seeing Eye". In this magazine article, Lewis's thoughts were sparked off by a Russian astronaut's report that he had not found God in outer space. This report revealed much about modern misconceptions of reality. "Looking for God – or Heaven – by exploring space," wrote C.S. Lewis, "is like reading or seeing all Shakespeare's plays in the hope that you will find Shakespeare as one of the characters or Stratford as one of the places. Shakespeare is in one sense present at every moment in every play."

"Christina dreams" For Lewis and his friends in the early 1920s, this was a shorthand for the idea that dreams of love can make a person incapable of true loving, dreams of heroism inculcate cowardice, etc. Lewis as a young atheist firmly supported the idea, and Owen Barfield*, in the process of converting to anthroposophy*, did not. Barfield linked such dreams to the material employed in art. The age was saturated by the new psychology and such introspection as theirs was characteristic. Lewis explained, in his preface to the 1950 edition of *Dymer**, that he and his friends wrestled with the problem of wishful thinking or fantasy*. "The 'Christina Dream', as we called it (after Christina Pontifex in Butler's novel) was the hidden enemy whom we were all determined to unmask and defeat." The Samuel Butler novel referred to was *The Way of All Flesh* (1903), a satirical attack on religious smugness and its devastating impact on family life.

Christmas, Father In *The Lion, the Witch and the Wardrobe**, this familiar figure appears in Narnia* as the White Witch's* curse of perpetual winter begins to break with Aslan's* reappearance. Her boast had been that it would be ever winter but never Christmas. Father Christmas is a portent of change. Also he gives magical presents to three of the four Pevensie children* who will become kings and queens of Narnia.

Some critics, including Lewis's close friend Roger Lancelyn Green*, felt that including this character left a discordant note in the story. He was unable, however, to convince Lewis he should be left out. Why did Lewis include Father Christmas? Michael Ward argues persuasively that Lewis had a strong artistic purpose for doing so: he embodies the theme of the dominance of the planet Jupiter in the the story. He is a quintessential jovial figure, with his red cheeks and bright red clothing. Father Christmas helps to convey "the spirit of the book". Ward argues that each story carries a distinctive quality or atmosphere deriving

C

from the particular planet that dominates it. See also: **gifts of Father Christmas**
Further reading
Michael Ward, *Planet Narnia* (2008).

The Chronicles of Narnia Seven tales for children by C.S. Lewis that cover almost half of the last century and over two and a half millenia of Narnian* years, from its creation to its final days. In chronological order the titles are: *The Magician's Nephew**, *The Lion, the Witch and the Wardrobe**, *The Horse and His Boy**, *Prince Caspian**, *The Voyage of the "Dawn Treader"**, *The Silver Chair**, and *The Last Battle**. In reading order, it is probably best to enjoy *The Lion, the Witch and the Wardrobe* first, as here are set out all the basic "supposals" from which all the stories come.

chronological snobbery C.S. Lewis believed that one of the strongest myths of the modern world is that of progress. Change is considered to have a value in itself. We are increasingly cut off from our past (and hence a proper perspective on the strengths and weaknesses of our own age). He expressed this concern with the myth of progress in his inaugural lecture at Cambridge University, *"De Descriptione Temporum"**. In their many discussions in the 1920s, Owen Barfield* demolished what Lewis dubbed as his own "chronological snobbery". Lewis explains this snobbery in *Surprised by Joy** as

> the uncritical acceptance of the intellectual climate common to our own age and the assumption that whatever has gone out of date is on that account discredited. You must find out why it went out of date. Was it ever refuted (and if so by whom, where and how conclusively) or did it merely die away as fashions do? If the latter, this tells us nothing about its truth or

falsehood… Our age is also "a period," and certainly
has, like all periods, its own characteristic illusions.

chronoscopes Instruments of the magician Coriakin* in *The
Voyage of the "Dawn Treader"**, for observing and measuring time.

The church As a child Lewis was baptized into the Anglican
communion, attending St Mark's*, Dundela, on the outskirts
of Belfast*, belonging to the Church of Ireland. After a period
as a confessing atheist, he gradually returned to a faith in Christ
(as told in his autobiography, *Surprised by Joy**). He resumed
worshipping in the Church of England until his death. Lewis
was careful to avoid promoting any one denomination in his
public writing, lecturing, and broadcasting, championing what
the Puritan writer and preacher Richard Baxter called "mere
Christianity"*. This led him to emphasize common ground
or "great-tradition" Christian faith. As a result, followers
among all orthodox Christian groupings have benefited from
his writings, most dramatically evangelicalism in the United
States, but also Roman Catholic and Eastern and Russian
Orthodox believers.

In private, the Anglican Lewis saw himself as not especially
High or Low Church. Features of his devotional life belonged
to both High and Low. His close Roman Catholic friend J.R.R.
Tolkien* noticed elements of his Northern Irish Protestant
upbringing in his constitution, dubbing this his "Ulsterior
motive". Lewis had affinities with puritanism, in its richest
sense, and also with a restrained High Church sacramentalism.
He was committed to a regular church attendance at his local
church, which was Holy Trinity (Anglican) Church, Headington
Quarry, Oxford*.

City Ruinous A ruined city close by Harfang* in the northern
wastelands in *The Silver Chair**. According to the Green Witch*,

a king who once dwelt there had the following words inscribed on the ruins: "Though under Earth and throneless now I be, / Yet, while I lived, all Earth was under me." The Green Witch's Underland* lay under it. Only the words "UNDER ME" remain. The letters are so large that Jill Pole* and Eustace Scrubb* walked through one of the letter Es, thinking it a trench. Only from the high vantage point of Harfang are the letters recognizable.

classes of Narnian creatures Doctor Cornelius*, Caspian's* tutor in *Prince Caspian**, sets out nine classes of beings (reminiscent of the hierarchies of medieval classification): walking trees, visible naiads*, fauns*, satyrs*, dwarves*, giants*, gods, centaurs*, and talking beasts*. Because Digory Kirke* brings evil into the newly created world in the form of Jadis*, it is decreed that humans should try to set things right. Accordingly, kings and queens of Narnia* are to be human, so they are highest in terms of sovereignty. As rational beings, however, humans and talking beasts are equal. One volume title cleverly suggested by Lewis's publisher points to this fact – *The Horse and His Boy**. Shasta* is as much Bree's* boy as Bree is Shasta's horse.

Clipsie The little daughter of the Chief Voice*, the leader of the Dufflepuds*, in *The Voyage of the "Dawn Treader"**. She speaks the spell that makes the Dufflepuds invisible.

Clodsley Shovel In *Prince Caspian**, a loyal Old Narnian* mole met by Caspian*. He leads the loyal moles to the Great Council*.

Cloudbirth A centaur* and renowned healer who tends the burned foot of Puddleglum*, in *The Silver Chair**.

Coalblack The horse of Prince Rilian* in *The Silver Chair**.

Coghill, Nevill (1899–1980) Nevill Coghill was Merton Professor of English Literature at Oxford* University from 1957 to 1966. After serving in the First World War, he read English at Exeter College, Oxford, and in 1924 was elected a fellow there. He was a friend of C.S. Lewis's from undergraduate days, and like him came from Ireland. His Christianity influenced Lewis as a young man. He was admired for his theatrical productions, and for his translation of Chaucer's *Canterbury Tales* into modern English couplets.

Col According to Lewis's sketch of Narnian* history, a Prince Col leads a company of Narnians to settle in the fertile, uninhabited region later called Archenland*. The younger son of King Frank V of Narnia, Col becomes Archenland's first king. In *The Magician's Nephew**, Lewis inconsistently states that Archenland's first king is the second son of King Frank* I.

Cole In *The Horse and His Boy**, Cole fights along with his brother Colin* against the Calormenes*.

Colin In *The Horse and His Boy**, Colin fights, together with his brother Cole*, for King Lune* against the troublesome Calormenes*.

The Collected Poems of C.S. Lewis (1994) A collection, by Walter Hooper*, of *Spirits in Bondage** (1919), *Poems** (1964), and seventeen other short poems. Eleven previously unpublished poems appear in the collection. Most of the latter are reproduced from the Lewis family papers*. Included in the work is a previously unpublished introductory letter by Lewis that sums up his attitude to his own poetry, particularly the isolation he felt as a poet. See also: **poetry of C.S. Lewis**

Colney Hatch A once well-known "lunatic asylum" near London, from the mid-nineteenth through to the twentieth century. In

The Magician's Nephew*, Jadis* is dubbed by someone in the crowd the "Hempress of Colney 'Atch".

The Consolation of Philosophy, Boethius Lewis listed this ancient work as one of ten books that particularly influenced his thinking and vocational attitude (see: **reading of C.S. Lewis**). Boethius was an Italian nobleman born in Rome in 480. He wrote the *Consolation* while in prison in Pavia, south of Milan, awaiting execution. King Theodoric the Great put him to death in 524 or 525. In the *Consolation,* a woman appears to the prisoner, and tells him she is his guardian, Philosophy, come to console him in his misfortunes and point out their remedy. There follows a dialogue exploring the questions that have troubled humanity such as the origin of evil, God's omniscience, and human free will. The "Consolations" are alternately in prose and verse; a method afterwards imitated by many authors (including Lewis in parts of *The Pilgrim's Regress**). Most of Boethius's verses are suggested by passages in the writings of the Roman philosopher Seneca, considered at that time the greatest moral authority in the West outside Christianity. The success of the work was enormous; it was soon translated into Greek, Hebrew, German, French, and Anglo-Saxon, the latter version by Alfred the Great – an important work of Anglo-Saxon prose. The *Consolation* was one of the most important works in the medieval world. It was by a Christian writer exploring how far the virtuous pagan* mind could reach without special revelation in the form of Christianity. It displays an enormous respect for philosophy.

context, C.S. Lewis in The subject of Lewis's context is a complex one. Key elements come out if we focus upon Lewis's formative years, roughly the 1920s and 1930s. His work is illuminated by his early life, and by the intellectual currents surrounding his scholarship. Lewis's originality of thought might easily suggest that he concocted his ideas with the minimum of help from others. In fact, he benefited from several key contemporaries, such as Owen Barfield*, from the wider scholarly community, and from long, searching hours spent in Oxford's* Bodleian Library (see: **reading of C.S. Lewis**).

In the twenties, particularly in Lewis's Oxford, idealism* predominated in philosophy, with realists counter-attacking. As an atheist at that time, Lewis was at first staunchly opposed to idealism. He was an out-and-out realist and naturalist (see: **naturalism and supernaturalism**).

Lewis taught philosophy for the year 1924 to 1925 in University College, before getting his teaching post at Magdalen College in English literature. The prevailing philosophy that was taught at Oxford University in the twenties had its roots in the nineteenth century. It also, on the English language and literature side, still emphasized the study of language. The language teacher at his best was embodied in J.R.R. Tolkien*, who left Leeds University in 1925 to take up the post of Rawlinson and Bosworth Professor of Anglo-Saxon at Oxford. Lewis and he met in 1926 and soon became friends. It was this friendship (see: **friendship of J.R.R. Tolkien and C.S. Lewis**), along with those with Hugo Dyson* and Owen Barfield, that was the basis of the Inklings*. Lewis took on many of Tolkien's concerns, such as the serious writing of fantasy*, and shared his passionate love of language, evidenced in his *Studies in Words** (1960). At one time Lewis and Tolkien planned to collaborate on a book on language. Lewis affectionately was to fictionalize his philologist friend in the figure of Elwin ("Elf-friend") Ransom* in *Out of the Silent Planet** (1938).

In the preface to his *The Allegory of Love**, references are made to three members of the Inklings, Tolkien, Dyson, and Barfield – to whom the book is dedicated, and to whom Lewis acknowledges the greatest debt, after his father. Lewis pays particular tribute to Barfield for demolishing what he calls elsewhere his "chronological snobbery"*.

C

Dyson and Tolkien also shaped Lewis's thinking and approach to literature, particularly in the 1930s and 1940s. Tolkien was of colossal importance to Lewis – indeed, their friendship is comparable to that between William Wordsworth and Samuel Taylor Coleridge. In the formative years of the twenties, however, Barfield's influence was much greater. Dyson was a friend from undergraduate days who played a key role in helping Tolkien to persuade Lewis that, as he saw it, Christianity was based upon fact in a way that fully engaged the imagination as well as the reason. Tolkien's influence increased in the thirties as Barfield's declined.

The first important area of Tolkien's influence on Lewis was his Christianity. When they first met, Lewis was not a Christian, and previously had been a naturalist* (as recorded in *Surprised by Joy**). Tolkien's Christian faith is a complex matter, and Lewis inherited some of its cast. Essential to Tolkien's Christianity is his view of the relation of myth* and fact, and how myth became fact*. This view can be seen as a theology of romance*. Related to Tolkien's view of myth become fact is his distinctive doctrine of sub-creation*, the view that the highest function of art is the creation of convincing secondary or other worlds.

What emerges from Lewis's bookish background is a richness of thought, imagination*, and writing that has influenced literary criticism (see: **literary critic, C.S. Lewis as a**), science fiction, children's literature, literary approaches to the Bible*, and Christian apologetics throughout the West.

Cor A twin son of King Lune* of Archenland* who is lost in Calormen*, to the south, for many years. There he has the name Shasta. The Narnian* tale of how he returns to Archenland, learns his true identity, and gains his Calormene wife, Aravis*, is retold in *The Horse and His Boy**. To them is born Ram the Great*, the most notable of all the kings of Archenland. Cor's identical twin is named Corin*. See also: **Shasta**

Coriakin A magician who, like Ramandu*, was once a star* of the sky, in *The Voyage of the "Dawn Treader"**. As a punishment for an unnamed wrong, Aslan* gives him the difficult task of governing the Dufflepuds*. He is elderly, with a waist-length beard, garbed in a red robe, and crowned with oak leaves. His many instruments reflect his scientific interests.

Corin In *The Horse and His Boy**, the younger twin brother of Cor* – who is lost for years in Calormen*. He would have been heir to the Archenland* throne had Cor not been restored, but is quite content not to become king. He is nicknamed "Thunder-Fist" because he is a great boxer.

Cornelius, Doctor A half-dwarf who is the tutor of Caspian*, later King Caspian X, in *Prince Caspian**. He is loyal to the Old Narnia* and teaches the young prince the true history of the kingdom. As a true scholar, he is never without pen and ink.

Corradin A member of Rabadash's* assalt against Anvard*, who is slain by King Edmund* in *The Horse and His Boy**.

cosmic war In a letter written on 8 May 1939 Lewis observed: "My memories of the last war haunted my dreams for years." War for him was an image of a permanent cosmic war between good and evil. In "Learning in War-Time"* he commented: "War creates no absolutely new situation; it simply aggravates the permanent human situation so that we can no longer ignore it."

It is not surprising that this perpetual cosmic war features prominently in Lewis's writings. This is particularly true of his first theological fantasy*, *The Pilgrim's Regress**. Significantly, John Bunyan's *The Pilgrim's Progress* and *The Holy War* influenced this. These allegories reflect a similar belief in the great battle for a person's soul. Instead of Christian in *The Pilgrim's Progress*, the central figure in *The Pilgrim's Regress* is John*, loosely based on C.S. Lewis himself. Like in *The Pilgrim's Progress*, the quest* can be mapped. Indeed, Lewis provides his reader with a *Mappa Mundi**, in which the human soul is divided into north and south, the North* representing arid intellectualism and the South* emotional excess. A straight road passes between them. The story illuminates the intellectual climate of the 1920s and early 1930s, and its geography of thought applies much more widely.

On the *Mappa Mundi* provided by Lewis it is significant that there are military railways both to the north and south. He observes in his preface to the third edition that "the two military railways were meant to symbolize the double attack from hell on the two sides of our nature. It was hoped that the roads spreading out from each of the enemy railheads would look like claws or tentacles reaching out into the country of Man's Soul."

Lewis's map of the human soul anticipates his reflections in *The Abolition of Man**, given fictional form in *That Hideous Strength**, in which he posits the danger of "men without chests"*. He comments in the preface that "We were made to be neither cerebral men nor visceral men, but Men. Not beasts nor angels but Men – things at once rational, and animal."

Relevant to Lewis's theme of cosmic war is a phenomenon pointed out by Professor Tom Shippey, author of *The Road to Middle-earth* (1982). He showed links between several apparently disparate writers just after the Second World War. The writers were linked in struggling with the appalling reality of evil in the modern world, a theme that forced them to create new forms and abandon the received canons of what constitutes a proper novel and fiction. The writers and their books, as highlighted by Shippey, are: William Golding's *The Lord of the Flies* (1954), Tolkien's* *The Lord of the Rings* (1954–1955), Lewis's *That Hideous Strength* (the final part of his science-fiction trilogy), George Orwell's *Animal Farm* (1945) and *Nineteen Eighty-Four*

(1949), and T.H. White's *The Once and Future King* (published 1958 but written long before).

Further reading

T.A. Shippey, "Tolkien as a Post-War Writer", *Scholarship and Fantasy: Proceedings of The Tolkien Phenomenon* (1993).

The Cowley Fathers The popular name for a religious community in the Church* of England founded in 1866, and officially called the Society of St John the Evangelist, Oxford. The Fathers met in their Mission House next to the Church of St John the Evangelist in the Oxford* suburb of Cowley, to the south-east of the city. Lewis, as part of his private devotions, made regular confessions to one of the Fathers, Walter Adams, between 1940 and Adams's death in 1952.

Cruels In *The Lion, the Witch and the Wardrobe**, hair-raising supernatural beings called to Aslan's* execution by the White Witch*.

Cruelsland A northern region depicted on the *Mappa Mundi** in *The Pilgrim's Regress**.

Cullen, Mary Cook–housekeeper at the Lewis's Belfast* home, Little Lea*, between 1917 and 1930. She was affectionately nicknamed "The Witch of Endor" by Albert Lewis and his sons.

Cupid and Psyche See: *The Golden Ass*; **Psyche**; *Till We Have Faces*

Cure Hardy A picturesque village with sixteenth-century almshouses and a Norman church, in *That Hideous Strength**. The steam train on the branch line from Edgestow* passes through here on its way to the terminus at St Anne's*. Its existence is jeopardized by a N.I.C.E.* plan to divert the River

Wynd into a reservoir in the narrow valley in which the village lay. This is to supply water to Edgestow when it is expanded into a major centre of population. The plan is another example of the Institute's disregard for "outdated" values like beauty.

D

Daaran A nephew of Queen Orual* of Glome* and prince of Phars* in *Till We Have Faces**.

Dancing Lawn The setting of the Great Council* of Caspian* and his Narnian* friends, west of the River Rush*, in *Prince Caspian**. The neat circle of grass is ringed by elms. It is the favoured site of feasts and councils in Narnia.

Dar Brother of Darrin in *The Horse and His Boy**, he fights in defence of Anvard* against the Calormenes* led by Rabadash*.

Dark Island An island that appears to the voyagers first as a dark spot in the ocean, in *The Voyage of the "Dawn Treader"**. Here, in the darkness permanently engulfing the island, dreams come true (dreams we have while sleeping, including nightmares, not idle daydreams). Lord Rhoop* is rescued from this place of despair, and Lucy* calls upon Aslan* to lead them out of the darkness.

***The Dark Tower and Other Stories* (1977)** A collection of two unfinished narratives, and three short stories, two of which appeared in *The Magazine of Fantasy and Science Fiction*. One fragment, "The Dark Tower", seems to have been written after *Out of the Silent Planet** and before *Perelandra**, and is about time rather than space travel. It owes much to David Lindsay's* *A Voyage to Arcturus* (1920). Lewis abandoned it as unsatisfactory. The other fragment, "After Ten Years"*, was unfinished because of illness and age, and perhaps his grief over the death of Joy

Davidman Lewis*. It is a historical fiction that shows the promise of his accomplished novel *Till We Have Faces**.

Darrin Brother of Dar in *The Horse and His Boy**, he fights in defence of Anvard* against the Calormenes* led by Rabadash*.

Daughter of Eve In the Chronicles*, the name by which female humans are formally addressed. The Narnian* throne may only properly be occupied by Sons of Adam and Daughters of Eve. See also: **Son of Adam**

Davidman, Joy See: **Lewis, Helen Joy Davidman**

"Dawn Treader" In *The Voyage of the "Dawn Treader"**, the galleon in which the children, Edmund and Lucy Pevensie* and their cousin Eustace Scrubb*, sail almost to Aslan's Country*, which lies beyond World's End*. Shaped like a dragon, it has green sides and a purple sail. Pauline Baynes* provided a useful cut-away illustration of the ship for the book. There are two long, large hatches fore and aft of the tall mast. In fair weather they are left open to allow air and light to penetrate the ship's belly. Below deck there are benches for rowing (for when the wind failed and for manoeuvring in and out of harbour). Cabins are in the ship's stern. Caspian's* is the finest, which he gallantly hands over to Lucy for her use. Instead, he takes the lowest cabin, sharing it with Edmund and Eustace. The name of the ship is highly significant for the story, which is about the journey eastward toward Aslan's Country. The ship treads toward dawn, to the uttermost east.

Deathwater Island In *The Voyage of the "Dawn Treader"**, to the east of Burnt Island*, and not more than twenty acres in size. The voyagers discover that it is rocky and rugged with a tall central peak. Its only flora is perfumed heather and coarse grass. Only seagulls appear to live there.

Two streams are found, one of which flows from a small mountain lake guarded by cliffs. To the horror of the visitors, anything dipped into the lake turns to solid gold! This explains the naked gold statue lying in its waters. It is the transformed body of one of the missing Seven Lords*, Restimar*. Reepicheep* gives the island its name as a result of this grisly discovery. See also: **Narnia: geography**

"*De Descriptione Temporum*" (1954) C.S. Lewis's inaugural lecture as Professor in the newly formed Chair of Medieval and Renaissance Literature at Cambridge University. It was delivered on 29 November 1954. The lecture reveals his sympathies with an earlier age, even though he was always concerned as a writer to communicate with a modern reader. He recognized that his assumptions and ideas were distasteful to many modern people. Lewis argued that he was in fact a relic of Old Western* Man, a museum piece, if you like; that even if one disagreed with his ideas, one must take account of them as being from a rare (and therefore valuable) specimen of an older world.

"*De Descriptione Temporum*", which has some striking parallels with cultural analyst Francis Schaeffer's essay *Escape From Reason* (1968), argues that the greatest change in the history of the West took place sometime early in the nineteenth century, and ushered in a characteristically modern mentality. For Lewis, Christians and ancient pagans* have more in common with each other than either has with the modern world. The change can be observed in the areas of politics, the arts, religion, and the birth of the machines. The machine had in fact been absorbed into the inner life of modern people as an archetype. Just as older machines are replaced by new and better ones, so too (believes the modern) are ideas, beliefs, and values. This notion that newer is better, the myth of progress, owes much the "the myth of universal evolutionism", which in fact predated Darwin.

D

The theme of this lecture complements his book *The Abolition of Man**, and like that book is illustrated by his science-fiction story, *That Hideous Strength**.

The Deeper Magic A deeper principle than the natural moral order that sustains the world in *The Chronicles of Narnia**. This is a principle resembling the concept of grace (a hidden Christian theme in the stories), which fulfils and perfects the older law (see: **The Deep Magic**). Thus this Deeper Magic allows a willing victim to die in place of a traitor. This is why Aslan* is able to die in Edmund's* place. The Witch Witch* sees the aspect of the Deeper Magic that fulfils the demands of the moral order that is the foundation of Narnia*, but fails to see its dramatic impact, which is to overturn her grip of winter over Narnia and allow Aslan to return to life and continue his rule.

The Deep Magic The moral order by which the world of Narnia* is made and sustained in *The Chronicles of Narnia**. One of its inner laws is that unless the White Witch* is given blood for every treachery committed, all Narnia will fall apart, perishing in fire and water. The Deep Magic has affinities with Old Testament law. See also: **The Deeper Magic**

Deep Realm Part of the lands lying under Narnia*, deeper than the Marches of Underland, but with Bism* below it. See also: **Underland**

demons See: **angels**; *The Screwtape Letters*

Denniston, Arthur and Camilla In *That Hideous Strength**, a young Christian couple who join the company of Elwin Ransom* at St Anne's*. They provide an important contrast with the marriage of Mark* and Jane Studdock*. Arthur is a

83

brilliant sociologist and fellow of Northumberland College at Edgestow* University. He was the chief rival for Mark Studdock's job when he had applied to Bracton College* several years earlier – but wasn't the "right sort of man" for the progressive element at Bracton. Mark and he had originally been friends as undergraduates but had grown apart because of Mark's desire for success and the lure for him of the "inner ring"*. Like Lewis, Arthur and Camilla liked weather of all descriptions. Jane was surprised to discover this when she was invited on a picnic with them on a foggy autumn day. Arthur explained: "That's why Camilla and I got married… We both like Weather. It's a useful taste if one lives in England."

Deplorable Word A secret word that is known only to the great kings in *The Magician's Nephew**. When spoken, it destroys all living things except the speaker of the word. Jadis* utters the word in Charn* during a battle with her sister, creating a frozen enchantment that includes herself. She is awakened when Digory Kirke* strikes the bell he discovers.

Descent into Hell, **Charles Williams** (1937) Writing to Charles Williams* on 9 September 1937, Lewis remarks that *Descent into Hell* is "a thundering good book and a real purgation to read". Williams's publisher, T.S. Eliot, wrote about him on the dust jacket of the Faber Standard Edition of the novel (words he adapted from a BBC* broadcast reproduced in *The Listener*): "He had a kind of extended spiritual sense: he was like a man who can perceive shades of colour, or hear tones, beyond the ordinary range. The theme of all his novels is the struggle between good and evil; and as an interpreter of the mystical experience he was unique in his generation… There are pages… which describe, with a frightful clarity, the deterioration and damnation of a human soul; and pages which describe the triumphant struggle towards salvation."

Lewis included his friend's novel among a list of the top ten books that influenced his thinking and vocational attitude (see: **reading of C.S. Lewis**). It explores Williams's characteristic themes of exhange and substitution, themes that are worked out in the parallel stories of one individual's salvation (Pauline Anstruther's) and another's damnation (the academic historian Lawrence Wentworth's). Lewis identified with the particular temptations that afflict the academic. Williams's novels, poetry, and personality had an enormous impact upon Lewis's thinking and writing (on, for instance, *A Preface to Paradise Lost**, *That Hideous Strength**, and *Till We Have Faces**). Williams's preoccupation with the theological implications of love also, no doubt, partly influenced the choice of subject and writing of *The Four Loves**, an interest Lewis had shown pre-Williams in *The Allegory of Love**.

Further reading
T.S. Eliot, "The Significance of Charles Williams", *The Listener*, 19 December 1946.

Destrier Caspian's* horse, a dumb beast*, in *Prince Caspian**. After bolting during a thunderstorm, it returns to its stables in Miraz's castle*, revealing Caspian's escape.

The devil, devils See: **angels**; *The Screwtape Letters*

Devine, Dick (Lord Feverstone) In *Out of the Silent Planet**, Professor Weston's* fellow conspirator in a plan to kidnap a human sacrifice for the rulers of Malacandra*. The two use a country house near Sterk*, called The Rise, where a rocket ship has been built in Weston's laboratory. By coincidence, Devine had been at school at Wedenshaw with Elwin Ransom*, his victim (where Ransom disliked him as much as anyone he could remember, a dislike that was mutual). He was also at Cambridge University at the same time as Ransom. Ransom had been puzzled at the appointment of this flashy and over-confident man to a fellowship at Leicester College, Cambridge, and further puzzled by his ever-increasing wealth. Devine eventually became "something in the city" and later even an MP, to Ransom's astonishment.

Devine funds Weston's experiments with space travel, and has plans for an ocean-going yacht, expensive women, and a big place on the Riviera with ill-gotten wealth from Malacandra's mineral resources. Behind his self-indulgent life there are genuine abilities, revealed when he saves the spacecraft returning from Mars by his persistence at the controls during its dangerous flight.

More emerges about him when he reappears in *That Hideous Strength** after the war as Lord Feverstone MP, now a fellow of Bracton College* and deeply implicated in the evil plots of the N.I.C.E.* Though apparently likeable with his infectious laugh, his ruthlessness is revealed in his verbally brutal treatment of elderly Canon Jewel in the Committee Meeting, which determined the fate of ancient Bragdon Wood*. Politically, he is totalitarian to the heart, taking, he claimed, the view of a military thinker Carl von Clausewitz, that total war is the most humane in the long run (redefining "humane" in the process). He graphically represents Lewis's theme of the abolition of mankind and of human values (see: ***The Abolition of Man***). To Jane Studdock*, he is "that man with the loud, unnatural laugh and a mouth like a shark, and no manners". There is something shifty about him. Mark Studdock* notices that he never looks a person in the face.

As the stranglehold of the N.I.C.E. tightens, Devine is appointed Emergency Governor at Edgestow*. He enjoys the spectacle of the massacre at the great banquet at Belbury*. After slipping away to Edgestow, he is fittingly engulfed in its destruction.

Dialectica A region charted in the *Mappa Mundi**, in *The Pilgrim's Regress**.

diaries Both Lewis and his brother, Major Warren ("Warnie") Lewis*, kept diaries, though the latter did much more, writing over a million words and filling twenty-three journals (see: ***Brothers and Friends***). Lewis only appears to have kept a significant diary between 1922 and 1927 (see: ***All My Road Before Me***). A significant record of Lewis's early domestic life appears in the unpublished Lewis family papers*.

Dick A spirit, one of the solid, heavenly inhabitants, in *The Great Divorce**. The narrator (Lewis) overhears a conversation between Dick and a wraith of a bishop, visiting the hitherlands of Heaven*. Dick had been a clergyman on earth. Ironically the bishop chides him for entertaining the "narrow-minded" belief in a literal heaven and hell toward the end of his life. When Dick replies, "Wasn't I right?" the bishop is shocked.

Diggle In *The Last Battle**, the spokesman of a company of dwarves* who survive the Last Battle only to be thrown into the stable at Stable Hill*. These dwarves believe in nothing but themselves.

Digory Kirke See: **Kirke, Digory**

Dimble, Dr Cecil In *That Hideous Strength**, a fellow in literature of Northumberland College, at Edgestow* University; a Christian, like C.S. Lewis, who doesn't suffer fools gladly. An elderly man, he has lived in Edgestow for twenty-five years, and is a close friend of Elwin Ransom*. He was Jane Studdock's* tutor during her last years as an undergraduate. In his house there is a constant danger of the conversation taking a literary turn, in which King Arthur and the Matter of Britain might come up, as he has a deep knowledge of Arthurian legend. He is prone to speculate aloud, letting his thoughts take him wherever their logic leads. Cecil Dimble is scrupulously polite, even with those he dislikes, such as Mark Studdock*. Even then, his conscience has troubled him for years about lack of charity toward Jane's husband. He suffers from a habitual self-distrust.

When the N.I.C.E.* requisition their cottage, the Dimbles join Ransom's community at The Manor at St Anne's*. His shrewd mind is a great help to Ransom in interpreting the enemy's moves, and he is also practical, able to search for Merlin* despite knowing better than almost anyone the dangers involved. His fluent knowledge of Old Solar*, the Great Tongue, is especially valuable in communicating with the magician. According to N.I.C.E. intelligence, Dimble poses no threat – they see him as purely an academic in a worthless discipline, and impractical, unknown to anyone except a few scholars in his own subject, a nonentity. In this respect Cecil Dimble parallels the humble hobbit Frodo Baggins in J.R.R. Tolkien's* *The Lord of the Rings*, confounding the wisdom of wicked powers by having a strategic role in the battle of good against evil.

Dimble, "Mother" Margaret ("Margery") The wife of Cecil Dimble*, in *That Hideous Strength*; a humorous, easy-natured, and childless woman, grey-haired and double-chinned.. She likes her husband's pupils of both sexes at Edgestow* University, but has particularly mothered generations of women students. Their homely house consequently is "a kind of noisy salon all the term". Lewis draws her character with affection, creating a figure with affinities to the young Green Lady* of Perelandra*, essentially "a kind of priestess or sybil... grave, formidable and august". She helps Jane Studdock* and introduces her to the community at St Anne's*.

The Discarded Image: An Introduction to Medieval and Renaissance Literature (1964) C.S. Lewis's professional study of medieval allegory* led him to think hard and deeply about the truth of the main medieval picture of reality. This also meant considering the position of various world models in our thinking about truth, knowledge, and reality. He believed our modern picture of reality (with galaxies expanding outwards from the Big Bang, for instance) is a complex imaginative model, as is a medieval picture with celestial hierarchies and a sun that encircles planet Earth.

The Discarded Image arose out of a series of lectures C.S. Lewis gave many times to Oxford* undergraduates on the medieval world image, which provided a background to literature up to the seventeenth century. Like John Milton before him, C.S. Lewis saw that if the medieval world model did not literally portray reality, if it was in a sense fictional, then it could still be used imaginatively. Milton employed it in his great epic *Paradise Lost*, even though he was well aware of the scientific revolution in thought created by Galileo and Copernicus. In the twentieth century, Lewis employed the medieval world model in his science-fiction trilogy* and *The Chronicles of Narnia**. Lewis helps his reader (of all ages) to feel the imaginative power of this model. It has an integrated picture of the heavens*, the earth, and mankind itself, with the human being as a miniature world, a microcosmos.

C.S. Lewis concludes *The Discarded Image* by hoping that no one thinks that he is recommending a return to the medieval model. He has only sought a proper regard for world models, respecting each and making an idol of none. Each age inevitably has its own "taste in universes". Thinking of chronological snobbery*, Lewis added: "We can no longer dismiss the change of Models as a simple progress from error to truth. No Model is a catalogue of ultimate realities, and none is a mere fantasy. Each is a serious attempt to get in all the phenomena known at a given period, and each succeeds in getting in a great many. But also, no less surely, each reflects the prevalent psychology of an age almost as much as it reflects the state of that age's knowledge."

Our world model will eventually change, like others before it. Lewis suggested that the change was more likely to come from a change in the mental temper of a future age than from some dramatic discovery about the physical universe. This change in mentality will shape questions asked of nature*, and thus what is considered evidence in support of a world model. See also: **literary critic, C.S. Lewis as a; imagination**
Further reading
Owen Barfield, *Saving the Appearances: A Study in Idolatry* (1957).

divine love See: *The Four Loves*

D.L.F. In *Prince Caspian**, an abbreviation of "Dear Little Friend", a nickname given to Trumpkin* the dwarf* by Edmund*.

dog-fox A talking dog-fox (male fox) in *The Lion, the Witch and the Wardrobe**, present at a party in the woods in which all the party-goers are turned into stone by the White Witch*.

door in the air In *Prince Caspian**, a portal between Narnia* and this world created by Aslan* to allow the exodus of those Telmarines* who wished to return to the South Sea island from which they came. The children Peter*, Edmund*, Susan*, and Lucy* use the same portal to return to the railway station from which they were called into Narnia.

Doorn The chief among the Lone Islands* in The *Voyage of the "Dawn Treader"**, a group of islands some 400 leagues to the east of Narnia*. These islands had been under Narnian rule since the ninth king of Narnia, Gale*, freed the islanders from a

D

dragon. The town of Narrowhaven* is Doorn's major settlement. Caspian* and the other voyagers are displeased to discover Narrowhaven is now a centre of a slave trade* to Calormen*. After skilfully deposing the Governor, despite inferior forces, Caspian gives Lord Bern* the post.

dragon In *The Voyage of the "Dawn Treader"**, an old and dying dragon is discovered by Eustace Scrubb* on Dragon Island*. (It is thought to be one of the lost Narnian* Lords – Octesian*, for whom the party of voyagers is searching – transformed into the hideous shape.) Upon his death, the unpleasant Eustace himself becomes a dragon, and only Aslan* is able to restore him to his boy nature.

Dragon Island Discovered and named by Caspian* of Narnia* in *The Voyage of the "Dawn Treader"**, it lies to the east of the Lone Islands*. It is named after a sad dragon* who lived and dies there, and who was thought to be the transformed shape of the missing Narnian* Lord, Octesian*. The mountainous island has deep bays rather like Norwegian fjords, ending in steep valleys that often have waterfalls. Cedars and others trees cover what little level land exists. Beside the ill-fated dragon, a few wild goats live there. See also: **Narnia: geography**

Drinian Caspian's* loyal captain of the *"Dawn Treader"** in *The Voyage of the "Dawn Treader"**, and a lord of Narnia*. In *The Silver Chair**, he is featured in the court of his king. He is a trusted friend of Prince Rilian*, and advises him not to pursue his quest* to find the serpent who killed his mother.

dryads Wood nymphs* who live in trees and preside over woods in classical mythology. They live and die with the trees they animate. In *The Chronicles of Narnia** they are sometimes referred to generically as wood people or tree people*. In *The

*Lion, the Witch and the Wardrobe** the winter spell of the White Witch* makes them disappear, and in *Prince Caspian** they are also subdued by the modernising New Narnians* of Miraz*. They are awakened by Aslan*. In *The Last Battle**, many die as their trees are cut down by order of the false Aslan instigated by Shift* the Ape. The term "dryad" in Greek derives from the word for oak tree, *drus*. Sometimes they are called hamadryads or Silvans in the Narnian stories.

Duffers See: **Dufflepuds**

Duffle In *The Horse and His Boy**, a practical and kind red dwarf* who feeds and looks after Shasta* when he first enters Narnia*. He is the brother of Rogin and Bricklethumb*.

Dufflepuds Encountered on the Island of Voices* in *The Voyage of the "Dawn Treader"**, these monopods (one-footed creatures) had been made invisible by a spell. Lucy Pevensie* is persuaded to find the spell in the magician's book to make them visible again. They have a humorous way of talking about the obvious. The name is a combination of their original title, Duffers, and the new name of Monopods*, given them by the voyagers. See also: **dwarves**

dumb beasts Originally, at the very beginning of the creation of Narnia*, all animals were dumb, but Aslan* chose some of them to receive the gift of speech. Smaller talking animals* are noticeably larger in stature than their dumb relations. When Ginger* the Cat is made dumb by Aslan, this is the worst that can happen to a talking beast*. Dumb beasts may be eaten for food, but never talking beasts.

Dumnus A faun* in *Prince Caspian**. With other fauns he dances around Prince Caspian*.

D

dust from Atlantis A box from Atlantis* in *The Magician's Nephew**, given by Mrs Lefay* to Uncle Andrew* to destroy. Instead, he opens it and uses its dust to make the rings* that allow transportation to other worlds.

The Dwarf A wraith on a trip from the Grey Town to the outskirts of heaven* in *The Great Divorce**. Back on earth he had been Frank, husband of Sarah Smith* from Golder's Green. The Dwarf is accompanied by a tall ghost, the "Tragedian", representing the theatrical, posing side of Frank. Sarah fails to persuade the Dwarf to enter heaven, and all that remains is the tall, unreal ghost.

dwarves Three kinds of dwarves live in Narnia*. In Norse mythology there are black and white dwarves, the former associated with evil. In Narnia there are black dwarves* (like Nikabrik*), red dwarves* (such as Duffle*, Rogin, Trumpkin*, and Bricklethumb*), and Dufflepuds* (who were transformed by magic from their earlier form into monopods). Doctor Cornelius*, Caspian's* tutor, is a half-dwarf. The red dwarves have the most talent for happiness, enjoying wild dances, opulent feasts, and brightly coloured garments. In *The Silver Chair**, Trumpkin* is regent to Caspian. In *The Lion, the Witch and the Wardrobe**, the White Witch's* sleigh is driven by a dwarf, reflecting an alliance between her and some of the dwarves, probably black ones.

dying God See: **Balder**

***Dymer* (1926; new edition 1950)** An anti-totalitarian poem that has some similarities with *Spirits in Bondage** (1919), written while Lewis was still an unbeliever in Christianity. It is included in *Narrative Poems**. The hero, Dymer, escapes from a perfect but inhuman city into the soothing countryside. Various adventures overtake him. In contrast to Dymer's idealism*, a revolutionary group rebel against the Perfect City in anarchy, claiming Dymer's name. Fresh in Lewis's mind when he wrote were the bloody events of the Russian Revolution and his native Ulster. He regarded popular political causes as "daemonic".

In *Dymer* the young C.S. Lewis attacks Christianity bitterly, regarding it as a tempting illusion that must be overcome and destroyed in one's life. Christianity is lumped together with all forms of supernaturalism*, including spiritism. By the time Lewis wrote *Dymer*, he had rejected current realist philosophy in favour of idealism*, in a form consistent with his atheism.

Dyson, H.V.D. "Hugo" (1896–1975) A member of the Inklings*, Dyson was seriously wounded at Passchendaele in the First World War, before reading English at Exeter College, Oxford* University. He was scarred both physically and mentally by war, as Lewis observed in a letter: "a burly man, both in mind and body, with the stamp of war on him" (22 November 1931). As an undergraduate, Dyson heard Tolkien* read "The Fall of Gondolin" (part of *The Silmarillion*) to the Essay Club at Exeter College. On a night in 1931, he helped Tolkien to persuade Lewis to take an important step towards his eventual conversion to Christianity. Dyson initially lectured in English at Reading University, near enough to Oxford to keep in touch with fellow Inklings. There he pioneered a Combined Humanities course in 1930. He also encouraged the development of a School of Fine Arts, and was considered a distinctive and outstanding lecturer. Like Charles Williams*, he gave lectures to the Workers' Educational Association. He poured more of himself into teaching than into his writing – he was involved in very few publications. He was, in 1945, elected fellow and tutor in English literature at Merton College, Oxford. He retired in 1963.

Dyson was cool about Tolkien's constant reading of *The Lord of the Rings* to the Inklings. He appears in fictional form in Tolkien's unfinished "The Notion Club Papers" as Arry Loudham. His theatrical nature contributed an important dimension to the Inklings, and he was very important to Lewis in providing emotional support. He featured as an aging writer in John Schlesinger's film *Darling* (1965), starring Julie Christie and Dirk Bogarde. He also gave several lectures for BBC* television on Shakespeare.

E

The Eagle and Child Familiarly known as the Bird and Baby, this central Oxford* public house was frequented by the Inklings* on Tuesdays, and later Mondays, over many years. The pub still exists, adorned with Inklings memorabilia. Although they also visited other pubs in central Oxford, this one has entered Oxford folklore and is a necessary venue for all on the C.S. Lewis trail. In Edmund Crispin's crime novel, *Swan Song* (1947) his detective Professor observes, "There goes C.S. Lewis; it must be Tuesday." Inspector Morse, in Colin Dexter's thrillers, frequently visits the Eagle and Child.

Earthmen Gnome* creatures in *The Silver Chair** who live in the Green Witch's* realm of Underland* – called by them the Shallow Lands*. They originally come from Bism*, deep below the earth's surface. At the time of their slavery to the Witch, they all look sad. Physically, they differ greatly from each other – some have tails, round faces, long, pointed, trunk-like or blobbed noses, beards, or horns on their foreheads.

"The Easley Fragment" This is a fragment, around 5000 words, of what has been dubbed Lewis's "Ulster novel", never completed. Warnie Lewis* included it in the Lewis family papers*. The central character is a young medical doctor, Easley, facing illusion and reality. Apparently poor relatives in Belfast* have misused him and his widowed mother. On the ferry crossing to Belfast he learns from a cheating businessman that the relatives are in fact people of substance, living among "the most substantial people". Later, Easley argues in Belfast with the perverted Reverend Bonner about evil and hell. The plot is likely to have been inspired by Lewis's distressing experiences with Dr John Askins*, who was subject to ravings and delusions as death approached.

Eastern Mountains In *The Pilgrim's Regress* * John* (the pilgrim) is born on the Western edge of the Eastern Mountains, in Puritania*. His visions of an island lead him across the world depicted in the *Mappa Mundi*. When John at last finds the island of his vision, he discovers that it is, in fact, the other side of the Eastern Mountains he knew in childhood.

Eastern Sea (Eastern Ocean) A great ocean washing the shores of all the countries on the east in *The Chronicles of Narnia*. See also: **Narnia: geography**

Edgestow In *That Hideous Strength*, a small Midlands university town more beautiful, in C.S. Lewis's opinion, than either Oxford* or Cambridge. Before the arrival of the N.I.C.E.*, "no maker of cars or sausages or marmalade ha[d] yet come to industrialize the country town". The university itself is tiny, having only four colleges, including Bracton*, and has a fine Norman church. Mark* and Jane Studdock* live in a flat on a sandy hillside suburb above the central and academic part of Edgestow. The Dimbles* also live there. Their typically English country cottage is requisitioned by the N.I.C.E., along with Bracton College property south of the River Wynd, including Bragdon Wood*. The Birmingham road is to the east, while Worcester is found to the west, and Stratford-upon-Avon to the east, not great distances away. Edgestow lies at the heart of ancient Logres (the spiritual and true England), and Merlin* had once worked in what was now Bragdon Wood. The N.I.C.E. engineer a great riot in the town, allowing their institutional police to take control. At this time, and later, very many of its citizens flee as refugees, which saves them from its destruction that purges the evil that the N.I.C.E. have brought.

Edmund, King See: **The Pevensie children**

education C.S. Lewis makes many references to education in his fiction. Experiment House*, for instance, in *The Voyage of the "Dawn Treader"**, embodies his dislike of modern educational methods. In his opinion Mark Studdock*, in *That Hideous Strength**, is characteristic of many of Lewis's contemporary intelligensia – uneducated by classical standards. Judged only by his satire, however, Lewis would seem intensely prejudiced. This is misleading. His powerful essay *The Abolition of Man** suggested that anti-human values were being unwittingly embodied in some typical school textbooks of his time.

Lewis nowhere more clearly put forward his vision of education than in his early essay "Our English Syllabus" in *Rehabilitations and Other Essays**. He confesses: "Human life means to me the life of beings for whom the leisured activities of thought, art, literature, conversation are the end, and the preservation and propagation of life merely the means. That is why education seems to me so important: it actualizes that potentiality for leisure, if you like for amateurishness, which is man's prerogative... Man is the only amateur animal; all the others are professionals... The lion cannot stop hunting, nor the beaver building dams... When God made the beasts dumb He saved the world from infinite boredom..."

Efreets Terrifying evil spirits summoned to the Stone Table* for Aslan's* execution in *The Lion, the Witch and the Wardrobe**. The word is a variant of *afreet*, a demon in Islamic stories.

eldila Lewis's angel*-like beings, or Archons (rulers or lords), who serve the Old One through Maleldil the Young* in Lewis's science-fiction trilogy*. Elwin Ransom* first comes across them on Malacandra* in *Out of the Silent Planet*. They are barely discernable to human eyes, though their voices are audible. Ransom learns from a sorn* that the eldila (singular, eldil) were placed on Malacandra from its creation to rule it. The overall ruler of the eldila on a planet is called the Oyarsa, and has some similarity to classical gods associated with Mars, Venus, Mercury, and other planets. The Oyarsa also steer their planets through Deep Heaven. Earth (or Thulcandra*, the Silent Planet) is atypical in having a Dark Oyarsa who has turned away from Maleldil. Earth is consequently in quarantine from the rest of the universe. See also: **The planets**

Emeth the Calormene *Emeth* is Hebrew for "truth", and Emeth in *The Last Battle** symbolizes*, for C.S. Lewis, what is best in human knowledge unenlightened by Christ. He is a Calormene* who attains to the New Narnia* because he is able to acknowledge Aslan* when the moment of truth arises. Aravis*, whose story is more fully told, is a similar virtuous pagan in *The Horse and His Boy**. Orual* is a somewhat similar figure in *Till We Have Faces**. See: **paganism and mysticism in Lewis**

Emperor-over-sea In *The Chronicles of Narnia**, a metaphorical term for the father of Aslan*, representing God* the Father of the biblical Trinity. Aslan's Country* lies over the Eastern Ocean*, on the borderland of all created worlds, including this world.

Endicott, Lizzie Lizzie Endicott was C.S. Lewis's nurse, who told him stories from her roots in County Down, stories of Irish lore about leprechauns and their crocks of buried gold; the faerie folk; and Cuchulain, the champion of Ulster. One day, when drying the young child and his older brother, Warren*, she threatened to spank their "pigieboties" or "piggiebottoms" because of their idling. This greatly amused the boys, who decided that Warren was the "Archpiggiebotham" and Lewis the "Smallpiggiebotham". "APB" and "SPB" they remained to each other for the rest of their lives. See also: ***Surprised by Joy***

English Literature in the Sixteenth Century, Excluding Drama

(1954) The volume of *The Oxford History of English Literature* written by C.S. Lewis. The book is based upon embryonic lectures he gave at Cambridge University in 1944. As well as providing a thorough history of the period, the book is notable for its introduction, "New Learning and New Ignorance", which adds to the themes laid out in *The Discarded Image** and his inaugural lecture to the Chair of Medieval and Renaissance Literature at Cambridge, "*De Descriptione Temporum*"*. He points out, for example, a transformation in the concept of magic that happened with the influence of a new empiricism. This new empiricism eventually led to the rise of modern science.

Lewis's introduction is of great interest to theologians, philosophers, and historians of ideas, as well as literary students. He points out that, in this period, "a Protestant may be Thomistic, a humanist may be a Papist, a scientist may be a magician, a sceptic may be an astrologer". He regards the idea of historical periods as a mischievous conception but a methodological necessity, and points out the grave dangers of historicism*.

Writing this volume allowed him to expound one of his favourite authors, Edmund Spenser, though space severely restricted him. Where he quotes from neo-Latin authors, he translates into sixteenth-century English, not simply "for the fun of it" but to guard against false impressions created by reading modern attitudes into the past.

C.S. Lewis concludes that the period "illustrates well enough the usual complex, unpatterned historical process; in which, while men often throw away irreplaceable wealth, they not infrequently escape what seemed inevitable dangers, not knowing that they have done either nor how they did it." See also: **literary critic, C.S. Lewis as a**

enjoyment and contemplation A technical distinction key to Lewis's thinking that he derived from the philosophy of Samuel Alexander*. He expounds it briefly in *Surprised by Joy** to explain a basic mistake he made in understanding the processes of desire, or joy*. He confessed that all his introspection had been in vain. He was trying to do the impossible, which was to "contemplate" what he was in fact "enjoying".

A passage from Lewis's book *The Personal Heresy** (written with E.M.W. Tillyard) helps in explaining the distinction. He is speaking of focusing upon a poem rather than upon its author:

> Let it be granted that I do approach the poet; at least I do it by sharing his consciousness, not by studying it. I look with his eyes, not at him... To see things as the poet sees them I must share his consciousness and not attend to it; I must look where he looks and not turn round to face him; I must make of him not a spectacle but a pair of spectacles: in fine, as Professor Alexander would say, I must enjoy him and not contemplate him.

Enlightenment, Mr An allegorical* figure in *The Pilgrim's Regress**, representing the pilgrim John's* encounter with nineteenth-century rationalism. The Enlightenment itself emerged in eighteenth-century France, its agenda being to institutionalize a belief in human reason's ability to understand all things. See: **naturalism and supernaturalism**

Erimon A lord of Caspian* IX, in *Prince Caspian**, executed by the usurping Uncle Miraz* on a trumped-up charge of treason.

Erlian The father of King Tirian*, in *The Last Battle**, with whom he is reunited in Aslan's Country*, in the real Narnia*.

eros (erotic love) See: *The Four Loves*

***Essays Presented to Charles Williams* (1947)** This posthumous tribute brings together essays by a number of Charles Williams's* friends, mainly from the Inklings*. In the first chapter, Dorothy L. Sayers* (the only non-Inkling) contributes "… And Telling You a Story", recounting her discovery of the poet Dante through Williams's *The Figure of Beatrice*. The next chapter is J.R.R. Tolkien's* seminal paper "On Fairy Stories", first delivered at St Andrews University in 1939. Equally important is Lewis's "On Stories", and Owen Barfield* follows it with a lucid account of the importance of metaphor, "Poetic Diction and Legal Fiction". Gervase Mathew* adds "Marriage and Amour Courtois in Late Fourteenth-Century England", and Warnie Lewis* writes about "The Galleys of France" from his rich knowledge of French history.

Lewis's preface superbly assesses Williams and speaks about his friendship with him, describing him as a "romantic theologian"; that is, someone who considers the theological implications of romanticism*. See: **The Inklings**; **theology of romance**

Essur A kingdom lying to the west of Phars*, in the novel *Till We Have Faces**, and separated from it by a high mountain range. Great forests and rushing rivers, and its richness in game, distinguish the country. It is also notable for a hot spring close to its capital. In recent times, the worship of Istra* (of which the name "Psyche" is the Greek form) had been introduced. The legends of Istra follow closely the events in the life of Princess Psyche* of Glome*. Apuleius's account of the myth of Cupid and Psyche* is virtually identical to that of the Istra legends.

Ettins Foolish, fierce, and savage stone giants who, in *The Silver Chair**, live in the rocks on Ettinsmoor. *Eten* is an old word for "giant". "Eotenas" are mentioned in the Early English poem *Beowulf.*

Ettinsmoor A desolate region of moorland, north of Narnia* and the River Shribble*, in *The Silver Chair**. Beyond Ettinsmoor lies the region of giants*. Years before the events recounted in the story, Caspian* X had fought the giants and forced them to pay tribute. See also: **Narnia: geography**

evacuees The children at the centre of events in *The Lion, the Witch and the Wardrobe** are evacuees from a wartime city who are billeted with Professor Digory Kirke*. During the Second World War Lewis, his brother, Mrs Janie Moore*, and Maureen Moore lodged evacuees at different times in their Oxford* home, The Kilns*. Two of them – Patricia Boshell (later Heidelberger) and Marie Bosc – arrived in September 1940. Patricia Boshell remembered, "My first impression of C.S. Lewis was that of a shabbily clad, rather portly gentleman, whom I took to be the gardener, and told him so. He roared – boomed! – with laughter. And then with a twinkle in his eye, he said, 'Welcome, girls.'" Later in the war June Flewett (later Freud) moved to The Kilns to help Mrs Moore and eventually stayed nearly two years. She was just sixteen when she arrived, with no opinion, as she put it, of her intellectual ability. "Lewis," she recalls, "was the first person who made me believe that I was an intelligent human being and the whole time I was there he built up my confidence in myself and in my ability to think and understand." Lewis began a draft of what later became *The Lion, the Witch and the Wardrobe* after the arrival of the evacuees, though he didn't pick up the story again until after the war.
   Further reading
   Stephen Schofield (ed.), *In Search of C.S. Lewis* (1983).

Eve in Narnia See: **Adam and Eve in Narnia**

***The Everlasting Man*, G.K. Chesterton (1925)** G.K. Chesterton* was a significant influence upon Lewis, and Lewis listed Chesterton's *The Everlasting Man* as one of ten books that particularly shaped his thought and vocational attitude (see: **reading of C.S. Lewis**).

Like Lewis in many of his writings, Chesterton was concerned to undeceive modern people, restoring a true view of things (see: **undeception and recognition**). Lewis found this process worked well in fantasy*. In *The Everlasting Man*, Chesterton sought such a restoration through the medium of prose argument that soon transforms into vision.

The Everlasting Man is an attempt to stand outside the human race and thus to see humans as the strange beings we really are, and to step outside Christianity and see for the first time what Chesterton believed to be its uniqueness among the religions of the world. Lewis and Tolkien* had a similar aim to Chesterton in exploring paganism*, which was to allow their readers to step outside the modern world and thus to see it in its true light.

Chesterton explains his purpose: "I desire to help the reader to see Christendom from the outside in the sense of seeing it as a whole against the background of other historic things; just as I desire him to see humanity as a whole against the background of natural things. And I say that in both cases when seen thus, they stand out from their background like supernatural things." With this purpose in mind he divides his book into two parts. The first part concerns "the main adventure of the human race in so far as it remained heathen; and the second [is] a summary of the real difference that was made by it becoming Christian".

The first part, therefore, is really a preparation for the second. It shows the Christian faith not as one religion among many but as the religion without rival. It uniquely binds into one both philosophy (or thought) and mythology (or poetry), by giving us a God who is the central presence in the strangest story in the world. These ideas of Chesterton in *The Everlasting Man* lay behind the arguments used by Tolkien and Dyson* to persuade Lewis to adopt the Christian faith – they convinced him that myth had become fact in the Gospel. See also: **myth became fact**

Ewart, Sir William Quartus and Lady Cousins of Lewis's mother, Flora, who lived near Little Lea* in Glenmachan (called "Mountbracken" in *Surprised by Joy* *). Sir William was a Belfast* linen manufacturer. The young C.S. Lewis greatly admired the beauty and grace of one of their daughters, Grundeda. She and her sisters, Hope and Kelsie, would often visit Little Lea and play with the Lewis brothers. They also gave tennis parties at Glenmachan attended by Lewis and Warnie*.

Experiment House The experimental school attended by Eustace Scrubb* and Jill Pole* in *The Silver Chair* *. It partly presents a satire on modern educational methods and is partly based on grim memories of C.S. Lewis's own school experiences. See also: **education**

An Experiment in Criticism **(1961)** Though literary criticism*, this book should be read by all who take reading seriously. As C.S. Lewis's mature reflections on fiction, story, and myth*, it helps the reader to understand what he was trying to do in his own fiction and poetry. He is also concerned with the function of the imagination*.

Lewis argues that literature exists for the enjoyment* of readers and books therefore should be judged by the kind of reading that they evoke. Instead of judging whether a book is good or bad, it is better to reverse the process and consider good and bad readers. When you have an idea of what a good reader is, you then can judge a book by the way in which it is read. A good book cannot be read in the same way as a bad one.

Good reading has something in common with love, moral action, and the growth of knowledge. Like all these, it involves a surrender, in this case by the reader to the work being read. Good readers are concerned less with altering their opinion than in entering fully into the opinions and worlds of others.

"The good reader," argues C.S. Lewis, "reads every work seriously in the sense that he reads it whole-heartedly, makes himself as receptive as he can." The poet Shelley had said: "What is love? Ask him who lives, what is life; ask him who adores, what is God?" C.S. Lewis seems to add, "Ask him who is a reader, what is literature?"

Lewis presents the evidence of a good reader, himself, in *An Experiment in Criticism*. He concludes by talking about the specific good or value of literature in terms of its content or meaning*. (He had previously discussed literary qualities, including narrative ones.) This value or good is that

> it admits us to experiences other than our own... Those
> of us who have been true readers all our life seldom fully
> realize the enormous extension of our being which we
> owe to authors... In reading great literature I become a
> thousand men and yet remain myself. Like the night sky
> in the Greek poem, I see with a myriad eyes, but it is still
> I who see. Here, as in worship, in love, in moral action,
> and in knowing, I transcend myself; and am never more
> myself than when I do.

See also: **literary critic, C.S. Lewis as a**

F

fact See: **myth became fact**

fantasy See: **imagination**

Farrer, Austin (1904–1968) A distinguished theologian and close friend of C.S. Lewis. He was Chaplin and Fellow of Trinity College, and Warden of Keble College, Oxford* University, and considered to be one of the most brilliant people at Oxford in his day.
> **Further reading**
> Philip Curtis, *A Hawk Among Sparrows: A Biography of Austin Farrer* (1985).

Farrer, Katherine (1911–1972) Wife of Austin Farrer*, writer, and friend of C.S. Lewis, and particularly of Joy Davidman Lewis*.

Farsight The talking eagle in *The Last Battle**, who reports the downfall of Narnia* to King Tirian*.

fauns Borrowed by C.S. Lewis from classical mythology, where they are rural semi-deities who are human from the waist up, and have the horns, legs, and tail of a goat. They play wild music on reed pipes, inducing a sleepy, trancelike state. They are more graceful than dwarves*, but roughly their height. The most famous faun in *The Chronicles of Narnia** is Mr Tumnus*. The first published Narnia* story, *The Lion, the Witch and the Wardrobe**, originated from a mental picture of a faun carrying parcels and an umbrella through a snowy wood.

Featherstone, Anne A fellow pupil of Lucy Pevensie* in *The Voyage of the "Dawn Treader"**. Jealous of Lucy's friendship with Marjorie Preston*, she manipulates Marjorie into pretending that Lucy is not her friend. Lucy magically overhears the conversation, revealing the pitfalls of eavesdropping.

Felimath One of the Lone Islands*, inhabited by sheep, in *The Voyage of the "Dawn Treader"**. It looks like a low green hill in the ocean. It may be based on Lewis's childhood memory of Rathlin Island, off the holiday resort of Ballycastle, County Antrim. See also: **The Lone Islands**

Felinda A city of the long-dead world of Charn*, in *The Magician's Nephew**. It is possible that the name evokes "cruel beauty" (*fel*, from Middle English, "cruel", and *linda*, from Spanish, "beautiful"), much like Jadis* herself.

Fenris Ulf See: **Maugrim**

fire-berry A berry that looks like a live coal, in *The Voyage of the "Dawn Treader"**, brought from the valleys of the sun to renew Ramandu* by a bird of morning*. The way the fire-berry is laid in his mouth is reminiscent of the coal of fire laid on Isaiah's lips by the seraphim after his vision of God* in the Temple (The Bible*, Isaiah 6).

fire-flowers These are said to grow in the mountains of the sun, in *The Voyage of the "Dawn Treader"**. They provide the cordial contained in Lucy's* flask of healing* (given to her by Father Christmas* in *The Lion, the Witch and the Wardrobe**).

five black dwarves A group of revolutionary dwarves in *Prince Caspian**, opposed to King Miraz*, who live in a cave together. They are allied to Caspian* against the tyrant rather than working to restore the Old Narnia*. Indeed, under the instigation of Nikabrik*, they are willing to call on the help of evil hags and werewolves*. See also: **dwarves**

flask of healing Lucy's* gift from Father Christmas* in *The Lion, the Witch and the Wardrobe*. It is a healing cordial in a beautiful small diamond flask.

Fledge See: **Strawberry**

Fords of Beruna See: **Beruna, Fords of**

***The Four Loves* (1960)** The four loves of this title of a book by C.S. Lewis are set out as affection, friendship, eros, and charity (agape: divine love, or gift love). This anatomy of love was written by Lewis during his short but happy marriage to Joy Davidman Lewis*. He shows how each love is able to merge into another, or even become another. It is vital however not to lose sight of the real differences that give each love its valid character.

He argues that "we must join neither the idolaters nor the 'debunkers' of human love… Our loves do not make their claim to divinity until the claim becomes plausible. It does not become plausible until there is in them a real resemblance to God, to Love Himself."

Affection is the humblest and most widespread of the four loves. Most of whatever tangible and consistent happiness we find in our lives can be explained by affection. It is not a particularly appreciative love. This very lack of discrimination gives it the potential to broaden the mind, and to create a feeling for other people of all shapes and sizes. Lewis approved of a comment made by someone: "Dogs and cats should always be brought up together. It broadens their minds so." Affection seeps through the whole texture of our lives. It is the medium of the operation of the other loves.

Lewis constantly explored the virtues and dangers of affection in his fiction. In *The Great Divorce**, for example, the ghost of a mother still desires to possess her son after death. In the novel *Till We Have Faces**, the deep affection Orual* feels for her sister Psyche* turns into a destructive jealousy that she cannot distinguish from love.

Friendship is the least instinctive, biological, and necessary of our loves. Today it is hardly considered a love, and Lewis is unusual among contemporary Christian thinkers in devoting so much of his attention to this theme. Lewis points out that the ancients put the highest value upon this love, as in the friendship between David and Jonathan in the Bible*. The ideal climate for friendship is when a few people are absorbed in some common, and not necessary, interest. Lovers are usually imagined face to face; friends are best imagined side by side, their eyes ahead on their common interest. Friendship, as the least biological of the loves, refutes sexual explanations for its existence. It is also sharply different from membership of an inner ring*.

Friendship was deeply important to C.S. Lewis throughout his life. Arthur Greeves* was a lifelong friend, as was Owen Barfield*. Friendship formed the basis of the association of the Inklings*, core figures in which included J.R.R. Tolkien* and Charles Williams*. Lewis's brother, Warnie (W.H. Lewis*), was also his friend from childhood, and in Joy Davidman Lewis* he found a friend as well as a wife. He had other female friendships, too, including Sister Penelope* and Jane McNeill*. Friendship, reckoned Lewis, made good people better and bad people worse. Sharing a disinterested point of view was not itself good.

Eros is the kind of love that lovers are within or "in" – the state of being in love. It is different from mere physical, sexual desire in that eros primarily wants the beloved, not sex as an end in itself. In eros love, a person is taken out of the self, and thus is enlarged as a person. Eros would value the beloved above happiness and pleasure, and would wish to retain the beloved even if the result was unhappiness. Lewis characteristically felt that were we not human beings, we should find eros hard to imagine. As it is, we find it difficult to explain.

Lewis's friend Charles Williams explored eros, and in his thought, fiction, and poetry, developed a theology of romantic love. This deeply influenced Lewis, and eros is an important theme in *That Hideous Strength** (in the marriage of Jane* and Mark Studdock*) and in *Till We Have Faces** (in Psyche's* love for the god of the mountain, the Westwind*). It was to have been a theme of the unfinished novel *After Ten Years**.

Charity, or divine love, the fourth love, transcends all earthly loves in being a gift-love. All human loves, believed Lewis, are by nature (even unfallen nature) need-loves. If we are in fact created beings, we, by necessity, have to turn to God for our fulfilment and meaning. Lewis saw this pattern repeated throughout creation, in our dependence as human beings on other people and upon nature*. Our human loves, he cautioned, are potential rivals to the love of God, and can only take their proper place if our first allegience is to him. All of God's love for us and for his creation is gift-love, Lewis argued, as he has no need of the universe and its inhabitants for his existence and personal fulfilment.

As with several other of his books of popular Christian theology, Lewis concludes by looking to heaven* as the ultimate context of human life. The divine likeness in all our human loves (affection, friendship, and eros) is their heavenly, and thus permanent, element. Only what is heaven-like can enter heaven; all else, when shaken, will fall. Thus any love for someone or something that is allowed to be a proper love has a heavenly element and is, in fact, also a love for God. Our own loves, like our moral choices, judge us. When those that enter heaven see God, they will find that they know him already. See also: ***The Allegory of Love***.

four signs See: **signs, four**

The Fox Lysias, the Greek slave in *Till We Have Faces** engaged by King Trom* to teach his daughters. "The Fox" is one of his nicknames (others include "word-weaver" and "Greekling"). He has sons and a daughter in far-off Greece. The Fox is short, thick-set, and very bright-eyed, always full of great intellectual curiosity. His nickname derives from the fact that when he arrived in Glome*, whatever of his hair and beard was not grey was reddish. The Fox becomes Queen Orual's closest adviser, and teaches her to think like a Greek, as well as to read and write the language. She never however allows this to make her lose touch with the common people of Glome, and their worship of Ungit*.

The Fox follows the philosophy of the Stoics, and particularly Zeno and other Greek philosophers of the third century BC. He dismisses the stories of the gods as "only lies of poets… Not in accordance with nature." The world, The Fox believes, can be understood by the principles of right reason. He opposes the supernaturalism* that filled the air of Glome.

Fox, Adam (1883–1977) An early member of the Inklings*, a fellow of Magdalen College, Oxford* University, and Dean of Divinity there from 1929. In 1938 he was elected Professor of Poetry at Oxford. He became Canon of Westminster Abbey in 1942. Among his publications were *Plato for Pleasure* (1945), *Meet the Greek Testament* (1952), and *Dean Inge* (1960).

Frank, King See: **Frank the Cabby**

Frank the Cabby A Victorian London cab driver in Lewis's *The Magician's Nephew**. The character perhaps owes something to Diamond's father in *At the Back of the North Wind*, by George MacDonald*. Frank is accidently drawn into Narnia* as it is being created, and, with his cockney wife Helen, is the first to rule there. All humans in Narnia or its surrounding countries are descended either from Frank and Helen or from the Telmarines* who stumble into its world. Aslan* commanded that Narnia be ruled by Sons of Adam* and Daughters of Eve*. The name Frank alludes to openness and lack of disguise. See also: **Narnia: history**

friendship See: *The Four Loves*

friendship of J.R.R. Tolkien and C.S. Lewis, the The friendship of C.S. Lewis and J.R.R. Tolkien* was of such importance to the two men that it is likely that without their influence upon each other, there would be no *The Chronicles of Narnia** or *The Lord of the Rings*. Though they did not meet until 1926, after beginning to teach at Oxford* University, their earlier lives had many affinities.

Both had childhoods strikingly dominated by their imaginations*. Typically, Lewis in Belfast* created Boxen* and "Animal-land" while Tolkien in the English Midlands invented languages, and fell under the spell of existing languages like Welsh and, later, Gothic. Significantly, both lost their mothers early, Lewis at the age of nine, Tolkien just into his teens. Both started writing seriously during the First World War, in which Lewis was wounded and Tolkien lost two of his closest friends. Tolkien was several years older than Lewis, and had already taught in Leeds University before returning to Oxford to be a professor and meeting Lewis in 1926. Lewis later acknowledged that, with Hugo Dyson*, Tolkien had a great deal to do with Lewis's process of conversion to Christianity (see: **myth became fact**). Lewis's eventual acceptance of Christian faith deepened the friendship; a friendship only later eclipsed by Lewis's acquaintance with Charles Williams*, and what Tolkien called Lewis's "strange marriage" to Joy Davidman Lewis*. Part of Tolkien's reaction to the marriage was that Davidman was a divorcee, which troubled him because of his commitment to Roman Catholic teaching.

Tolkien was a central figure from the beginning in the Inklings*, the literary group of friends held together by Lewis's zest and enthusiasm. Tolkien's influence on Lewis, and the importance of Lewis to Tolkien, is a great and rich subject. Their association is comparable in importance to that of William Wordsworth and Samuel Taylor Coleridge.

Further reading
Colin Duriez, *Tolkien and C.S. Lewis: The Gift of Friendship* (2003); UK edition entitled *J.R.R. Tolkien and C.S. Lewis: The Story of Their Friendship* (2003).

G

Gale The ninth king of Narnia* in *The Chronicles of Narnia**, in descent from King Frank*. He delivers the population of the Lone Islands* of the Eastern Ocean* from a dragon. In gratitude they give the islands over to Narnian sovereignty. See also: **Narnia: history**

Galma An island off the coast of Narnia* in *The Voyage of the "Dawn Treader"**, about a day's sailing north-east of Cair Paravel*. King Caspian* X of Narnia stops here on his great journey across the Eastern Ocean*. Galma's governing duke marks the occasion with a great tournament.

Giant Allegorical* figure in *The Pilgrim's Regress** signifying the Spirit of the Age* who captures John*.

giants In *The Lion, the Witch and the Wardrobe**, the narrator mentions that giants of any sort are now extremely rare in England. In Narnia* there are many, usually on the side of good or bad. Giants particularly feature in *The Silver Chair**, with the visit of Eustace Scrubb*, Jill Pole* and Puddleglum* to Harfang*. Not all giants are stupid: in ancient times some had constructed an impressive bridge, and Harfang itself had been built by giants. Named giants include Pire*; Rumblebuffin*, with his honest, ugly face; and Wimbleweather*. The White Witch* has some giant blood in her. See also: **Ettins**

gifts of Father Christmas In *The Lion, the Witch and the Wardrobe** Father Christmas arrives when the White Witch's*

spell of perpetual winter weakens and Christmas comes. He gives presents rich in symbolism* to three of the four Pevensie children*, which they use in adventures, to fight, to warn, or for healing. Peter* is given a shield and sword, Susan* is presented with a bow and arrows and a small ivory horn, and Lucy* receives a little bottle of healing cordial and a small dagger. Edmund* misses out on a gift, as he has gone to the White Witch in betrayal of his brother and sisters. See also: **Christmas, Father**

Ginger the Cat An evil and clever cat who joins forces with the perverse Shift*, a talking ape, in *The Last Battle**. After meeting Aslan* face to face he loses the ability to speak. Near the end of his life, Lewis had a ginger tomcat, which he described as "a great Don Juan and a mighty hunter before the Lord".

Girbius A faun* in *Prince Caspian**.

Glamaria A region in the deep south of the world charted on the *Mappa Mundi** in *The Pilgrim's Regress**. The city of Magopolis is to be found in it.

Glasswater Creek A coastal inlet in *Prince Caspian**, that leads in the direction of the hill of the Stone Table*. (Note: C.S. Lewis is not using creek in the US, Australian, or New Zealand sense.)

Glenmachan House Home of C.S. Lewis's mother's cousin, Lady Ewart, and Sir William Quartus Ewart*, described in *Surprised by Joy**.

Glenstorm A centaur* in *Prince Caspian** who lives in a mountain glen. He is a particularly noble creature with glossy chestnut flanks and a golden red beard, as befits a prophet and stargazer.

G

Glimfeather A talking owl in *The Silver Chair** who is as big as a dwarf*. In the service of the now elderly King Caspian* X, he takes under his wing Jill Pole* and Eustace Scrubb*. Glimfeather aids them in their endeavour to find lost Prince Rilian* by carrying them one by one to a Parliament of Owls* and then, with another owl, to Marsh-wiggle* country to the north of Narnia*.

Glome Glome is a kingdom bordering on Phars* and Caphad*, described in C.S. Lewis's novel *Till We Have Faces**. The capital, also called Glome, is situated well back and west of the River Shennit, and a day's journey north-west of the border town of Ringal. The Royal Palace stands on a hillside above the city. The older part of the building is made of wood and the rest of painted brick. On the second floor is a small five-sided room sometimes used as a prison. Near the city lie stretches of mud, reeds, and plenty of wildfowl on each side of the River Shennit, which tends to flood during heavy rain.

About a mile beyond a ford that served the city is the temple of Ungit*, deity of Glome, whom the far-off Greeks called Aphrodite. Four great stones, twice the height of a man, are erected there in an egg-shaped ring. Within the ring, and in the brick and thatched temple, stands a shapeless stone, representing Ungit. She is considered to be the mother and sometimes wife of the Westwind*, god of the mountain, who dwells on the Grey Mountains. The foothills of these lie further north-east of the city, past the temple. Here Psyche* (or Istra*) is left as a sacrifice to the god. Psyche is the half-sister of Orual*, who becomes Queen of Glome.

The country's cattle and its silver mines play a leading role in its economy. See also: **sub-creation; Essur**

Glozelle In *Prince Caspian**, one of the lords of the usurper, Miraz*, who plans the tyrant's defeat by getting him to accept Peter Pevensie's* challenge to a duel.

Glubose In *The Screwtape Letters**, the tempter assigned to the crabbed mother of the patient looked after by the inexperienced Wormwood*. Wormwood's uncle, Screwtape*, urges him to liaise with Glubose to aggravate all the characteristics the patient dislikes in his mother.

gnomes The inhabitants of Underland* and Bism* in *The Silver Chair**. They are short, fat, white-faced, goblin-like creatures, but with no malice toward "overlanders", as they call those who live above the world's crust.

God C.S. Lewis wrote in his book *Miracles**: "There comes a moment when the children who have been playing at burglars hush suddenly: was that a real footstep in the hall? There comes a moment when people who have been dabbling in religion ('Man's search for God'!) suddenly draw back. Suppose we really found Him? We never meant it to come to that! Worse still, supposing He had found us?" (chapter 11.)

Throughout his life C.S. Lewis loved particular things, distinctiveness in people and places, books, and conversations. This was an affinity he shared with his mentor, George MacDonald*. In *Miracles**, which is key for understanding Lewis's view of God, he makes many connections between the deep reality of particular things and what he calls the underlying factuality of God.

Lewis observes that it is one thing to speak about beauty, truth, or goodness, and about God as a great force of some kind. People will listen in a friendly manner. But it is quite another matter if you talk about a God who commands, acts, and who has definite ideas and a pointed character.

Many say, Lewis points out, that God is beyond personality, and mean by this that God is impersonal, less than a person. If you want that kind of God, he suggests, there are many religions to choose from. Christians, on the other hand, find

God beyond personality because he is more than a person. It took C.S. Lewis many years of belief that there is no God before he finally came to believe that God was personal and reluctantly abandoned his atheism.

Lewis felt that people often hide from the idea of a definite, personal God by calling it crude or primitive. In fact, they reject the idea very often because the thought of a God who does things and makes demands is distasteful. Lewis became convinced that far from being impersonal, God is far more personal than people can imagine.

People realize God's concreteness and reality best, Lewis decided, not by merely thinking about him but by obeying and worshipping him. The prime purpose of life, he came to believe, is to "lose" ourselves and to enter the divine life. He said that it is the easy way out (for there is no cost) to think of God as a formless life-force surging through people, as Lewis was tempted to do when he eventually contemplated the possibility that God existed after all.

For Lewis, God is fact, rather than the result of a rational argument. To this fact of God, he believed, people bring to bear views of life and the world that they already hold. They interpret this divine fact, or even explain him away. Lewis is not afraid to call God a fact that is given to people, a definitive thing. Lewis felt that if people fully understood what God is, they should see that there is no question whether he is. In Lewis's vivid phrase, he is the "fountain" of facthood. To some people he is discoverable everywhere, to some nowhere.

Lewis felt that he had made a basic mistake when trying to imagine God as unchangeable, invisible, infinite, and eternal. People, he decided, are prone, as he had been, to miss God's overwhelming life, energy, joy*, and concreteness.

Lewis's view of God as the utterly concrete thing, the basic fact, was part and parcel of the supernaturalism* that marks all his writings after he abandoned atheism. In an age of increasing secularization, Lewis stands out in holding to the reality of the unseen world. For many people in the modern world, he has refreshed and renewed the reality of God.

Soon after his conversion to theism Lewis wrote about his progress, and later gave a fuller account in *Surprised by Joy**. He claimed that he was an "empirical theist". He meant that he had come to theism as a result of uncomfortable facts, not merely by reasoning in a theological or philosophical manner (though he did plenty of that). Lewis always stressed the danger that our theoretical reasoning – which has to be abstract – can easily draw us from the particularity of the world. To him, God is present to us first of all in given things, facts that resist being grasped fully in abstractions. Often, Lewis felt, picture language and stories came closer to grasping the tangible nature of reality.

The pre-Christian Lewis felt the concreteness of God first of all through stories and myths* – but his reason demanded that God's existence must be perceived in literal facts and events. This prepared him for finding God through the literal facts of Christ's incarnation, life, death, and resurrection. In other words, he became convinced these events were not merely a story, though they were like many good stories that he now saw God had been pleased to give to the human race. Such merely "good stories", felt Lewis, were real though unfocused shafts of divine light and truth. One such "good story" he fashioned himself, *Till We Have Faces**, is based upon an ancient myth.

Lewis believed that God has done three basic things to reveal himself to mankind. The first was to install within people a conscience. The second was to send what he dubbed "good dreams". By these he meant "those queer stories scattered all through the heathen religions about a god who dies and comes to life again and, by his death, has somehow given new life to men". The third was to give the scriptures to the Jewish people, followed by the incarnation of Christ and the writings of the New Testament. These three acts of God were closely related in Lewis's mind. For example, he believed that the Genesis creation story might possibly have been derived from earlier pagan* myths, although he believed that the biblical retelling was the one chosen by God, the "vehicle of the earliest sacred truth". For him, the creation account was not less true than history as we know it, but more so: its symbols (see: **symbolism**) portray the essence, the meaning*, of the historical event. This gives a three-dimensional rather than a two-dimensional picture of creation.

God as revealer was tied up for Lewis with people's innate sense of the fittingness of things. Fundamental to Lewis was the idea that we are meant to be moral, rational creatures, but that rationality is hard work – a lifetime's training of our thinking, emotions, imagination*, and behaviour. We have a sense of order that needs cultivating with loving care. For C.S. Lewis, the greatest objective fact people have to attend to is God himself. Like life, literature, those we love, our needy neighbour, and other aspects of reality, Lewis believed that God, as the source of reality, makes right and proper demands upon our attention. These aspects of reality cannot, however, be his rivals, no matter the strength of their demands.

It was vital for C.S. Lewis that belief in God does not undermine people's whole system of thinking, which leads them to regard certain things as true, as happens, he argued, with naturalism*. He states that a system that has no place or foundation for thought cannot itself be true. Such a system undermines the validity of the very process of thinking by which it comes to the conclusion that it is true.

Like George MacDonald, Lewis saw God essentially as "the glad creator" and hence regarded the incarnation as the central miracle, springing from God's involvement with his creation. Christian faith, beginning as it does with belief in concrete historical events, endorses and delights in the reality and "thereness" of the universe. By holding to the body's resurrection, Christianity "teaches that Heaven is not merely a state of the spirit but a state of the body as well: and therefore a state of Nature as a whole... The glad creator... has become Himself incarnate" (*Miracles*, chapter 16).

For many readers of C.S. Lewis, he is most memorable for creating fresh images of God, enabling them to see again the meaning of divine reality. These images include Aslan* (pre-eminently), the Emperor-over-sea*, Maleldil*, the Old One, the Landlord*, and even the pagan* insights of the character of the Westwind*, the god of the mountain in *Till We Have Faces*. Lewis's delight in God's creation was at the heart of his fantasy writing (see **imagination**), and his theology of romance*. See also: **theology, C.S. Lewis and; myth; nature; joy**.

God in the Dock See: ***Undeceptions: Essays on Theology and Ethics***

god of the Grey Mountains In *Till We Have Faces**, a god, in the mythology of the land of Glome*, who dwells in the Grey Mountains. He is also refered to as the Shadowbrute and the Westwind. As son of the goddess Ungit*, he is a debased image of Cupid, who appears in the classical myth of Cupid and Psyche*. The people of Glome sacrifice Princess Psyche to the god in appeasement for various calamities, and he takes her as his bride, placing her in his palace. He turns out to be a god of beauty rather than a hideous monster. See also: **Psyche's Palace**

Golden Age of Narnia The period when Peter Pevensie* is high king in Narnia* in *The Lion, the Witch and the Wardrobe**, and his brother and two sisters are king and queens under him. The Golden Age begins with the dissolution by Aslan* of the White Witch's* one-hundred-year spell of winter upon the land. It is during this celebrated period that Shasta* and Aravis* in *The Horse and His Boy* * escape from Calormen*. In *Prince Caspian* * it has come to symbolize* Old Narnia*, suppressed by the modernizing tyrant Miraz*.

The Golden Ass A collection of stories by the Latin writer Lucius Apuleius (c. AD 124–c. 170), divided into eleven books, and written in Carthage. The plot is simple. A young man sees an old sorceress transform herself into a bird after drinking a philtre. He also wishes for such a transformation, but mistakes the vial and turns into an ass. To become a man again, he must eat a certain species of rose. The author uses the pilgrimage of the donkey in search of them as a device to knit together a number of fantasies and stories. The most famous of all is "The Loves of Psyche". This inspired Lewis's *Till We Have Faces* *, in which he retells the haunting myth. In Apuleius, the tale occupies two entire books, and has inspired poets, painters, and sculptors, in many periods and countries.

Golden Tree A tree formed of gold in *The Magician's Nephew* *. It grows in the first fecundity of Narnia's* new creation from two half-sovereigns dropped by Uncle Andrew*.

Golg A gnome* in *The Silver Chair* * originally from Bism* but captured by Puddleglum* and the others in Underland* after the death of its self-styled queen (the Green Witch*). He directs them to the surface, where they re-enter Narnia*.

Golnessshire The country of lechery charted on the *Mappa Mundi* * in *The Pilgrim's Regress* *.

Great Council The council of war held against the usurper, Miraz*, in *Prince Caspian* * to decide a workable strategy. It was held on the Dancing Lawn*.

Great Desert The scorching wilderness in *The Horse and His Boy**, between Calormen* and Archenland*, crossed by Shasta*, Aravis*, Bree*, and Hwin* in desperate pursuit of freedom to the north.

The Great Divorce (**1945**) Like *The Screwtape Letters**, this story was first serialized in a religious periodical, and also concerns the relation of heaven* and hell. C.S. Lewis casts his story in the form of a dream, with himself as narrator, and does not wish his reader to think that information is being presented about the actual state after death. This of course does not mean that Lewis denies an actual heaven and hell. He is in fact concerned in this story to show their plausibility and reality.

The story opens in hell, with Lewis standing in a bus queue on a pavement in a long, shabby street. He had wandered for hours in similar, mean streets. Hell is an endless conurbation of perpetual twilight, where people move further and further away from each other. A new building just has to be thought in order to be made, but lacks sufficient reality to keep out the rain that constantly falls.

Anyone in hell who wishes can take a bus trip to heaven, or at least to its outlands. Lewis takes such a trip with a varied collection of ghosts. Upon arrival in heaven, the passengers find it painfully solid, hard, and bright in comparison to hell. Solid People* who have travelled vast distances to meet the ghosts try to persuade them to stay, pointing out that they will gradually adjust to heaven and become more solid as they forsake particular follies that hold them back from heaven. Much of the story is taken up with encounters between Solid People and ghosts, who were friends, relations, or spouses on earth. Lewis himself meets his master, George MacDonald*, who explains many mysteries of salvation and damnation to him. Lewis particularly questions him about his apparent universalism, the belief that all people will be saved. For Lewis, universalism is ruled out by the reality of human will. Hell is in fact chosen by the damned. Lewis's portrayal of the damned adds to Sartre's brilliant comment "Hell is other people", the reality that hell is also oneself.

Lewis handles the question of salvation and damnation very sensitively. Out of all the bus passengers, only one accepts the invitation to stay in heaven, after allowing a red lizard of lust perched on his shoulder to be destroyed by a colossal angel. Lewis's portrait of an apostate bishop strikes home painfully, exposing theological liberalism in his own church* denomination. The bishop almost cheerfully returns to hell to read a paper to its Theological Society.

In *The Great Divorce* (and also in *The Screwtape Letters**) Lewis highlights practical matters of the Christian life like family problems, selfishness, disagreement, greed, and the persistence of bad habits. Fantasy* proves a powerful medium for examining such matters, remembered long after a sermon is forgotten.

The "Great Knock" See: **Kirkpatrick, William T.**

The Great River The river leading to Aslan's How* in *Prince Caspian**, for which the children search. It runs its course from Lantern Waste* in the west, across Narnia*, into the Eastern Ocean*.

Great Snow Dance An annual dance in *The Silver Chair**, held on the first moonlit night after snow has fallen. It takes place north of the Great River*. The dancers (dryads*, fauns*, and dwarves*) move to the music of four fiddles, three flutes, and a drum. Dancers getting off-step are liable to be hit by well-aimed snowballs.

The "Great War" (between C.S. Lewis and Owen Barfield) What Barfield* called "an intense interchange of philosophical opinions" and Lewis described as "an almost incessant disputation, sometimes by letter and sometimes face to face, which lasted for years". The dialogue ensued soon after Barfield's acceptance of anthroposophy* around 1922 and trailed off by the time of Lewis's conversion to Christian faith in 1931. The dispute centred on the nature of the imagination* and the status of metaphor. It cured Lewis of his "chronological snobbery"*, making him hostile to modernism, and provided a rich background of sharpened thought for Barfield's important study *Poetic Diction** (1928).

Great Waterfall The source of the Great River* in *The Chronicles of Narnia**, on Narnia's* western edge. It flows over high cliffs into Caldron Pool*. In *The Last Battle**, travellers to Aslan's Country* swim up the waterfall and continue westward.

The Great Woods The huge forest in *The Chronicles of Narnia**, that extends west from the coast around Cair Paravel* to the Stone Table* (later, Aslan's How*) and south to the mountains bordering Archenland*. During the period of the Telmarine* suppression of Old Narnia* under Miraz* in *Prince Caspian**, the forest is feared and renamed the Black Woods*.

Green Lady See: *Perelandra*

Green, Roger Lancelyn (1918–1987) Biographer, with Walter Hooper*, of Lewis, a friend of his, and sometimes a visitor to the Inklings*. Lewis and his wife, Joy Davidman Lewis*, visited Greece with Green and his wife shortly before Joy's death. Green was a pupil of Lewis's who became a friend, and the two had a common taste in reading. He wrote an authoritative study of children's literature, *Tellers of Tales* (1946, updated 1953 and later), and composed many books for children. After hearing Lewis read early chapters of *The Lion, the Witch and the Wardrobe**, Green encouraged him to complete it. Many of Green's books introduce children to myth* and legend. *The Land Beyond the North* (1958) follows the Argonauts to the realm of Britain. His other fiction includes *From the World's End* (1948), his most mystical piece.

Greenroof A summer month in Narnia* in *Prince Caspian*, referring to the freshness of the trees.

The Green Witch The witch who tries to dominate Narnia* in *The Silver Chair*, during the reign of King Caspian* X. She appears to the travellers Jill Pole*, Eustace Scrubb*, and Puddleglum* as a tall, beautiful young woman wearing a green dress and hence is called The Lady of the Green Kirtle. The witch enchants and dominates Caspian's son, Rilian*, in her Shallow Lands*. Eventually she reveals her true nature as she transforms into a green serpent. See also: **White Witch**

Greeves, Joseph Arthur (1895–1966) A friend of Lewis's from teenage years who shared the secret of joy* and a similar taste in reading and all things "northern", such as Old Norse mythology. Arthur's skill was in visual art rather than words, though he was an appreciative reader of a life-long correspondence from Lewis (collected in *They Stand Together*). Arthur lived at a house called Bernagh*, almost opposite Lewis on the outskirts of Belfast*. Lewis continued to meet up with Arthur until his death. Between 1921 and 1923, Arthur Greeves studied at the prestigious Slade School of Fine Art in London. Later he exhibited with the Royal Hibernian Academy in Dublin. Lewis did not share his faith (Arthur came from a Christian Brethren background) until 1931, and later Arthur explored varieties of faith, concluding his life as a Quaker.

Gresham, David (b. 1944) Older son of Joy Davidman (see: **Lewis, Helen Joy Davidman**), and stepson of Lewis. In

1956, with his younger brother, Douglas, he joined the Lewis brothers living in The Kilns*. His mother was then seriously ill with cancer. He stayed on at The Kilns after her death in 1960, and gradually explored his Jewish roots. He continues to pursue the study of the Hebrew Bible and The Talmud, and is involved in furthering Jewish education.

Gresham, Douglas (b. 1945) Younger son of Joy Davidman (see: **Lewis, Helen Joy Davidman**). He tells the story of his life, including his memories as Lewis's stepson, in *Lenten Lands* (1988). His experiences as a boy are featured in the two film versions and play, *Shadowlands*, all based upon a script by William Nicholson. After his mother's death from cancer, Douglas eventually studied agriculture and moved to Tasmania with his wife, Meredith (Merrie). The family settled in County Carlow, Ireland, in 1993, to create a centre for Christian ministry, and now live in Malta. He is actively involved in the Lewis literary estate, co-produced three films adapting books from *The Chronicles of Narnia**, and lectures throughout the world. He has also written a biography of his stepfather, entitled *Jack's Life: The Life Story of C.S. Lewis* (2005).

Gresham, Joy Davidman See: **Lewis, Helen Joy Davidman**

Gresham, William Lindsay (1909–1962) Writer and first husband of Joy Davidman (see: **Lewis, Helen Joy Davidman**). Like Joy, he was for a time a Communist (serving in Spain in the Civil War) and later a convert to Christian faith. Unlike Joy he did not persist in this, but later in life moved to Scientology and then Buddhism. He successfully sold the film rights for his first novel, *Nightmare Alley* (1946). After many marital difficulties, Joy eventually agreed to a divorce. After the death of Joy in 1960, Bill Gresham travelled to England to see his two sons, and allowed them to stay with their stepfather,

C.S. Lewis. Tragically, in 1962, after cancer was diagnosed, he took his own life.

***A Grief Observed* (1961)** Originally published under a pseudonym, N.W. Clerk (see: **Nat Whilk**), this slim book sets out C.S. Lewis's pilgrimage through bereavement after losing his wife, Joy Davidman Lewis*. *A Grief Observed* complements his study *The Problem of Pain**. He wrote it as a kind of journal of grief. Whereas *The Problem of Pain* explores suffering generally and theoretically, the journal observes it specifically and personally (or existentially). Like the earlier book, *A Grief Observed* affirms the presence of God* in the deepest human darkness, even when he for long seems absent. Biographically, *A Grief Observed* reveals the quality of relationship between Lewis and Joy. He remembers: "She was my daughter and my mother, my pupil and my teacher, my subject and my sovereign; and always, holding all these in solution, my trusty comrade, friend, shipmate, fellow-soldier."

Griffle The chief of a band of dwarves* in *The Last Battle**, who believe that only they themselves are worth believing in and fighting for. This is after being disillusioned by Shift* and his trickery.

Gumpas The slave-trading* and bureaucratic governor of the Lone Islands* in *The Voyage of the "Dawn Treader"**, whom Caspian* replaces with the worthy Lord Bern*.

Gwendolen A pupil in a school in Telmarine*-controlled Beruna* in *Prince Caspian**. She disrupts her strictly disciplined class when she notices a lion outside (who turns out to be Aslan*, freeing the town). She is an example of a virtuous pagan* who welcomes Aslan, even though she has not known Old Narnia*.

H

Hag An accomplice of the surly dwarf* Nikabrik* in *Prince Caspian**. She has a nose and a chin that sticks out like nutcrackers, and dirty grey hair.

Handramit The fertile lowlands in the great artificial chasms of Malacandra* in *Out of the Silent Planet**.

Harandra The harsh outer surface or highland of Malacandra* in *Out of the Silent Planet**. The seroni (or sorns*) like to live here.

Hardcastle, Major "Fairy" In *That Hideous Strength**, the psychopathic controller of the Institutional Police of the N.I.C.E.* She gets sexual pleasure in sadism against her own sex and enjoys torturing Jane Studdock*.

Harfang The stronghold of wicked giants* north of Ettinsmoor* in *The Silver Chair**. The children, and even Puddleglum*, are persuaded they are friendly by the disguised Green Witch*. Marsh-wiggles* and man are considered delicacies for a feast.

Harfang stands on a small hill overlooking the ruins of the giant City Ruinous*. Among the crumbling ruined stone, pillars as tall as factory chimneys are to be found in places. Large sections of pavement can be seen from Harfang to bear the words "UNDER ME", all that remains of an ancient verse.

Harwood, Alfred Cecil (1898–1975) Friend of C.S. Lewis's. Harwood and Owen Barfield* became lifelong friends when the former was a scholar at Christ Church, Oxford* University.

Both were introduced to Lewis in 1919 through a mutual acquaintance, Leo Kingsley Baker*. Harwood became, like Barfield, an anthroposophist*. In 1931, Warren Lewis* described him in his diary as a "pleasant, spectacled, young looking man, with a sense of humour of a whimsical kind, to whom I took at sight… we found ourselves seeing everything with much the same eye". Lewis was godfather to his son, Laurence Harwood, whose memoirs are recorded in *C.S. Lewis, My Godfather: Letters, Photos and Recollections* (2007).

hastilude A dangerous type of spear play in *The Horse and His Boy* *, drawn by Lewis from medieval origins.

Havard, Dr Robert Emlyn "Humphrey" (1901–1985) Affectionately known as the "Useless Quack", and also "Humphrey", Havard was the doctor of C.S. Lewis, and member of the Inklings*. The son of an Anglican clergyman, Havard studied medicine after graduating in chemistry from Oxford* University in 1922 and became a doctor, writing research articles. In 1934 he took over a medical practice in Oxford with surgeries in Headington and St Giles (near the Eagle and Child* public house, haunt of the Inklings). He and Lewis took to each other instantly when they met. Soon after, he was invited along to the Inklings. Havard appears briefly as a character in *Perelandra**. In 1943 he volunteered for the Royal Navy Reserve, and became a naval surgeon. When he returned to Oxford (because of his wife's breast cancer) he was hailed as "the Red Admiral" by the Inklings because he now sported a red beard, and turned up to a meeting in uniform. "Hugo" Dyson* called him "Humphrey" because he couldn't remember his name. Havard converted to Roman Catholicism in 1931, influenced by Ronald Knox, the writer, priest, and Bible* translator. "Humphrey" had five children, and became a single parent when his wife succumbed to cancer in 1950.

Havard felt that Lewis's association with Charles Williams* strained the friendship between Lewis and Tolkien* (see: **friendship of J.R.R. Tolkien and C.S. Lewis**). He recalled: "Lewis was fascinated by Williams, and rightly; he [had] a very extraordinary charm. You couldn't be in the same room with him without being attracted to him." Havard felt that Williams had a "curious, rather mixed character". In some way he "wasn't fully integrated". On the friendship of Lewis and Tolkien, and its eventual cooling, Havard observed: "The surprising thing, really, is that they became such close friends, rather than that differences appeared and separated them."

Further reading
Robert E. Havard, "Philia: Jack at ease", James T. Como (ed.), *C.S. Lewis at the Breakfast Table and Other Reminiscences* (1979).
Also, the Oral History Project of the Marion E. Wade Center, Wheaton, Illinois, USA.

heaven Heaven, as C.S. Lewis saw it, is a literal place, though, in our present, fallen situation, it will not be discovered by searching through the universe in space rockets (that would be like trying to find Shakespeare by looking through the pages of one of his plays, Lewis pointed out). Heaven is a new nature* that God* has planned, the ultimate context of a fully human life, bodies and all. The theme of heaven's reality runs through Lewis's writings, particularly his fiction, and is closely linked with his characteristic theme of joy* or *sehnsucht*.

Before his conversion to Christianity, as an atheist, and even after he began believing in God, Lewis was uninterested in immortality, and only became convinced about life after death a year into his Christian life. He desired God himself, and the desire for heaven was a spin-off from this. As heaven is part of creation, he reasoned, it is not worthy of being an ultimate aim of human beings. Lewis, however, decided that it was no more mercenary to desire heaven than to wish to marry the person one loves. In this present life, he concluded, the situation is like being on the wrong side of a shut door, with heaven on the other side. Morning was one of Lewis's favourite images of heaven. He claimed that, while we respond to the "freshness and purity of morning", that doesn't "make us fresh and pure".

C.S. Lewis isolated five promises about heaven from the teaching of Christianity for its followers: that they will be with Christ; that they will be like him, sharing his glory; that they will be fed, feasted, and entertained. Finally, Lewis believed, there will be work to do in heaven and those that go there will be office bearers of responsibility in the universe.

Heaven, in Lewis's way of thinking, is founded upon the paradox that the more Christians abandon themselves to Jesus Christ, the more fully themselves they become. Thus, while redemption by Christ may improve people in this present life, the consummation of human maturity is unimaginable. In heaven, as Lewis saw it, both the individuality and society of persons will be fulfilled; there will be both diversity and harmony. Heaven is varied; hell monotonous. Heaven is brimful of meaning*; hell is the absence of meaning. Heaven is reality itself, hell a ghost or shadow. He particularly captures such a vision in his dream story, *The Great Divorce*.

Lewis believed that heaven is probably unimaginable, even though the biblical images take believers as far as they can. Parable, allegory*, and fiction are the closest that believers can come to speaking of heaven, he argued. This is why he explored heaven so much through fantasy*, as in *The Great Divorce*, *The Voyage of the "Dawn Treader"**, *The Last Battle**, and *Perelandra**. In his prose, he particularly speaks of heaven in *The Problem of Pain**, *Letters to Malcolm**, and in a published sermon, "The Weight of Glory".

In *The Last Battle*, the children saw the land of Narnia* die for ever and freeze over in blackness. They were filled with regret. Later, as they walked in a fresh morning light in Aslan's

Country*, they wondered why everything seemed strangely familiar. At last they realized that this was again Narnia, but now different – larger and more vivid, more like the real thing. It was different in the way that a real thing differed from its shadow, or waking life from a dream.

Hegeliana A region charted on the *Mappa Mundi** in *The Pilgrim's Regress**, representing Hegelian philosophy (from Hegel) and absolute idealism*.

Hermit of Southern March He looks after the wounded Aravis* and the talking horses in *The Horse and His Boy**, while Cor* continues his journey to warn King Lune* of the Calormen* danger. A tall, robed figure with a beard that reaches his knees, the hermit is 109 years of age and has a pool with the properties of a crystal ball. The "March" is a variant of mark, or boundary – the hermit lives on the southern border of Archenland*.

historicism See: **history**

history In much of his literary criticism*, C.S. Lewis was a literary historian. In an important essay, "Historicism" (1950), first published in book form in *Christian Reflections**, he expressed his attitude to the study of history. This essay contains both an affirmation and a denial concerning the meaning* of history.

On the one hand, Lewis believes absolutely that human history is "a story written by the finger of God". On the other hand, he firmly rejects all claims to know the inner meaning and patterns of history by means of mere rational observation of events. Writing history is of course worthwhile, but grand philosophies of history (historicisms) are doomed to futility. Such grand schemes have been worked out by thinkers such as Hegel, Marx, and even Augustine. Lewis comments: "If by one miracle, the total content of time were spread out before me, and if, by another, I were able to hold all that infinity of events in my mind and if, by a third, God were pleased to comment on it so I could understand it, then, to be sure, I could do what the Historicist says he is doing. I could read the meaning, discern the pattern."

C.S. Lewis more realistically wants instead to emphasize trust in God and an openness to ordinary human reality – the "primary history" in which God reveals himself in the moment by moment experience of life to each one who seeks him. That, for him, this view of history doesn't lead to scepticism about the value of culture is clear from another key essay, "Learning in War-Time"*, where he points out the abiding value of scholarship. See also: **literary critic, C.S. Lewis as a**

Hnohra The hross* in *Out of the Silent Planet** who teaches Elwin Ransom* the language and cultures of the beings on Malacandra*.

Hogglestock A talking hedgehog in *Prince Caspian**, who participates in the Great Council*.

Hooper, Walter (b. 1931) Described by *The Independent* (7 March 1994) as Lewis's other American (the first being Joy Davidman*), Walter Hooper was born in Reidsville, North Carolina. He was educated at the University of North Carolina at Chapel Hill. After serving in the US Army, he read theology at Virginia Theological Seminary. He taught English at Christ School, Arden, North Carolina, 1960–1961, and then at the University of Kentucky in Lexington, 1961–1963.

After corresponding for a while, Lewis invited Walter Hooper to visit him in Oxford*. They met on 7 June 1963, and Hooper attended his first meeting of the Inklings* a few days later. That summer, in poor health, Lewis gladly accepted

Hooper's offer of secretarial assistance. But the young American's stay at The Kilns* proved to be all too brief. "There followed the happiest period of my life," Mr Hooper told the author, "for Lewis was a thousand times more interesting than his books. But the privilege was of short duration. I was in Kentucky, teaching one final term before returning to Oxford, when Lewis died."

He did, however, return to Oxford in 1964, and Warren Lewis* invited him to edit his brother's literary legacy. He has worked from 1964 as the Literary Adviser to the C.S. Lewis Estate, during which time he has edited a number of Lewis's posthumous publications. In 1974 he and Roger Lancelyn Green* co-authored the authorized biography of Lewis. Formerly an Anglican, Walter Hooper became a Roman Catholic in 1988. He is the author of *C.S. Lewis: A Companion and Guide* (1996), and editor of the *Collected Letters of C.S. Lewis* in three volumes. Walter Hooper has undoubtedly contributed more than any other individual to Lewis's popularity throughout the world, by his unstinted devotion to the publication of Lewis's works, many of which would have otherwise been neglected. In 2009, Walter Hooper was given the Clyde S. Kilby Lifetime Acheivment Award by The Marion E. Wade Center, Wheaton College, Wheaton, Illinois.

Horn of Narnia Queen Susan's* gift from Father Christmas*, which she drops in the Lantern Waste* as she returns through the wardrobe. In *Prince Caspian** the horn has been passed on to Caspian*, who sounds it as a desperate call for help.

The Horse and His Boy (1954) Set in the period of Narnia's* Golden Age*, most of the story unfolds in the cruel southern land of Calormen*. Cor*, a lost son of King Lune* of the friendly country of Archenland*, north of Calormen, has been brought up by a poor fisherman. He is named Shasta*, and knows nothing of his true origin, but has a strange longing to travel to the northern lands.

The story also concerns a high-born Calormene* girl, Aravis*, who runs away from home to flee an unpleasant marriage. Both children independently encounter Narnian talking horses, in captivity in Calormen, who tell them about the freedom of Narnia's pleasant land, and who escape with the children. They meet up on the road.

When passing through Calormen's capital, Tashbaan*, Aravis uncovers a treacherous plot to conquer Archenland and Narnia, led by the spiteful Prince Rabadash*, foiled in his attempt to marry Queen Susan* of Narnia. With great courage, and some failures, the children warn the two northern countries of their danger. The Calormene plot fails, Cor is restored to his father, the two horses, Bree* and Hwin*, return to their talking companions in Narnia, and Cor and Aravis marry, to become king and queen of Archenland after Lune's death.

Several of the characters familiar to readers of *The Lion, the Witch and the Wardrobe** appear in this book, including most of the Pevensie children* and the faun* Mr Tumnus*. Both the sceptical horse Bree and the disdainful Aravis have to encounter Aslan*.

In this tale, perhaps more than any other, C.S. Lewis embodies his love of "Northernness", which he shared with J.R.R. Tolkien* and Arthur Greeves*. The book also reveals some of the extent to which the geography of the world of which Narnia is a part is drawn from the late medieval picture of reality that Lewis loved so deeply, as portrayed in his seminal study *The Discarded Image**.

House of Correction for Incompetent Tempters One of the many departments of hell in *The Screwtape Letters**. Tempters are initially trained at the Tempters' Training College*, run by Dr Slubgob*.

house of Professor Kirke This is a rambling country house in the south of England, with a river at the bottom of its garden. It is a long way from a railway station and a post office. In *The Lion, the Witch and the Wardrobe** it offers much for the evacuee* children, the Pevensies*, to explore on rainy days. A room of particular interest is empty except for a wardrobe* and a dead bluebottle, a large fly. The house is of historic interest, attracting many visitors, and strange stories are told about it, even stranger than the story of the children entering Narnia* through the wardrobe. As a child Digory Kirke* lives here, except for a period when his mother is ill and he stays with her in the London home of his aunt and uncle. He remembers having a pony there. His father eventually inherits the estate from his great uncle, and hence in time it becomes Digory's.

Some time after the adventure with the wardrobe, the house is destroyed. The reason is not revealed – perhaps there was a fire. After this, the professor, suddenly poor, moves to a small cottage with a spare bedroom. Peter* stays there while being coached for an exam, just as a young C.S. Lewis had stayed at the cottage of W.T. Kirkpatrick* while preparing for university entrance.

house of the magician In *The Voyage of the "Dawn Treader"**, Coriakin's* house discovered by the voyagers on the island inhabited by the Monopods* (see: **Island of the Monopods**). The two-storey house of grey stone is overgrown by ivy and is reached by a tree-lined avenue that runs through well-kept lawns. Its paved courtyard has a pump in its centre. A passage on the upper floor runs the length of the house, with seven rooms off it. The last, entered by Lucy Pevensie*, holds the magician's book along with a library. Another room is full of various scientific instruments.

House of the Tisroc A palace straight out of an Arabian tale in *The Horse and His Boy**. It stands on the brow of Tashbaan's* dominant hill, which it shares with the temple of Tash*. The palace's extensive gardens extend right down to the river's edge on the northern side of the city island.

hrossa Intelligent inhabitants of the planet Malacandra* in *Out of the Silent Planet**, who outwardly look like gleaming black animals, a little like an otter or seal, yet are a walking land creature. From the hrossa (singular, hross), Elwin Ransom* learns the language of Old Solar*. They are practical, food-gathering beings, with a penchant for poetry. See also: **talking animals; The planets**

Humanist, Mr An allegorical* figure in *The Pilgrim's Regress** representing a key player in the intellectual climate in which Lewis, as a young scholar, lived. He is one of the "cerebral" men John* the pilgrim meets in the north of the world. See also: *Mappa Mundi*

Hwin The talking Narnian* mare who plays an important part in the tale known as *The Horse and His Boy**. She helps Aravis* escape an unpleasant marriage. There are many delightful contrasts between her character and that of Bree*, the other talking horse in the book. Like Bree, she had been captured and taken to Calormen* and there had to keep her nature secret. She only speaks at first to dissuade her mistress, Aravis, from suicide.

Hyoi The hross* whom Elwin Ransom* first encounters on Malacandra* in *Out of the Silent Planet**. Much to Ransom's distress, Hyoi is later shot by one of the earth men. See also: **talking animals; The planets**

I

idealism, C.S. Lewis and In his journey from atheism Lewis turned at one stage to idealism. In his autobiography, *Surprised by Joy**, he recalls admitting that the stuff of the entire universe was ultimately mental. When thinking, our logical processes were "participating in a cosmic *logos*". (See: ***logos***.) Idealism in England was especially associated with T.H. Green (1836–1882), F.H. Bradley (1846–1924), and J.M.E. McTaggart (1866–1925). These idealists typically held that physical objects can have no existence apart from a mind that is conscious of them. Lewis's brilliant friend Owen Barfield*, with whom he had a formative "Great War"*, persuaded him eventually to accept some tenets of idealism. Lewis did not stay long here, however, and moved from idealism, via pantheism, to theism, and eventually to Christian belief.

Idealism in England was dramatically swept away by logical positivism. It had already been weakened by the realism of G.E. Moore (1873–1958) and Bertrand Russell (1872–1970). In the rest of Europe, idealism was disintegrated by secular and religious existentialism. Theologically, existentialism made a deep impression on the thought of Rudolf Bultmann (1884–1976), whose view on myth* in the Gospels was far from that which C.S. Lewis developed as a Christian.

The Idea of the Holy, **Rudolf Otto (1917)** Subtitled "An inquiry into the non-rational factor in the idea of the divine and its relation to the rational", this was the chief work of the German Lutheran theologian Rudolf Otto (1869–1937), who was professor of systematic theology at Marburg University

1919–1937. In it he explores the sense of the numinous*, which is, he believed, common to all strong religious experiences and beyond reason, knowledge, or any other term. Lewis powerfully summarizes Otto's main idea in the introduction to his *The Problem of Pain**. Otto's portrayal of the numinous made a major impact upon Lewis's thought and work. Indeed, he listed *The Idea of the Holy* as one of the ten books most influential upon his thinking and vocational attitude (see: **reading of C.S. Lewis**). As well as providing a phenomenology of the numinous, in the book Otto explores the numinous in the Old and New Testaments, in poetry and art, and in figures such as Luther and John Ruskin.

Ilgamuth One of the lords of Rabadash*, in *The Horse and His Boy**, slain by Darrin* of Archenland* in the Battle of Anvard*.

Ilkeen In *The Horse and His Boy**, the location in Calormen* of a lake and the beautiful palaces of wealthy Tarkaans, including Ahosta*.

The imagination (imaginative fantasy) Both imagination and fantasy are difficult to define. For C.S. Lewis, fantasy is a power and product of the imagination, just as thought is a power and product of the intellect. As thought is the reason in action, fantasy is the imagination at work. His view of nature* implied the reality of the supernatural* world and its myriad connections with the natural world. Hence his Christian fantasy not only concerns the supernatural, but illuminates the natural world. As he put it: "For me, reason is the natural organ of truth; but imagination is the organ of meaning." Reason involves abstractions, but imagination brings us into contact with the definite and real.

As well as a power and product of the imagination, fantasy is also to be found in a number of genres, such as science fiction, heroic romance (such as *The Lord of the Rings*), allegory*, apocalyptic (such as the biblical book of Revelation), and fairy story. Fantasy always draws attention to its fictional nature, so has to be well crafted to achieve its effects, and this is why Lewis viewed fantasy as imaginative invention. For him, fantasy was a prime vehicle for capturing the elusive quality of joy*, which is a strong theme throughout his fiction. See also: **meaning and imagination**

Further reading
C.S. Lewis, "Bluspels and Flananferes: A Semantic Nightmare", Walter Hooper (ed.), *Selected Literary Essays* (1969); C.S. Lewis, "Horrid Red Things", *Miracles* (1947).

The Inklings These were of group of male friends, all people of talent, who met together informally at least once a week to talk about ideas, to read to each other for pleasure and criticism on pieces they were writing, and to enjoy a good evening of "the cut and parry of prolonged, fierce, masculine argument".The Inklings embodied C.S. Lewis's ideals of life and pleasure. In fact, he was the life and soul of the party. Their important years as a writing group were from the early 1930s to near the end of the 1940s. The war years were especially significant, when Charles Williams* was resident in Oxford*. They also met even more informally as a conversation group in favoured Oxford pubs, commonly the Eagle and Child* in St Giles, until shortly before Lewis's death.

The group did not have any consistent documentation such as the careful minuting of J.R.R. Tolkien's fictional the Notion Club (see below). Humphrey Carpenter's pioneering study of the group drew on the key sources: the diaries* of Major Warren Lewis*, C.S. Lewis's letters* to his brother in the early months of the Second World War, Tolkien's long letters to his son Christopher while Christopher was serving in the RAF in South Africa, Lewis's introduction to *Essays Presented to Charles Williams*, and reminiscences by Inklings such as John Wain*, Commander Jim Dundas-Grant, Christopher Tolkien, and others.

The Inklings expanded from the deep friendship between Tolkien and Lewis (see: **friendship of J.R.R. Tolkien and C.S. Lewis**), a remarkable association comparable perhaps to that between William Wordsworth and Samuel Taylor Coleridge in literary significance. In his book *The Four Loves**, Lewis explains the process by which friendship, the least jealous of loves, expands: "In each of my friends there is something that only some other friend can fully bring out."

Humphrey Carpenter's book gives a long list of Inklings members, but, in a letter to Bede Griffiths in December 1941, Lewis has quite a short list. He is explaining his dedication to the Inklings in his recently published *The Problem of Pain** and lists Charles Williams*, Dyson of Reading (H.V.D. "Hugo" Dyson*), Warren Lewis, Tolkien, and Dr "Humphrey" Havard*. Lewis explains Tolkien and Dyson as the "immediate human causes of my own conversion" to Christianity. Remarkably, the name of Owen Barfield* does not appear in this list, though Lewis elsewhere mentions him as of the Inklings. In fact, Barfield was rarely able to join the Inklings meetings. On one occasion, Lewis grumbles that Barfield is visiting on a Thursday, which means he'll attend the Inklings and Lewis will have less time to himself with him! It was later that the Inklings swelled further to include Colin Hardie, Lord David Cecil*, John Wain, and others. Christopher Tolkien attended as soon as he was back from South Africa. It was upon this larger group that Tolkien drew inspiration for "The Notion Club Papers" (his unfinished fictional portrait of an Inklings-type group of friends, set in the future, in 1987), and it is likely that he read as much of it as he wrote to them. Warren Lewis records in his diary, Thursday 22 August 1946, about "Tollers" reading "a magnificent myth which is to knit up and concludes his Papers of the Notions Club". This would have been "The Drowning of Anadûnê" (now published with "The Notion Club Papers" in Tolkien's *Sauron Defeated*).

The death of Charles Williams in 1945 was a great blow to the group, particularly Lewis, and the 1950s marked a gradual cooling of the friendship between Lewis and Tolkien. The situation was not helped by Hugo Dyson vetoing Tolkien reading from the unfinished *The Lord of the Rings* at Inklings meetings. A further complexity in the friendship with Tolkien was introduced by Lewis's at first only intellectual friendship with Joy Davidman, but that is explored elsewhere in my *J.R.R. Tolkien and C.S. Lewis: The Story of Their Friendship* (see: **Lewis, Helen Joy Davidman**).

C.S. Lewis describes a typical meeting in a letter to an absent member – his brother – in 1939. The "new Hobbit" is a reference to the first volume of *The Lord of the Rings*. "On Thursday we had a meeting of the Inklings… we dined at the Eastgate. I have never in my life seen Dyson so exuberant – 'A roaring cataract of nonsense'. The bill of fare afterwards consisted of a section of the new Hobbit book from Tolkien, a nativity play from Charles Williams (unusually intelligible for him, and approved by all), and a chapter out of the book on *The Problem of Pain* from me." An extract from the "new Hobbit" – *The Lord of the Rings* – was standard: much of it was read to the Inklings, sometimes for better enunciation by Christopher instead of Tolkien senior.

The Inklings had somewhat of a modest and unassuming "Boswell", Warnie Lewis* (see: ***Life of Samuel Johnson***). He, more than anyone at the time, seemed aware of the uniqueness and identity of the Inklings, valuing the group partly because of his affection for his brother. From various reminisences of members, and a variety of documentation, it appears that other members of the circle – in addition to those listed by Lewis in his December 1941 letter, outlined above, like Tolkien, Charles Williams, and Dr Havard – were Owen Barfield, J.A.W.

Bennett*, Lord David Cecil*, Nevill Coghill*, Commander Jim Dundas-Grant, Adam Fox*, Colin Hardie, Gervase Mathew*, R.B. McCallum*, C.E. ("Tom") Stevens*, Christopher Tolkien, John Wain, and Charles Wrenn.

One of the favourite haunts of the Inklings, the Eagle and Child* public house, has been renovated since the group met there, but a plaque has been erected in memory. It reads: "C.S. LEWIS, his brother, W.H. Lewis, J.R.R. Tolkien, Charles Williams and other friends met every Tuesday morning, between the years 1939–1962 in the back room of this their favourite pub. These men, popularly known as the 'Inklings', met here to drink Beer and to discuss, among other things, the books they were writing."

Warnie Lewis was sceptical of the idea of the Inklings representing a school of literature or theology, a view shared by others such as Humphrey Carpenter. He is probably right to be so in view of the diversity of its members at one time or another. However, Lewis hankered for others who shared his core beliefs, and some of the main Inklings, including Williams, Tolkien, and even Barfield did, though Barfield never became a Christian in an orthodox sense, even though he joined the Church* of England later in life. He remained committed to anthroposophy*, which was a synthesis of views, including a belief in reincarnation.

Speaking in California in the spring of 1969, Owen Barfield remembered the way Lewis affected all the groups he was part of, including the Inklings. This was partly, unconsciously and unobtrusively, by the sheer force and weight of his personality and, as Barfield put it, "a rather loud voice when he was in high spirits". Lewis would set the tone and decide the topic of conversation. Barfield recalled that on one occasion, when the topic was not of interest to Lewis (it could have been politics or economics) he turned aside from the conversation, picked up a book, and proceeded to read it instead of talking.

Lewis also affected a group, irrespective of what was brought up, by always turning the subject around to the point where it was a moral issue or problem. If anyone did not think that a moral issue was involved, Lewis would remind him that there ought to be.

Barfield wondered if something happened to "the Romantic Impulse" during the life of the Inklings. He could discern four important threads, each largely identified with Lewis, Tolkien, Williams, or himself: (i) the yearning for the infinite and unattainable – Lewis's *sehnsucht* or joy*; (ii) in Barfield's words, "The conviction of the dignity of man and his part in the future history of the world conceived as a kind of progress towards increasing imanence of the divine in the human" (Barfield's own position); (iii) the idealization of love between the sexes, as in Charles Williams's thought and writings; and (iv) the opposite of tragedy, the Happy Ending, Tolkien's idea of the "eucatastrophe". See also: **theology of romance**

Further reading

Humphrey Carpenter, *The Inklings: C.S. Lewis, J.R.R. Tolkien, Charles Williams and Their Friends* (1978); John Wain, *Sprightly Running: Part of an Autobiography* (1962); Rand Kuhl, "Owen Barfield in Southern California", *Mythlore*, Vol. 1, No. 4, 1969; Gareth Knight, *The Magical World of the Inklings* (1990); Colin Duriez and David Porter, *The Inklings Handbook: The Lives, Thought and Writings of C.S. Lewis, J.R.R. Tolkien, Charles Williams, Owen Barfield and Their Friends* (2001); Diana Pavlac Glyer, *The Company They Keep: C.S. Lewis and J.R.R. Tolkien as Writers in Community* (2008); J.R.R. Tolkien, "The Notion Club Papers", Christopher Tolkien (ed.), *Sauron Defeated* (1992).

"The Inner Ring" An essay that first appeared in print in *Transposition and Other Addresses**. Its theme is illustrated in C.S. Lewis's science-fiction story *That Hideous Strength**. Lewis saw the lure of the inner ring as a perversion of friendship*, which "causes perhaps half of all the happiness in the world, and no Inner Ringer can ever have it". Unlike friendship, the desire to be on the inside of a group leads to a perpetual anxiety, even if achieved, whereas real friendship is "snug and safe" because it is free of this desire. Lewis believed that in most associations of business and profession there were inner rings as well as the official hierarchies. "You are never formally and explicitly admitted by anyone. You discover gradually, in almost indefinable ways, that it exists and that you are outside it; and then later, perhaps, that you are inside it." Inner rings provide a climate in which evil becomes easier. Until a person conquers the fear of being an outsider, an outsider they will remain. In *That Hideous Strength*, the lure of the inner ring of Belbury* on Mark Studdock* dramatically illustrates its danger.

Intelligence Department Part of the bureaucracy of hell in *The Screwtape Letters**. Although hell dislikes knowledge, which it regards as hateful and mawkish, a certain amount is necessary to have effective power on earth to upset the Enemy's plans. Devils* assigned to human patients pass information back to the Department. Screwtape* laments the inability of the Department to penetrate the purposes of the Enemy.

The Island Glimpsed by John* in *The Pilgrim's Regress**, the cause and object of his sweet desire, a longing involving joy*.

Island of the Monopods The estate of the magician Coriakin* in *The Voyage of the "Dawn Treader"**, and called the Island of Voices* by the seafarers. The lawns are well kept, like the grounds of Lewis's college in Oxford*, Magdalen. In the centre of the island, approached by an avenue of trees, is the warm stone house of the magician*, a long, two-storeyed building with many windows. The island is inhabited by Monopods*, who, until Lucy* reverses the spell of invisibility, cannot be seen – hence the name "the Island of Voices".

Island of Voices A low-lying island to the west of Deathwater Island* in the Eastern Ocean*, in *The Voyage of the "Dawn Treader"**. See: **Island of the Monopods**

Istra Psyche's* name in her native Glome* in *Till We Have Faces**. "Psyche" is the Greek form of her name, preferred by Psyche herself, Orual*, and The Fox*.

J

Jackle, Edith A tale-bearer and hanger-on to the gang of bullies in *The Silver Chair**, who terrorize Eustace Scrubb* and Jill Pole* at Experiment House*.

Jadis See: **The White Witch**

Jenkin, Alfred Kenneth Hamilton (1900–1980) As undergraduates attending University College, Oxford*, he and Lewis became fast and lifelong friends. He is referred to affectionately in *Surprised by Joy** and mentioned frequently in Lewis's diaries* (published as *All My Road Before Me**). Jenkin taught Lewis to enjoy the thisness or "quiddity" of things, an enjoyment that became a hallmark of Lewis's thought and writings (see: **nature**). In *That Hideous Strength**, Camilla and Arthur Denniston* enjoy all types of weather, as Jenkin did.

Jewel the Unicorn In *The Last Battle**, Jewel, a talking beast*, is the dearest friend of Tirian*, last king of Narnia*. They save each other's lives in war. Jewel's feelings as he enters the New Narnia* remade by Aslan* illustrate C.S. Lewis's constant and special theme of joy*.

John John is the contemporary Everyman or pilgrim in *The Pilgrim's Regress**, based loosely upon Lewis himself. The name possibly was borrowed from Lewis's model, John Bunyan.

joy Joy is a defining characteristic of romance (and thus fantasy*) in C.S. Lewis. His autobiography up to his conversion to

Christianity in 1931 is recorded in *Surprised by Joy**, and somewhat in his long allegory *The Pilgrim's Regress**. These tell us that his lengthy, varied, and reluctant pilgrimage was greatly influenced by a certain distinct tone of feeling that he discovered in early childhood, and which stayed with him on and off throughout his adolescence and early manhood.

This longing for beauty or joy he learned from gazing at the Castlereagh Hills of Belfast* from his nursery windows. Later reading of northern myths and sagas intensified this dissatisfaction. Significantly, in 1922, while still a non-believer, Lewis wrote a poem on this theme, "Joy", reprinted in *The Collected Poems**. Toward the end of his life Lewis personified the imaginative longing in a character in *Till We Have Faces**. This character is based upon the Psyche* of ancient Roman writing. Because myths* and other-worldly tales can often define this longing for beauty, Lewis defended and wrote this type of literature throughout his distinguished career, despite its lowly standing with the critics.

The relationship between love and zest for life and the desire for beauty constantly fascinated Lewis. The stories of George MacDonald*, which shaped his imagination*, are dominated by a joyful quality of holiness or goodness in life – but it was no platonic spirituality. MacDonald's stories (including his novels) concern the homely and ordinary, transformed by a new light. Lewis captured this exactly when he wrote: "The quality which had enchanted me in his imaginative works turned out to be the quality of the real universe, the divine, magical, terrifying and ecstatic reality in which we all live."

C.S. Lewis's own imaginative creations such as *The Chronicles of Narnia** sprang from this love of life. He seems to have been very preoccupied with Joy, as he called it, throughout the 1940s and early 1950s. The last chapter of *The Problem of Pain** (1940) speaks of it; a sermon, "The Weight of Glory" (1941), tries to define the desire; *The Voyage of the "Dawn Treader"** (1952) is

about the Narnian* mouse Reepicheep's* quest* for Aslan's
Country* at World's End*; *Surprised by Joy* (1955) traces the twin
threads of Lewis's thinking and his longing for beauty up to
his conversion to theism; and in *Till We Have Faces** (1956) the
princess Psyche has a love of this beauty that is stronger than
death. In *Transposition and Other Addresses** (1949) Lewis wrote:
"We do not want merely to see beauty... We want something
else which can hardly be put into words – to be united with
the beauty we see, to pass into it, to receive it into ourselves, to
bathe in it, to become part of it. That is why we have peopled
air and earth and water with gods and goddesses and nymphs
and elves."

Such joy, thought Lewis, inspired the writer to create fantasy.
In fact, what in German is called *sehnsucht*, seen as a yearning
or longing that is a pointer to joy, was for Lewis a defining
characteristic of fantasy. The creation of Another World is an
attempt to reconcile human beings and the world, to embody
the fulfilment of our imaginative longing. Imaginative worlds,
wonderlands, are "regions of the spirit". Such worlds of the
numinous* may be found in some science fiction, some poetry,
some fairy stories, some novels, some myths, even in a phrase
or sentence. Lewis claimed in his book *Of Other Worlds**: "To
construct plausible and moving 'other worlds' you must draw
on the only real 'other world' we know, that of the spirit" (see:
Romanticism).

Joy for C.S. Lewis is the key both to the nature of human
beings and to their creator. He saw this unquenchable longing as
a sure sign that no part of the created world, and thus no aspect
of human experience, is capable of fulfilling fallen mankind.
He became convinced that human beings are dominated by a
homelessness, and yet by a keen sense of what home means.

In *Surprised by Joy* Lewis reported his sensations of joy,
including responses to natural beauty and literary or artistic
responses, in the belief that other people would recognize

similar experiences of their own. Even some who cannot do so through Lewis's autobiographical account, however, respond to this experience when reading his fiction.

C.S. Lewis came to see joy was a foretaste of ultimate reality, heaven* itself, or (the same thing in his Christian view) our world as it was meant to be, unspoilt by the fall of mankind, and one day to be remade. "Joy," wrote Lewis, "is the serious business of Heaven."

In attempting to imagine heaven, Lewis discovered that joy is, as he put it, "the secret signature of each soul". He speculated that the desire for heaven is part of our essential (and unfulfilled) humanity:

> There are times when I think we do not desire heaven; but more often I find myself wondering whether, in our heart of hearts, we have ever desired anything else… Are not all lifelong friendships born at the moment when at last you meet another human being who has some inkling (but faint and uncertain even in the best) of that something which you were born desiring, and… you are looking for, watching for, listening for? You have never had it… It is the secret signature of each soul… (*The Problem of Pain*, chapter 10)

C.S. Lewis's portrayal of joy can be seen as providing valuable data of a key human experience, data that has philosophical and religious importance. It was also central to his popular defence of the Christian faith. See also: **heaven**

K

Ketterley, Andrew See: **Andrew, Uncle**

Ketterley, Letitia ("Letty") The aunt of Digory Kirke* in *The Magician's Nephew**, who is caring for his dying mother, the sister of Letty and his Uncle Andrew*. She is unimpressed by Jadis* the witch, who, in response, hurls her across the room.

Kidrash Tarkaan The lord of the Calormen* province of Calavar* and father of Aravis* in *The Horse and His Boy**, who tries to marry her off to the ugly and aged new Grand Vizier, Ahoshta* Tarkaan. It is claimed in Calormen that he is a descendant of the god Tash*.

The Kilns Lewis's home in Oxford* from 1930 until his death in 1963. Prior to moving there, he had lived at many other addresses since first arriving in the city as an undergraduate in 1917. The Kilns occupied eight acres and was still relatively new when Lewis established a household in it with Mrs Janie Moore* and her daughter, Maureen. His brother, Warnie Lewis*, also joined them there when on leave, moving in permanently at the end of 1932 upon taking early retirement from the British Army. At that time the property boasted a tennis court, large unruly grounds including a pond large enough for swimming in, a greenhouse, and the ruins of brick kilns. The pond (which still exists today as part of a nature reserve) is a flooded quarry from which clay for brick-making had been taken.

The house is now owned by the C.S. Lewis Foundation of Redlands, California, and has undergone extensive renovation, retaining its period character.

Kirke, Digory Digory appears as a boy in *The Magician's Nephew**, then as a grown-up in *The Lion, the Witch and the Wardrobe** and *The Last Battle**. As a boy he and his dying mother lodge with his Uncle Andrew* in late Victorian London. With his neighbour, Polly Plummer*, he travels to other worlds by means of magical rings*, and is present at the creation of Narnia* by Aslan*, the talking lion. By the beginning of the Second World War, he is an elderly professor who owns a country house of historical interest. The Pevensie children* arrive as evacuees*, and stumble across a way into Narnia through his wardrobe*, built of wood that grew from a magical Narnian apple. Later, he becomes poor, and, his house destroyed, he is forced to tutor students, including Peter Pevensie, in a small cottage. He perhaps owes something to the Professor in T.H. White's *Mistress Masham's Repose*, admired by Lewis. Digory's surname might be an affectionate tribute to Lewis's own tutor, W.T. Kirkpatrick*. Lewis had already used the name "Kirk" before in *The Pilgrim's Regress** for Mother Kirk*, representing the church*.

Kirke, Mabel Mother of Digory* in *The Magician's Nephew** and younger sister of Andrew Ketterley* and Letitia Ketterley*. She is dying and being nursed by her sister. (Her husband is forced by his employment to stay in India.) Digory brings an apple for her from the Land of Youth*, and she miraculously recovers. Later she, her husband, and Digory are able to return to living in the country, and they take Uncle Andrew with them.

Kirkpatrick, William T. (1848–1921) Lewis's tutor from 1914–1917, dubbed by him the "Great Knock" because of the impact of his stringent logical mind on the teenager. Kirkpatrick was the retired head teacher of Lurgan College, in Northern Ireland, where Albert Lewis*, C.S. Lewis's father, had studied. He lived in Bookham, Surrey, England, where Lewis lodged happily during the tutelage. Lewis held a great affection for Kirkpatrick, describing him as the person who came closer to being "a purely logical entity" than anyone else he had ever met. Kirkpatrick's method was to combine language study with first-hand experience of major works; he guided Lewis in German, French, Italian, Latin, and Classical Greek. His rationalism and atheism reinforced Lewis's own beliefs at that time, though Lewis's imagination* continued to have an independent, contradictory life (for instance, he discovered George MacDonald's* *Phantastes** during this period).

Kirkpatrick made his mark on Lewis's fiction, and can be seen in some characteristics of the learned Professor Digory Kirke* and in the sceptical Ulsterman Andrew MacPhee in *That Hideous Strength**.

L

***

Lady Liln The beautiful wife of Olvin* in *The Horse and His Boy*, the fair-haired king of Archenland*.

The lamb A form Aslan* takes in World's End*, near his country (see: **Aslan's Country**) in *The Voyage of the "Dawn Treader"*, on the borderlands of all worlds, providing a clue to his identity as redeemer of the world.

lamp post, lantern The lamp post stands at the western edge of Narnia* in both *The Magician's Nephew* and *The Lion, the Witch and the Wardrobe*, marking a way to the world of humans, according to the White Witch*. The portal between Narnia and our world via the wardrobe* is nearby to the lamp post, as is the place where Digory Kirke*, Polly Plummer*, and the others earlier stand and observe as Narnia is created by the song of Aslan*. In fact, the lamp post originates from a bar of a London lamp post torn off by Jadis*, which she still clutches in that other world and hurls at Aslan. It grows, like everything grows, in the first fecundity of that new creation.

The Landlord In *The Pilgrim's Regress*, John* first hears of the Landlord in his childhood Puritania*, and perceives the giver of rules to be a despot, before his understanding grows as a result of his pilgimage through the modern world. The Landlord is sovereign over Puritania and the other regions of John's world (depicted in the *Mappa Mundi*).

Land of Youth The place west of Narnia* in *The Magician's Nephew* where Digory Kirke* obtains at the request of Aslan* a magic apple. From the apple grows a tree that provides an apple the boy is able to take back to his dying mother. In Celtic mythology, the Land of Youth (Tir-na-nÓg) is in the realms of heaven*.

Lantern Waste The area in *The Magician's Nephew** in which the children enter an empty world and see Narnia* created by Aslan*. A Victorian London lamp post grows here from the piece of lamp post* brought by the White Witch*. In later years children again enter Narnia near here, through a wardrobe* in the story *The Lion, the Witch and the Wardrobe**. Lantern Waste is west of Beaversdam*. See also: **Narnia: geography; Narnia: history**

Lapsed Bear of Stormness A talking bear in *The Horse and His Boy** that regresses to the behaviour of a dumb beast*, attacking travellers. Prince Corin* becomes known as "Thunder-Fist" after successfully boxing with the bear and reforming him.

Lasaraleen Tarkheena An old friend of Aravis*, in *The Horse and His Boy**, who helps her to escape from the great Calormen* city of Tashbaan*.

The Last Battle **(1956)** Based upon biblical prophecies of the end of the world, this story tells the end of one world of which Narnia* is a part, how all worlds are linked, and how the great talking lion Aslan* is the key to this link. Thus *The Chronicles of Narnia** draw to their conclusion, and the consistency of their other-worldliness is established. It won the high-ranking Carnegie Medal for the best children's book of its year.

As in all the stories, children from our world are in Narnia to help or to rule. In this case, Eustace Scrubb* and Jill Pole* are the first to come. One of the strangest features of *The Last Battle*, a twist reminiscent of Charles Williams*, is that all the principal characters from our world who come into Narnia are already dead as a result of a train accident. There are some similarities with Lewis's *The Great Divorce**, in that events after death are imagined, and a vision of heaven* is presented.

The Last Battle tells of the passing of Narnia and the beginning of the New Narnia*. It recounts the attempt of Shift* the talking ape to delude the creatures of Narnia that Aslan* has returned. Shift drapes Puzzle*, a simple donkey, in a lion skin found floating in the river. He then persuades the talking animals* that Puzzle is Aslan returned, and that he, Shift, is his spokesperson. Worse, he forms an alliance with Narnia's traditional enemy, Calormen*.

Young King Tirian*, the last of the Narnian rulers, and seventh in descent from Rilian*, hears of evil things happening – talking trees cut down, Narnian animals enslaved – and cannot believe that Aslan has returned and that this is his will. With his loyal unicorn, Jewel*, he resists the Calormenes* and is captured. Like several before him in previous ages, he calls for help from our world. Eustace and Jill are sent in answer to his prayer. The true Aslan also returns.

In our world, Professor Digory Kirke* and Polly Plummer*, the very first visitors to Narnia (as recounted in *The Magician's Nephew**), had called together those who had been in Narnia (See: **Seven Friends of Narnia**). There is a train crash that kills those who answer the call, and are in an arriving train or awaiting it at the station. All go into Narnia, though only Eustace and Jill are active participants in the final battle against evil, helping Tirian, Jewel, and the loyal Narnians. The visitors see Aslan's judgment of all the inhabitants of Narnia and its other countries, and then are called "further up and further in" to a New Narnia. They discover that it is now permanently linked to their own, familiar world of England, also transfigured. They would never again have to part from Aslan, though now they see him in a new form.

L

Last Sea The stretch of ocean in *The Voyage of the "Dawn Treader"**, between World's End Island* and World's End*, in which light takes on an intensity that is both physical and spiritual.

"Learning in War-Time" An important essay that first appeared in book form in the collection *Transposition and Other Addresses** (1949). C.S. Lewis argued that nothing – not even war – can rightfully occupy the whole of our lives, except God* himself. People are not defined by any of their temporal functions. War might require dying for, but it should never be lived for. Since the fall of mankind, war is a permanent human state. All aspects of believers' lives are to be given to God, including scholarship. This gives all parts of life their proper place and allows them to be good in an ultimate sense, he believed. See also: **cosmic war**

"The Lefay Fragment" This fragment, named after the appearance in it of Mrs Lefay*, was written to explain various elements in *The Lion, the Witch and the Wardrobe**, such as the lamp post* and how Narnia* came to be. This posed a difficult artistic problem. In the fragment, Digory Kirke* is rather like Curdie in George MacDonald's* *The Princess and Curdie* when he shoots a white pigeon and feels sorry afterwards. In Digory's case, he cuts a limb of his friend, the oak tree, to impress a girl, Polly Plummer*. As a result he loses his gift of understanding the speech of living things, animals, and trees, and is bereft when he discovers the truth: "The only life he had ever known was a life in which you could talk to animals and trees. If that was to come to an end the world would be so different for him that he would be a complete stranger in it." Lewis abandoned it after a few thousand words as, artistically, it didn't work as a Narnia story – perhaps because the magic is in this rather than another world. The fragment reveals much about Lewis's creative processes – he wrote intuitively, inspired by vivid mental pictures. In many cases he was able to sustain the story from such a beginning, but sometimes not, as in this case and that of another fragment, "The Dark Tower"*, which was intended as another story about Elwin Ransom* in his science-fiction sequence.

Lefay, Mrs In *The Magician's Nephew**, the fairy godmother of Uncle Andrew*. She passes on to him a box of dust from Atlantis* to destroy, but he keeps it. She is probably named after the sinister Morgan Le Fay of Arthurian legend. Like Andrew Ketterley and Jadis*, she sees herself above "ordinary, ignorant people". In Lewis's abandoned "The Lefay Fragment"* she also appears, but as Digory Kirke's* eccentric but benevolent fairy godmother.

The Leopard Lucy's* favourite Narnian* constellation in *Prince Caspian** and *The Voyage of the "Dawn Treader"**, appearing in the summer sky along with the Ship and the Hammer. See also: **astronomy of Narnia**

letters of C.S. Lewis C.S. Lewis's letters have been published as the *Collected Letters* in three volumes, edited by Walter Hooper*. The series is a significant addition of the corpus of Lewis's major writings, because of the quality of his letters, and the addition of very many previously unpublished ones. Earlier selections of his correspondence include *Letters of C.S. Lewis* (1966), which has a memoir by his brother, W.H. Lewis*, and grew out of Warnie's very important unpublished biography, available to read at The Marion E. Wade Center, Wheaton College, Wheaton, Illinois. There is another copy at Oxford's Bodleian Library*.

Letters to An American Lady (1967), edited by Clyde S. Kilby, is a collection of letters to a woman Lewis never met, Mary Willis Shelburne. The largest collection outside the *Collected Letters* is *They Stand Together: The Letters of C.S. Lewis to Arthur Greeves (1914–1963)**, edited by Walter Hooper. This is made up of letters to one of Lewis's closest Ulster friends, Arthur Greeves*. *Letters to Children* (1985), edited by Lyle W. Dorsett and Marjorie Lamp Mead, contains a foreword by Douglas Gresham*, Lewis's stepson. In 1988, *Letters: C.S. Lewis and Don Giovanni Calabria: A Study in Friendship* was published, edited and translated from Latin by Martin Moynihan. A revised and enlarged edition of the *Letters* edited by W.H. Lewis was brought out in 1988, edited by Walter Hooper. It contained some changes to Warnie's sometimes rather free editing. This is therefore not strictly a complete replacement for the 1966 volume, which is worth obtaining if possible.

Letters to Malcolm: Chiefly on Prayer (1964) Malcolm is an imaginary friend of C.S. Lewis, to whom he writes twenty-two letters on the theme of prayer, and much else, including heaven* and the resurrection of the body. In the book, Lewis writes as having known Malcolm from undergraduate days. Some have felt that Lewis's theological writings lack an experiential depth (or a shyness of spiritual experience). This last book concerns one of the most experiential subjects of the Christian life, and Lewis handles it with great power. From the moment of his conversion to theism Lewis was a thoroughgoing supernaturalist*, and thus the question of petitionary prayer made in time to a God* outside space–time was a central one to him. He saw it as God's prerogative to change actual events in the light of the prayers of his people.

The letter format allowed C.S. Lewis to explore and speculate on prayer in a manner impossible in a more didactic book. Prayer, for Lewis, was necessary for any understanding of the relationship between man and God:

> This "real world" and "real self" are very far from being rock-bottom realities. I cannot, in the flesh, leave the stage...; but I can remember that these regions exist.

And I also remember that my apparent self... under his grease-paint is a real person with an off-stage life... And in prayer this real I struggles to speak, for once, from his real being, and to address, for once, not the other actors, but – what shall I call Him? The Author, for He invented us all? The Producer, for He controls all? Or the Audience, for He watches, and will judge, the performance?

Lewis, Albert (1863–1929) The father of C.S. Lewis and a gifted Belfast* Corporation county solicitor, 1889–1928. When his wife, Flora Lewis*, died of cancer, Albert Lewis was unable to cope with his grief, and sent the nine-year-old C.S. Lewis off to England to boarding school, to an establishment his son later called "Belsen"*. Relations between Mr Lewis and his two sons were often strained. C.S. Lewis portrays his father as having little talent for happiness, and withdrawing into the safe monotony of routine. A.N. Wilson, however, believes the picture Lewis painted of his father as a "comic character" to be one-sided. The richest heritage he gave to Lewis was, literally, a houseful of old books that the gifted boy explored unimpeded. Lewis acknowledges this debt in *Surprised by Joy** and in his preface to *The Allegory of Love** (see: **reading of C.S. Lewis**).

Albert Lewis shared an interest in writing with his son, and a gift for rhetoric, including recounting "wheezes" (pithy observations often of humourous events). Lewis as a child was taken by Albert and Flora Lewis to worship at nearby St Mark's*, Dundela, on the outskirts of Belfast, where there is a stained glass window placed in memory of their parents by the Lewis brothers. Albert's Irish brogue was a constant source of amusement to his sons – throughout their lives they often refered to him as the "P.B." or the "Pudaita-bird", after the way he pronounced "potato". Like his wife long before him, Albert Lewis succumbed to cancer in 1929.

Lewis, Clive Staples Known to his friends and family as "Jack" (he didn't like "Clive Staples"), Lewis was born in the outskirts of Belfast* on 29 November 1898, and died in his Oxford* home, The Kilns*, almost sixty-five years later on 22 November 1963. He was equally a scholar and a storyteller. An account of his early life, his conversion from atheism to Christianity, and his awareness of joy* and longing for a fulfilment outside his own self is told in his autobiography *Surprised by Joy** and his allegory *The Pilgrim's Regress**.

His published letters (see: **letters of C.S. Lewis**) and *Brothers and Friends: The Diaries of Major Warren Hamilton Lewis** give vivid insights into his life. A selection from his diaries*, *All My Road Before Me**, records the years between 1922 and 1927. Jack Lewis was devoted to his brother, W.H. "Warnie" Lewis*. The two were brought together by their common interest in creating imaginary worlds as boys, particularly Boxen*, and also by their mother's death. Mrs Flora Lewis* died when Jack was nine. Their father never got over the loss and relations between him and his sons became more and more strained as time went on, particularly with Jack.

In the year of his mother's death from cancer, Lewis was sent off to Hertfordshire to join his brother at a school he was later to dub "Belsen"*. The brutal head teacher there was certified insane several years later. In 1910 Jack was moved first to Campbell College*, Belfast, and the next year to "Chartres"* (Cherbourg House) in Malvern, and later Malvern College* ("Wyvern"), Worcestershire. He was never happy, however, until he was finally sent in 1914 to a private tutor in Bookham, Surrey, W.T. Kirkpatrick*.

His brother Warnie wrote in his introduction to *Letters of C.S. Lewis*: "The fact is he should never have been sent to a public school at all. Already, at 14, his intelligence was such that he would have fitted in better among undergraduates than schoolboys; and by his temperament he was bound to be a misfit, a heretic, an object of suspicion within the collective-minded and standardising Public School system." Characteristically, Jack's first article – for a school magazine – was entitled "Are Athletes Better Than Scholars?"

His private tutorage under the Irishman W.T. Kirkpatrick was one of the happiest periods of Lewis's life. Not only did he rapidly mature and grow under the stringent rationality of this teacher, but he discovered the beauty of the English countryside and fantasy* writers such as William Morris. Full of the discovery of George Macdonald's* *Phantastes**, Lewis wrote about its power to Arthur Greeves*, his lifelong Ulster friend, in 1915: "Of course it is hopeless for me to try and describe it, but when you have followed the hero Anodos along that little stream to the faery wood, have heard about the terrible ash tree... and heard the episode of Cosmo, I know that you will quite agree with me." In *Surprised by Joy*, Lewis describes the effect as "baptising his imagination".

The First World War had broken out, and its shadow loomed over Lewis's peace. Warnie was already on active duty. Lewis was not old enough to enlist until later in the war. He spent his nineteenth birthday at the front line. In spring 1918, he was wounded in action and was eventually discharged after a spell in hospital. During all this time he had been writing poetry and preparing a book of poems, *Spirits in Bondage**, for publication.

At the Front he had lost a billet mate called "Paddy" Moore. Before his death, Lewis had promised him that should anything happen to him, he would take care of Paddy's mother and sister.

Lewis in fact looked after Mrs Janie Moore* until her death in 1951, and it is possible that he had an intimate relationship with her up to his conversion to Christian faith, as emphasized by his biographer A.N. Wilson. This is also deemed likely by his biographer George Sayer*, and Walter Hooper*. Owen Barfield* felt the likelihood to be about fifty-fifty. There is no conclusive evidence for this, however, and Lewis's moral beliefs and the death in battle of Mrs Moore's son make his explanatory story of her being his adoptive mother plausible. Her troublesome personality was more a thorn in the flesh to Warnie, particularly later in his acquaintance with her, than it seemed to be to him.

By 1923 Lewis had confirmed his brilliance by gaining a triple First at Oxford* University. He won a temporary lectureship in philosophy at University College (see: **idealism, C.S. Lewis and**). Then Magdalen College appointed him as a fellow, lecturing and tutoring in English (see: **literary critic; C S Lewis as a**). He was an Oxford don until 1954, when Cambridge University invited him to the new Chair of Medieval and Renaissance Literature, where he described himself as an "Old Western Man" in his inaugural lecture (see: **The Old West**). C.S. Lewis's pupils included such figures as the critic Kenneth Tynan*, George Sayer, the poet John Betjeman*, Harry Blamires*, and novelist and poet John Wain*.

In the early Oxford days Professor J.R.R. Tolkien* became one of Lewis's lifelong friends. They would criticize one another's poetry, drift into theology and philosophy, pun, or talk English Department politics.

Tolkien's deep friendship with C.S. Lewis was of great significance to both men (see: **friendship of J.R.R. Tolkien and C.S. Lewis**). Tolkien found in him an appreciative audience for his burgeoning stories and poems of Middle-earth, a good deal of which was not published until after his death. Without Lewis's encouragement over many years, admitted Tolkien, *The Lord of the Rings* would have never appeared in print. Lewis equally had cause to appreciate Tolkien. His views on myth* and imagination*, and the relation of both to reality, eventually helped to convince a very sceptical Lewis (who had not long before been a firm atheist) to convert to Christianity. Seeing mind to mind on both these issues formed the strong foundation of their remarkable friendship. The Inklings*, the group of literary friends around Lewis, grew out of this rapport.

A.N. Wilson, in his biography *C.S. Lewis*, remarks that at the very beginning of their association, it "must have seemed clear to him at once that Tolkien was a man of literary genius". On Tolkien's side, thinking with sadness in 1929 of his marriage, he wrote: "Friendship with Lewis compensates for much."

After the war, the American *Time* magazine published a perceptive cover feature on Lewis (8 September 1947) that was partly responsible for increasing his appeal in the United States. The article was researched in the later war years, and partly based on an interview with Lewis's friend and Inkling Charles Williams*.

In 1953 Lewis met an American woman, Helen Joy Davidman Gresham (see: **Lewis, Helen Joy Davidman**), with whom he had corresponded for some time. She was a poet and novelist who had been converted from atheism and Marxism to Christianity partly through reading Lewis's books. When she was free to remarry, and was dying of cancer, Lewis married her. He never got over her death in 1960, and his grief was combined with constant worry about his brother's alcoholism. The last book he sent to press, *Letters to Malcolm: Chiefly on Prayer**, affirmed his hope in heaven*.

Further reading
Roger Lancelyn Green and Walter Hooper, *C.S. Lewis: A Biography* (1974, 2002); George Sayer, *Jack: C.S. Lewis and His Times* (1988); A. N. Wilson, *C.S. Lewis: A Biography* (1990); Alan Jacobs, *The Narnian* (2005); Colin Duriez, *C.S. Lewis: A Biography of Friendship* (2013).

Lewis family papers When Warnie Lewis* moved into The Kilns* (first on leave from the Army, then permanently), he began the enormous task of dealing with the family papers (letters*, diaries*, photographs, and various documents), typing and arranging the material in what ended up being eleven volumes. They are entitled *The Lewis Papers: Memoirs* *of the Lewis Family: 1850–1930.* The volumes were completed in 1935 and bequeathed by Warnie Lewis to The Marion E. Wade Center, Wheaton College, Wheaton, Illinois, as a result of his friendship with pioneering Lewis scholar Clyde S. Kilby. They include a fragment of Lewis's uncompleted Ulster novel, "The Easley Fragment"*.

Lewis, Flora Hamilton (1862–1908) C.S. Lewis's mother was the daughter of the church rector at St Mark's*, Dundela, Belfast*, the Lewis family church. Today a stained glass window in memory of C.S. Lewis's parents can be seen in the church, put there by the Lewis brothers. In various examinations leading up to a BA, Flora gained First Class honours in geometry, algebra, and logic and Second Class honours in mathematics, at Queen's University, Belfast (then called the Royal University of Ireland). Lewis recalled that neither of his parents "had the least taste for… that kind of literature to which my allegiance was given the moment I could choose books for myself. Neither had ever listened for the horns of elfland. There was no copy either of Keats or Shelley in the house, and the copy of Coleridge was never (to my knowledge) opened. If I am a romantic," he concludes, "my parents bear no responsibility for it." The grim, uncushionable blow of his mother's death from cancer took away all that was stable in the nine-year-old C.S. Lewis's life. His father, unable to cope with his grief, almost immediately sent him off to a boarding school that Lewis savagely nicknamed "Belsen"*, in *Surprised by Joy**. A dying mother appears in the Narnia* tale, *The Magician's Nephew**, but her story has a happy ending.

Lewis, Helen Joy Davidman (1915–1960) C.S. Lewis's wife, and subject of his book *A Grief Observed**, written after her death from cancer at the age of forty-five. Joy Davidman was a poet and novelist (see: ***Anya***) from a New York Jewish family, and she also published a theological study of the Ten

Commandments, *Smoke on the Mountain*. Lewis's attraction to her was at first merely intellectual, that of friendship. She was at that time on the verge of divorce, with two young sons. Joy had been converted from Marxism to Christianity partly through reading C.S. Lewis.

Some time after meeting Lewis, Joy Davidman came to live in Oxford* with her sons. She and Lewis became on close terms. In retrospect he wrote, "Her mind was lithe and quick and muscular as a leopard. Passion, tenderness and pain were all equally unable to disarm it. It scented the first whiff of cant or slush; then sprang, and knocked you over before you knew what was happening." They married, in a civil ceremony to give her British nationality, in April 1956.

In the autumn of 1956 they learned that Joy had terminal cancer. It was sudden, unexpected news, and Lewis was deeply shocked. Cancer was an old acquaintance. Her two boys were about the same age as the Lewis brothers had been when their mother died; the parallels were uncomfortable. A bedside Christian wedding ceremony took place on 21 March 1957. Joy came home to The Kilns* to die.

After prayer* for healing, she had an unexpected reprieve. By July she was well enough to get out and about. The next year they had a fortnight's holiday in Ireland. The remission was the beginning of the happiest few years of both their lives. Lewis confessed to Nevill Coghill*: "I never expected to have, in my sixties, the happiness that passed me by in my twenties."

Lewis's brother, Warnie*, points out that the marriage fulfilled "a whole dimension to his nature that had previously been starved and thwarted". It also put paid to a bachelor's doubt that God* was an invented substitute for love. "For those few years H. and I feasted on love," Lewis recalled in *A Grief Observed*, "every mode of it – solemn and merry, romantic and realistic, sometimes as dramatic as a thunderstorm, sometimes as comfortable and unemphatic as putting on your soft slippers."

L

The cancer eventually returned, but the Lewises were able to have a trip to Greece in the spring of the year of her death, a journey much desired by both of them. The story of the happiness that had come to Lewis so late in life, and subsequent bitter bereavement, has been made into two successful films and a play based around a script by William Nicholson, entitled *Shadowlands*. The earliest film, for the BBC*, is the closer to reality. The dramatic licence used in all versions has created much debate, but they each are extraordinarily poignant. Many in their audiences have been inspired to read Lewis for the first time. The original research for *Shadowlands*, undertaken by Brian Sibley, was historically accurate, and became the basis for his book of the same name (1985).

Recently, Joy Davidman's writings have come into focus, with attention starting to bear upon her poetry and novels. A milestone in this has been the publication of a large selection of her letters, compiled and edited by Don W. King. A large sequence of accomplished sonnets she wrote concerning her love for C.S. Lewis has been discovered, and archived in The Marion E. Wade Center, Wheaton College, Wheaton, Illinois.

Further reading
Lyle Dorsett, *Joy and C.S. Lewis* (1988); Douglas H. Gresham, *Lenten Lands: My Childhood with Joy Davidman and C.S. Lewis* (1989); Don W. King (ed.), *Out of My Bone: The Letters of Joy Davidman* (2009); Brian Sibley, *Shadowlands* (1985).

Lewis, Warren Hamilton "Warnie" (1895–1973) Lewis's only brother, a lifelong friend, and a member of the Inklings* from its inception. Like his brother he was a gifted writer, producing a number of books on French history. He contributed to *Essays Presented to Charles Williams*. His diaries* provide a unique and essential insight into Lewis's life and meetings of the Inklings. A selection has been published as *Brothers and Friends* (1982), but only in North America.

Warnie Lewis began his military career when he entered the Royal Military Academy shortly before the outbreak of the First World War. After the war he served in Sierra Leone, and Shanghai, before retiring from the army in 1932 with a pension. He joined the unusual household run by his brother and Mrs Janie Moore* at The Kilns*, in Oxford*. This short section cannot do justice to his brother's immeasurable importance to Lewis, an importance that can be seen through Warnie's elegantly written diaries. He devoted himself to the task of editing the Lewis family papers* and, after C.S. Lewis's death, prepared a powerful memoir of his brother, now housed in The Marion E. Wade Center, Wheaton College (with a copy in the Bodleian Library*, Oxford). An abridged version of the *Memoirs* is published in *Letters of C.S. Lewis* (1966, 1988) (see: **letters of C.S. Lewis**).

Life of Samuel Johnson, James Boswell (1791) The *Life of Samuel Johnson* resulted from the association of James Boswell, the natural documenter, and Dr Samuel Johnson, the eighteenth-century man of letters. Lewis listed it as one of the ten books that most influenced his thought and vocational attitude (see: **reading of C.S. Lewis**). It is a biography perhaps unique in literature, and at once became a classic. In Boswell, hero worship and appreciation became an artform. Boswell's documentary brilliance merges with Johnson's towering literary talent. Johnson, like Lewis, was larger than life, in personality and endlessly active intellect, and he looms large in almost every sentence of this hypnotically admiring book. Boswell seems to forget no detail of speech or manner. As Helen Rex Keller remarks, "Boswell begins with Johnson's first breath (drawn it seems, with difficulty), and will not let him draw a later breath without full commentary." Here is a taste of Boswell from some brief extracts:

We dined at Elgin, and saw the noble ruins of the Cathedral. Though it rained much, Dr. Johnson examined them with a most patient attention.

Next day, Sunday, July 31, I told him I had been that morning at a meeting of the people called Quakers, where I had heard a woman preach.

JOHNSON: "Sir, a woman's preaching is like a dog's walking on his hind legs. It is not done well, but you are surprised to find it done at all."

JOHNSON: Well, we had a good talk.
BOSWELL. Yes, Sir; you tossed and gored several persons.

JOHNSON:A man, indeed, is not genteel when he gets drunk; but most vices may be committed very genteelly: a man may debauch his friend's wife genteelly: he may cheat at cards genteelly.

James Boswell (1740–1795) was a member of Samuel Johnson's London Literary Club and the two men travelled to Scotland together, their journeys recorded in Boswell's *Journal of the Tour to the Hebrides* (1785). Born in Edinburgh, Boswell studied law but soon centred his ambitions on literature and politics. Boswell's long-lost personal papers became public in 1949, and his journals are of particular interest.

Lilith In *The Lion, the Witch and the Wardrobe**, an ancestor of the White Witch*. She is a figure from Babylonian and Hebrew imagination, in mystical tradition the first wife of Adam, particularly vindictive to babies and children. C.S. Lewis's mentor, George MacDonald*, explores the symbolic* figure in his fantasy* *Lilith* (1895).

Lilygloves A chief mole in *Prince Caspian**, a talking animal*, who helped to plant an orchard at Cair Paravel*. At the time of the events recorded in the book, the orchard has run wild for centuries.

Lindsay, David (1876–1945) His *A Voyage to Arcturus* (1920) is today recognized as one of the classics of science fiction, though its first edition sold under 600 copies, making it difficult for Lindsay to sell subsequent work. C.S. Lewis, hearing of it, found difficulty in obtaining a copy. When he did, it greatly influenced his own science-fiction trilogy*, and his unfinished *The Dark Tower and Other Stories**. Writing of *Out of the Silent Planet** in 1944, Lewis responded in a letter to an enquiry about influences on his work: "The real father of my planet book is David Lindsay's *A Voyage to Arcturus*, which you also will revel in if you don't yet know it. I had grown up on [H.G.] Well's [sic] stories of that kind: it was Lindsay who first gave me the idea that the 'scientifiction' appeal could be combined with the 'supernatural' appeal... His own spiritual outlook is detestable, almost diabolist I think, and his style is crude: but he showed me what a bang you could get from mixing these two elements."

Lindsay's "Tormance", in far-off Arcturus, perhaps gets its name from a contraction of "torment" and "romance". In an essay, "On Stories", which appeared in *Essays Presented to Charles Williams**, Lewis wrote that David Lindsay's "Tormance is a region of the spirit. He is the first writer to discover what 'other planets' are really good for in fiction. No merely physical strangeness or merely spatial distance will realize that idea of otherness which is what we are always trying to grasp in a story about voyaging through space: you must go into another dimension. To construct plausible and moving 'other worlds' you must draw on the only real 'other world' we know, that of the spirit."

L

David Lindsay's other tales of fantasy* were *The Haunted Woman* (1922), *Sphinx* (1923), and *Devil's Tor* (1932). He also wrote a historical novel, *The Adventures of M. de Mailly* (1926). In 1970 a memorial volume, *The Strange Genius of David Lindsay*, appeared, including articles by Colin Wilson and E.H. Visiak (who finds parallels between *A Voyage to Arcturus* and Milton's *Paradise Lost*).

The Lion, the Witch and the Wardrobe (1950) This is the first tale of Narnia* that C.S. Lewis wrote. Its inspiration owed something to evacuee* children who lodged in Lewis's Oxford* home, The Kilns*, and began with a picture that he saw in his head of "a faun carrying an umbrella and parcels in a snowy wood". Four children, Peter, Susan, Edmund, and Lucy Pevensie*, are evacuated from wartime London to stay with Professor Digory Kirke* (who, as a boy, had visited Narnia, as recounted in *The Magician's Nephew**). In one room of his vast house is a bulky wardrobe*, made out of a tree that grew from a Narnian seed. Through this wardrobe the children enter a snowy wood in Narnia's Lantern Waste*. Three of them join forces with the talking animals* who are loyal to Aslan*, the great talking lion, creator of Narnia. Edmund, however, turns traitor and goes over to the White Witch*, who has Narnia in her spell, so that it is always winter and never Christmas. Aslan pays the terrible cost of Edmund's treachery by sacrificing his own life to break the witch's magic. Narnia is freed, Aslan returns to life, the witch is destroyed, and the creatures that she had turned to stone are unpetrified by the lion. See also: **Narnia: history**

literary critic, C.S. Lewis as a C.S. Lewis was an outstanding literary critic, being invited to the newly created Chair of Medieval and Renaissance Literature at Cambridge University in 1954 as a result of his work on these periods. Prior to that, he was for almost thirty years a fellow and tutor in English at

Magdalen College, Oxford* University. His main works of literary criticism are: *The Allegory of Love: A Study in Medieval Tradition** (1936), *Rehabilitations and Other Essays** (1939), *The Personal Heresy: A Controversy** (1939, with E.M.W. Tillyard), *A Preface to Paradise Lost** (1942), *Arthurian Torso** (1948, with Charles Williams*), *English Literature in the Sixteenth Century, Excluding Drama** (1954), *Reflections on the Psalms** (1958), *Studies in Words** (1960), *An Experiment in Criticism** (1961), *The Discarded Image: An Introduction to Medieval and Renaissance Literature** (1964), *Studies in Medieval and Renaissance Literature* (1966), *Spenser's Images of Life** (1967, edited by Alistair Fowler), and *Selected Literary Essays* (1969).

Literature is more than mere written language. R. Wellek and A. Warren's definition in *Theory of Literature* is useful: "The term 'literature' seems best if we limit it to the art of literature, that is, to imaginitive literature... We recognize 'fictionality,' 'invention,' or 'imagination' as the distinguishing trait of literature." Older views of the nature of literature, in nineteenth-century literary criticism for instance, have a wider perspective than this, and thus a larger canon, but did recognize the importance of the aesthetic element in literary works.

What is C.S. Lewis's place in literary criticism? Generally, literary theories have perhaps had one of three dominant emphases: they been author-centred, text-centred, or reader-centred. It is worth making a simple thumbnail sketch of these positions to see C.S. Lewis's contribution to criticism and continuing value as a critic more clearly.

Traditionally, criticism was concerned with what is extrinsic to the literary text, its origin, authorship, original setting, and the like. It has needed to know about the activities and thinking of the author. This has been described by later critics as the "intentional fallacy", and part of it by C.S. Lewis as "the personal heresy" (see: **The Personal Heresy**). Traditional criticism interpreted the meaning* of a piece of literature by concentrating on the author and his or her social and cultural world. Questions of origin and authority are central, standing in the stream of Western metaphysical tradition.

In the 1940s and 1950s the so-called "New Criticism" shifted from an extrinsic to an intrinsic regard for the text. It moved away from authorial intent to an emphasis on the autonomy of the literary work. The New Criticism was rooted in the thought of T.S. Eliot, I.A. Richards, and William Empson. As a trend, it included several American scholars and F.R. Leavis in Britain.

The trend takes its name from John Crowe Ransom's *The New Criticism* (1942). It sees the text as self-sufficient, with the author's intention and background being unimportant. The literary text is typically perceived as an artifact or "verbal icon". A parallel in the modern novel is John Fowles's (and others') rejection of an all-knowing narrator. The New Criticism requires a close reading of the text, and has been deeply influential in English studies.

Another text-centred movement is structuralism. Structuralism is actually rooted in linguistics, but has affected many disciplines, as described by Jean Piaget in his book *Structuralism* (1968, English translation 1970). It is a general theory about human culture. It sees all aspects of culture characterized by signs, the meaning of which lie in their interrelatedness. Metaphor is key to all human thought from the cave man to our present Information Age, being based upon our human ability to recognize similarity in difference. Literature is particularly important to structuralism because its "material" is language itself. Instead of appreciating the originality and genius of an author, the concern of structuralist criticism is with the writer's actual transformations of deep structures or pre-existing meanings.

In contrast, reader-centred theories emphasize the reader's role in creating the meaning of the literary text. Softer views within this camp are interested in the objective interaction between the reader and the text, rather like the analogy of an orchestra performing a musical score. Just as the music lives as it is performed, the text is realized as it is read. There are therefore good and bad readers, ideal readers, competent readers. Feminist or Marxist criticism (or other ideologies) can fall into a reader-centred approach, as can psycho-analytical and gender criticism. This approach has drawn attention to the "pre-understanding" or world view of the reader in coming to the text.

An important movement in literary criticism is deconstruction. This is part of a wider postmodernist trend seeking the dismantling of all Western metaphysics, including Christian theism. As in the thought of Don Cupitt, "God" is a symbol* of human aspirations and has no objective reference – there is no thing or person called God* that exists. Deconstruction questions the basis of author-, text-, and reader-centred approaches. It rejects any univocal, unambiguous view of meaning*. Jacques Derrida was a central force behind deconstruction. He links the "myth" of authorial presence in a text with *author*-ity. Concepts of authority need to be abandoned. Literary meaning is an "endless labyrinth". He exalts writing over speech, seeing earlier literary critics as speech-centred and thus "logocentred".

Deconstruction is characteristic of postmodernism. Its abandonment of Western metaphysics, particularly theism, is expressed for example by Roland Barthes in his essay "The Death of the Author": "Literature (it would be better from now on to say writing), by refusing to assign a 'secret', an ultimate meaning, to the text (and to the world as text), liberates what may be called an anti-theological activity, an activity that is truly revolutionary since to refuse to fix meaning is, in the end, to refuse God and his hypostases – reason, science, law." Not only is God dead, as prophesied by the philosopher Nietzsche, but also the author and, ultimately, the critic.

L

In the kind of movements sketched above, literary criticism has become an important part of the shaping of contemporary culture. Can C.S. Lewis's own work in this area still contribute to this momentous debate?

Though Lewis died in 1963, his literary criticism has much to contribute today. He still offers a sturdy defence of a literary criticism based upon theism, and what he would call "Old Western values" (see: **The Old West**). He would see much contemporary criticism as helping the cause of those working for the abolition of mankind (see: *The Abolition of Man)*, in dismantling transcendent, objective values. More remarkable, he also avoids the extremes of reader-, author-, or text-centredness, while appreciating the importance of all these three dimensions of literary meaning.

The critic David Lodge sums up Lewis's position as a historical approach to literature. For him, C.S. Lewis's literary criticism

> shows a remarkable range of interest and expertise,
> but Lewis was probably best known and admired
> for his work on medieval literature… C.S. Lewis in
> many ways represented the "Oxford" tradition of
> literary criticism at its best: relaxed, knowledgeable,
> enthusiastic, conservative… It is clear that he regarded
> the study of literature as primarily a historical one,
> and its justification as the conservation of the past. *De
> Descriptione Temporum* expresses eloquently, learnedly and
> wittily this conception of the subject and Lewis's doubts
> about its viability in the future.

"*De Descriptione Temporum*"* was C.S. Lewis's inaugural lecture at Cambridge. However, Lewis is not simply a literary historian. His historical work had a double purpose: to shed light on the textual meaning (for example, its iconography) rather than the author's personality, society, or other extrinsic feature, and to value a historically distant text as a remarkable window into a previous cultural world. That world was the fruit of corporate human imagination* and power, containing values that we need to take into account. We need perspectives on the narrow limitations of our own world model of today.

As regards the reader, in his seminal *An Experiment in Criticism** Lewis attacks the evaluative criticism of F.R. Leavis and others. He rejects their "good" and "bad" literature, in favour of "good" and "bad" readers. Good readers attend to and receive the text rather than using it for some end. Literary texts are intended to have readers. Some texts may be too poor to merit the attention of readers, but where a good reader finds nourishment in a text, one can be sure that meaning is captured there: presence, transcendence, authority, power, insight, and understanding.

Much of C.S. Lewis's critical work was on Edmund Spenser, Geoffrey Chaucer, the Arthurian tales, John Milton, and Dante, as well as on myth*, allegory*, world models, meaning*, story, metaphor, linguistics, and fairy stories. He also wrote key essays on John Bunyan, Jane Austen, Percy Bysshe Shelley, and William Morris, many of them collected in *Selected Literary Essays*.

Through all his work Lewis advocates and demonstrates the close reading of texts, where readers and critics have a first-hand experience of an author's work. Lewis argues that "we invariably judge a critic by the extent to which he illuminates reading we have already done". Such close reading ought to be in the original languages, if possible. It was important therefore, believes Lewis, for a student and reader of English literature to be acquainted with Anglo-Saxon. As well as classical languages, Lewis was able to read German, French, and Italian, and this enriched his critical work.

Complementary to this textual concern is a historical engagement. He is always interested in the intellectual and cultural currents of a period. Lewis feels that the extrinsic features of the literary work are essential to consider, such as its world view, including the model of reality and the universe it embodied, and authorial intention. For him this does not mean that the text is a personal, cultural, or moralistic expression, or simply a quarry for anthropologists, theologians, psychologists, and sociologists. The work, according to Lewis, is *poiema* as well as *logos**, something made as well as something said. Therefore as a unique entity it should be taken on its own terms.

He emphasizes the interrelationship of literary works, particularly in what he perceives as a unified period before the rise of the stranglehold of modernism, a period he sees as stretching from ancient pagan times to sometime in the nineteenth century. Literary works illuminate each other, contributing to a symbolic* language and iconography. Lewis is not a narrow specialist. He is at ease in a number of disciplines, such as philosophy, classics, and history, but usually humble about the extent of his knowledge when he steps out of his professional field, as when he writes popular theology.

Related to this wideness of view is his preoccupation with Christianizing paganism*, and with a rehabilitation of premodernist literature and values. For Lewis there is a vast ancient continuity. So he is not simply rehabilitating the medieval period but the entire premodernist period. He has a strong polemical purpose. Lewis paints the inner world using allegory, symbol, or myth – just like the medievals and the earlier ancient Western world. His fiction and literary work are therefore of a piece. He believes that, with skill, contemporary literature can take us into the literature of the Old West, by our recognizing likeness, going from the more familiar to the less. A child for example may read *The Voyage of the "Dawn Treader"** and later discover that Homer's *The Odyssey* is familiar.

In his literary criticism, Lewis maintains both continuity and discontinuity with the present (he is a premodernist who has a postmodern appeal). He is thus valuable in giving a transcendent perspective on our times. His early rejection of "chronological snobbery"* allowed this freedom. His preoccupation with story, and metaphor as a condition of all good thinking, was fought out in opposition to modernism and its characteristic naturalism*. These interests are highly palatable in our postmodernist era. Yet at the same time his work refuses to be reduced to a postmodernist position; he is unashamedly premodernist in his chosen beliefs and tastes. Another (and related) feature of his work that appeals to a postmodernist climate is his hallmark emphasis upon particularity – the distinctiveness that exists in people, places, and books.

To him the symbolic and imaginative are supremely important. They were a significant factor in his move from atheism to Christianity, and in his professional life thereafter. He advocates what might be called a symbolic perception of reality. The flair of his criticism is notable: it is elegantly written, with a timeless element. Furthermore, his literary and related criticism fuels his imaginative writing. There are often parallels for instance, between his works of criticism and particular fictions. The pattern is established in the inspiration that *The Allegory of Love* (started in 1928) gives to the writing of *The Pilgrim's Regress** (1933): his *A Preface to Paradise Lost** (1942) naturally leads to *Perelandra** (1943); *The Abolition of Man** (1943) theoretically treats the themes of *That Hideous Strength** (1945); his many explorations of myth* and pre-Christian paganism result in *Till We Have Faces** (1956); and it could perhaps be argued that his consideration of Spenser's *The Faerie Queene* over many years provides a pattern for the imaginative eclecticism yet coherent unity of the Narnian Chronicles* (1950–1956). See also: **theology, C.S. Lewis and; theology of romance**
    Further reading
    Tremper Longman, *Literary Approaches to Biblical Interpretation* (1987); David Lodge (ed.), *20th Century Literary Criticism: A Reader*

L

(1972); Bruce L. Edwards, *A Rhetoric of Reading: C.S. Lewis's Defense of Western Literacy* (1985); Doris T. Myers, *C.S. Lewis in Context* (1994).

Little Lea Leeborough House, Lewis's childhood home from 1905, described in detail in his autobiography, *Surprised by Joy**. It is located in Strandtown, on the outskirts of Belfast*. When the Lewis family moved there, the house was set in open countryside with an uninterrupted view of Belfast Lough. Now it is in a suburban area. Bernagh*, home of Arthur Greeves*, and Glenmachan*, residence of the Ewarts*, were nearby. The "little end room" in the attic area was of particular importance to the young Lewis brothers, providing a haven for writing, reading, and drawing.

logos In *An Experiment in Criticism*, C.S. Lewis contrasts *logos* (as, something said) with *poema* (as, something made, from which comes our word "poetry") in a work of literature. He also readily uses the term elsewhere, as a classical and medieval scholar, and a philosopher. The word comes from the Greek verb *legein*, which means "to say" something substantial. In early philosophy, *logos* connected rational explanation, description, and discourse with the rationality of the world, in a broad range of meanings. In Jewish and Christian thought, *logos* became identified with the Word – the divine power to bring all things into being, and to govern them, by way of speech that embodied wisdom.

The Lone Islands A group of islands comprising Felimath*, Doorn*, and Avra*, and visited by the travellers in *The Voyage of the "Dawn Treader"**. Ancient King Gale* of Narnia* had once rid these islands of a dragon and, in gratitude, was given them to be part of Narnia. They lie 400 leagues to the east of that land in the Eastern Ocean*. See also: **Narnia: geography; Narnia: history**

love See: ***The Four Loves***

Lucy, Queen See: **The Pevensie children**

Lune, King The jolly father of Shasta* (Cor*) and Corin*, in *The Horse and His Boy*, and king of Archenland* during the Golden Age* of Narnia*. He rules from the strategic castle at Anvard*. He enjoys dressing in old, comfortable clothes, a quality admired by Lewis, for whom uncomfortable dress was a sign of spiritual restriction.

Lysias See: **The Fox**

M

McCallum, Ronald Buchanan (1898–1973) A member of the Inklings* and a fellow and tutor of history of Pembroke College, Oxford* University, until 1955, when he was elected Master of Pembroke.

MacDonald, George (1824–1905) The Scottish writer was born in Huntly in rural Aberdeenshire, the son of a weaver. C.S. Lewis regarded his own debt to him as inestimable. Like Lewis, MacDonald lost his mother in boyhood, a fact that touched his thought and writings. His views on the imagination* anticipated those of Lewis and J.R.R. Tolkien*, and inspired G.K. Chesterton*. MacDonald was a close friend of Charles Dodgson (Lewis Carroll) and John Ruskin, the art critic. His insights into the unconscious mind predated the rise of modern psychology. Like Lewis and Tolkien, he was a scholar as well as a storyteller. George MacDonald made a memorable appearance in C.S. Lewis's *The Great Divorce**, for Lewis regarded him as his "master".

MacDonald's sense that all imaginative meaning* originates with the Christian creator God* became the foundation of C.S. Lewis's thinking and imagining. Two key essays, "The Imagination: its Functions and its Culture" (1867) and "The Fantastic Imagination" (1882), remarkably foreshadow Tolkien's famous essay "On Fairy Stories" (1947). (Tolkien's views on imagination's role in knowledge significantly helped to persuade C.S. Lewis to convert to Christianity.) As an adolescent, Lewis had stumbled across a copy of MacDonald's *Phantastes** (1858), resulting in what he decribed as a baptism of his imagination.

George MacDonald wrote nearly thirty novels, several books of sermons, a number of abiding fantasies* for adults and children, short stories, and poetry. His childhood is beautifully captured in his semi-autobiographical *Ranald Bannerman's Boyhood* (1871). He never lost sight of his humble childhood and adolescence, when he had lived in a cottage so small that he slept in an attic. He was a happy boy, riding, climbing, swimming, and fishing, and reading while lying on the back of his beloved horse. We catch many glimpses of the countryside he knew and loved in his writings.

MacDonald entered Aberdeen University in 1840, and had a scientific training. For a few years he worked as a tutor in London. Then he entered Highbury Theological College and married. He was called to a church in Arundel, Sussex, where he fell into disfavour with the deacons, who reduced his small salary to persuade him to leave. Some of the poorer members, however, rallied around with offerings they could ill afford. Then he moved to Manchester for some years, preaching to a small congregation and giving lectures. The rapidly growing family was always on the brink of poverty. Fortunately, the poet Lord Byron's widow, recognizing MacDonald's literary gifts, started to provide financial help. The family moved down to London, living in a house then called The Retreat, near the Thames at Hammersmith, later owned by William Morris.

Many famous writers and artists came to visit the MacDonalds, as well as people who shared a concern for London's desperate and crowded poor. One such friend was Charles Dodgson, who let the MacDonald children hear his story, *Alice in Wonderland*. As a result of their enthusiasm he decided to publish it. One of MacDonald's sons, Greville, remembered calling a cab for the poet Alfred, Lord Tennyson.

For a time George MacDonald was Professor of Literature at Bedford College, London. Because of continued ill health the family eventually moved to Italy, where MacDonald and his wife were to remain for the rest of their lives. There were, however, frequent stays in Britain during the warmer months, and a long and successful visit to the United States on a lecture tour. One of his last books, *Lilith* (1895) is among his greatest, a fantasy with the same power to move and to change a person's imaginative life as *Phantastes*.

In her book *The Stars and the Stillness: A Portrait of George MacDonald*, Kathy Triggs points out the paradox of a leading nineteenth-century writer being virtually forgotten today, and hazards some reasons for this. Today's is a post-Christian world where MacDonald's values are alien. Television and other claims on our time deprive us of the leisure to tackle his lengthy novels. Yet, she posits, people lose out on so much if they neglect to read him; his theological insights are still needed today. He was the master of ageless symbolism* in his imaginative work: a fact that so captured C.S. Lewis, bringing him face to face with the quality of holiness, though he didn't acknowledge it for many years.

The poet and critic W.H. Auden observed: "To me, George MacDonald's most extraordinary, and precious, gift is his ability, in all his stories, to create an atmosphere of goodness about which there is nothing phony or moralistic. Nothing is rarer in literature." It was this quality of goodness that attracted Lewis from the beginning, and he tried to emulate it in writing *The Chronicles of Narnia**.

Further reading
Greville MacDonald, *George MacDonald and His Wife* (1924); C.S. Lewis (ed.), *George MacDonald: An Anthology* (1946); Rolland Hein, *The Harmony Within: The Spiritual Vision of George MacDonald* (1982); Kathy Triggs, *The Stars and the Stillness: A Portrait of George MacDonald* (1986); William Raeper, *George MacDonald* (1987); Michael Phillips, *George MacDonald* (1987).

Macgowan, John (1726–1780) A Baptist minister and author of *Infernal Conference: Or, Dialogues of Devils*, a forerunner of C.S. Lewis's *The Screwtape Letters**, though Lewis may never have read it but merely have been told about it. There are striking similarities of aim; one devil is the uncle of another, and Lewis's preface echoes Macgowan's introduction. John Macgowan wrote several other popular works, including *Death: A Vision* and a life of the biblical character Ruth.

McNeill, Jane Agnes (1889–1959) A close family friend of C.S. Lewis's in childhood. She was the daughter of the head teacher of Campbell College*, briefly attended by Lewis. Both Lewis brothers dedicated books to her, C.S. Lewis's choice being *That Hideous Strength**. Was it a coincidence that a leading character is called Jane?

Macready, Mrs Professor Digory Kirke's* formidable housekeeper in *The Lion, the Witch and the Wardrobe**, in his large country house.

The Maenads These appear in *Prince Caspian*.* In classical mythology they are the female members of Bacchus's* boisterous company.

***The Magician's Nephew* (1955)** This tale tells of the creation of Narnia* by Aslan*. It also tells us about the late Victorian childhood of Professor Digory Kirke*, who owns the big country house with the wardrobe* in *The Lion, the Witch and the Wardrobe**, and about how the London gas lamp post* comes to be in Narnia at all. Also it speaks of the origin of the White Witch*, and explains the arrival of evil in Narnia – showing evil as older than that world.

Digory and his dying mother are staying with his Uncle Andrew* and Aunt Letty (Letitia) Ketterley* in London, his father being in India. He makes friends with Polly Plummer*, his neighbour, and the two are tricked into an experiment with magic rings* by the uncle, a mad scientist.

At first they find themselves in the dying world of Charn*, blighted by Jadis*, the White Witch, whom Digory awakes from a spell, despite warnings from Polly. They are unable to leave her behind as they return to London with the aid of the rings. There Jadis wreaks havoc, until the children are able to whisk her back to the Wood Between the Worlds*, but not before she has wrenched off a handle from a lamp post, intending to use it to punish those who opposed her. The trio, along with Frank*, a London hansom cab driver, his horse, and Uncle Andrew, end up in an empty world of Nothing, in time to hear Aslan's creation song. At the words and music of the lion's song, mountains, trees, animals, and other creatures come into being to make Narnia and the world of which it is part. The sequence is reminiscent of passages from J.R.R. Tolkien's* *The Silmarillion*, parts of which Lewis was familiar with in unfinished form.

Aslan gives Digory the opportunity of undoing the evil he had brought into Narnia. His task is to find a magic apple, the seed of which would produce a tree to protect the young world from Jadis for many years. Polly joins him on the adventure, which requires journeying into the mountains of the Western Wild* to find a delightful valley. In a garden there, on a hilltop, grows an apple tree with the magic apples. To help them, Frank the Cabby's horse, Strawberry*, renamed Fledge by Aslan, is transformed into a flying and talking horse to carry them.

Upon the children's return, Aslan allows Digory to bring back an apple from the tree that immediately sprang up from the apple's seed, in order to restore his dying mother. (Lewis's own mother, Flora Lewis*, died when he was a boy in Edwardian Belfast*.)

In the fecundity of new growth associated with Narnia's creation, the metal pole brought by the witch grows into a lamp post in Lantern Waste*, and a great apple tree grows from the core of the magic apple eaten by Mrs (Mabel) Kirke*.

Later, after the great tree falls, Digory has it made into a large wardrobe, the very same wardrobe* that features in *The Lion, the Witch and the Wardrobe*.

Main Road An allegorical* feature of the country depicted on the *Mappa Mundi** in *The Pilgrim's Regress**. In the story John* the pilgrim usually strays to the north of the road (the intellectual rather than the emotionally-centred part of the world).

Malacandra The name for Mars in Old Solar*. See: ***Out of the Silent Planet; The planets***

Maleldil the Young The name by which God's* son was known in Old Solar* in *Out of the Silent Planet**, he who had become incarnate as a rational creature on the Silent Planet, Earth.

Malvern College A fee-paying boarding school, the academic reputation of which persuaded Albert Lewis* to send his sons there. Warren Lewis*, as the elder, went there first, followed by C.S. Lewis after a very brief and unhappy spell at Campbell College*, Belfast and a period at a preparatory school beside Malvern College. The college gets its name from the Malvern Hills, on the flanks of which it is built, and from which a great deal of rural Worcestershire can be seen. C.S. Lewis calls it "Wyvern". Though unhappy at Malvern, Lewis benefited enormously from its teaching, and particularly valued the "Grundy" (the college library), and an English teacher he nicknamed "Smewgy" (Harry Wakelyn Smith). Because of his misery, Albert Lewis arranged for him to be privately tutored by W.T. Kirkpatrick*.

Further reading
C.S. Lewis, *Surprised by Joy: The Shape of my Early Life* (1955);
George Sayer, *Jack: A Life of C.S. Lewis* (1994).

M

Mappa Mundi This map is found inside *The Pilgrim's Regress**. Theologian J.I. Packer describes the world it depicts as "the personal world of wandering and return that the story explores". In his preface to the third edition, Lewis explains the map as a scheme of "the Holy War as I see it". It depicts "the double attack from hell on the two sides of our nature" (the mind and the physical sensations). Packer points out that the idea of the Holy War, drawn from John Bunyan and others, as well as Lewis's war experience, not only informs *The Pilgrim's Regress,* but "gives shape and perspective to Lewis's output as a whole". The attack on the soul from North* and South* represent, in Lewis's words, "equal and opposite evils, each continually strengthened and made plausible by its critique of the other". The Northern people are cold, with "rigid systems whether sceptical or dogmatic, Aristocrats, Stoics, Pharisees, Rigorists, signed and sealed members of highly organized 'Parties'". The emotional Southerners are the opposite, "boneless souls whose doors stand open day and night to almost every visitant, but always with the readiest welcome for those... who offer some sort of intoxication... Every feeling is justified by the mere fact that it is felt: for a Northerner, every feeling on the same ground is suspect."

Both tendencies actually dehumanize us, a thesis Lewis explored in *The Abolition of Man**. To remain human we have no choice but the straight and narrow, the "Main Road"*: "With both the 'North' and the 'South' a man has, I take it, only one concern – to avoid them and hold the Main Road... We were made to be neither cerebral men nor visceral men, but Men."
See also: **cosmic war**
Further reading
J.I. Packer, "Living truth for a dying world: the message of C.S. Lewis", Alister E. McGrath (ed.), *The J.I. Packer Collection* (1999).

Mars See: *Out of the Silent Planet*

Marsh-wiggles Long and frog-like creatures in *The Silver Chair**, who are occupied with most of the watery and fishy work in Narnia*. The most famous Marsh-wiggle is Puddleglum*. His habit of gloomy prognostication is affectionately drawn from C.S. Lewis's groundsman at The Kilns*, Fred Paxford*.

Master Bowman The sailor in the company who shoots the dreadful Sea Serpent* in *The Voyage of the "Dawn Treader"**.

materialism See: **naturalism and supernaturalism**

Mathew, Gervase (1905–1976) One of the Inklings*, and a contributor to *Essays Presented to Charles Williams**. Educated at Balliol College, Oxford* University, he joined the Catholic order of Dominicans in 1928 and was ordained a priest in 1934. He lectured in modern history, theology, and English at Oxford, and wrote books on Byzantium and medieval England.

Maugrim An enormous wolf and Captain of Jadis's* secret police in *The Lion, the Witch and the Wardrobe**. (In American editions of *The Lion, the Witch and the Wardrobe* before 1994, he is called Fenris Ulf.) Maugrim owes his creation to Fenris Wolf, or the Wolf of Fenrir, of Norse mythology. Fenris Wolf was the gigantic offspring of Loki and the giantess Angrboda. The wolf was fated to be chained until the doom of the gods, when it would escape and devour Odin. Vidarr would then savagely kill the beast. It is in keeping with the nature of Narnia* that Maugrim is a talking wolf. The wolf is a characteristic evil figure of fairy stories. He is slain by Peter*.

Mavramorn One of the Seven Lords* in *The Voyage of the "Dawn Treader"**, for whom the voyagers search. They find him sleeping under a spell on World's End Island*.

M

---

mazers Historic drinking bowls made of hardwood, often carved or ornamented with silver. They are fashioned out of mazer wood, that is, wood from gnarly trees. They are used in *Prince Caspian** at the feast celebrating the victory of the Old Narnians* over the tyranny of Miraz*.

meaning and imagination The question of meaning (both of reality itself and of language) is a key theme running throughout the writings of C.S. Lewis. For him, meaning was intimately tied up both with the role of the imagination, and the fact that, in his view, the entire universe is a dependent creation of God*. He saw reason as the organ of truth, and imagination as the organ of meaning. Reason and imagination each had their own integrity, one he attempted to respect in his fiction and theoretical writings. He was also concerned with their interrelationship, both within a mature person and in their complementary roles in the pursuit of knowledge. He particularly stressed the dependence of even the most abstract of thinking upon imagination.

Lewis, like Tolkien*, believed that in some real sense the products of imagination in the arts could give true knowledge. Myth* could become fact*. In writing fantasies like *The Chronicles of Narnia** and *The Hobbit*, they felt that they were discovering inevitable realities that were not the product of theories of the conscious mind (even though rational control is not relinquished in the making of good fantasy*). This attitude prompted both men to create consistent secondary worlds, or sub-creations*, like Middle-earth and Perelandra*. Fiction, for C.S. Lewis, was the making of meaning; it reflects the greater creativity of God when he originated and put together his universe and us. Meaning is at the core of real things and events. Natural objects are not mere facts. Human beings are not merely personalities. Objects, events, and people are real insofar as they are in relationship to other objects, events, and persons, and ultimately in relationship to God, according to Lewis. With persons, this relationship is more than that of an object to God its creator; it involves personal characteristics like choice. The complex web of relationships that is the hallmark of reality confers objects, events, and people with meaning. In themselves, they do not mean: they refer elsewhere to their meaning.

The heart of Lewis's Christian view of meaning is captured by the Dutch Christian philosopher Herman Dooyeweerd: "Meaning is the mode of being of all that is created. This universal character of referring and expressing, which is proper to our entire created cosmos, stamps created reality as meaning, in accordance with its dependent non-self-sufficient nature. Meaning is the being of all that has been created and the nature even of our selfhood. It has a religious root and a divine origin." A similar view seems to have been held by the scientific and social thinker, Michael Polanyi, at least in equating meaning and being as a consequence of a theistic view of the universe. Polanyi spoke at the Oxford University Socratic Club* on occasions. Owen Barfield* wrote much on the subject of meaning, and his influence can be seen in Lewis's thought and writings.

C.S. Lewis has sometimes been accused of crude rationalism: the belief that reason alone is enough to convince us that A is true and B is false. He, however, saw reason itself in the light of the primacy of meaning (that is, in the light of the reference of all things, events, and people to God). In *Miracles**, he posits that when we analyse our thinking as an actual event, two levels are evident. On one level are the physical facts about the actual state of our brain at the time – the natural state of that particular bit of the universe. Our thinking, as an event, is obeying the laws of physics and chemistry, and mechanistic principles. The other level is the meaning to which these physical facts point, providing the character of the event that enables it to be called thinking. We always think about something; our thoughts refer to or mean something other than themselves as events.

As a literary critic*, C.S. Lewis also saw literary works in the light of the primacy of meaning. A good literary work takes us into meanings not normally or often perceived by us (or even its author). These meanings give the work its character, even though the actual literary arrangement of the work, with all the skill that that involves, is a necessary condition for receiving the meanings.

It is on the relationship between concept and meaning, and thought and imagination, that C.S. Lewis makes his most distinctive contribution to understanding. He argues that good imagining is as vital as good thinking, and either is impoverished without the other. Lewis set out some key ideas in an essay in *Rehabilitations and Other Essays**:

> For me, reason is the natural organ of truth; but imagination is the organ of meaning. Imagination, producing new metaphors or revivifying old, is not the cause of truth, but its condition... The truth we [win] by metaphor [can] not be greater than the truth of the metaphor itself; and... all our truth, or all but a few fragments, is won by metaphor. And thence, I confess, it does follow that if our thinking is ever true, then the metaphors by which we think must have been good metaphors.

There are a number of suggestive ideas in the essay, many of which Lewis developed and refined in later years, leading to his definitive statement about literature, *An Experiment in Criticism**. Some of the basic ideas are as follows. (1) There is a distinction between reason and imagination as regards roles – reason is to do with theoretical truths, imagination is to do with meanings. (2) There are standards of correctness, or norms, for the imagination, held tacitly and universally by human beings. (3) Meaning is a condition of the framing of truth; poor meanings make for poor thoughts. (4) The framing of truths in propositions necessitates the employment of metaphors supplied by the imagination. Language and thought necessarily rely upon metaphor. One of the most controversial and difficult points here is that meaning is somehow a condition of thought in a manner obviously different from how the physical brain is. A footnote in Barfield's *Poetic Diction** sheds light on this, if "poet" is read as "the imagination": "Logical judgments, by their nature, can only render more explicit some one part of a truth already implicit in their terms. But the poet makes the terms themselves. He does not make judgments, therefore; he only makes them possible – and only he makes them possible." Imagination is the maker of meaning, the definer of terms in a proposition, and as such is a condition of truth.

The place of metaphor in thinking was central to C.S. Lewis's beliefs. In *Miracles*, he points out that to speak of anything beyond the perceptions of our five senses, metaphorical expression is required; this is as true in the fields of psychology, economics, philosophy, and politics as it is in the fields of religion and poetry. To speak of what is beyond the senses, he argues, is inevitably to talk "as if they could be seen or touched or heard (e.g. [we] must talk of 'complexes' and 'repressions' as if desires could really be tied up in bundles or shoved back; of 'growth' and 'development' as if institutions could really grow like trees or unfold like flowers; of energy being 'released' as if it were an animal let out of a cage)".

Meldilorn In *Out of the Silent Planet**, the habitation of the ruling Oyarsa, the great eldil*. Meldilorn is an island on a sapphire lake set within a border of purple forest. It lies in the Marsian handramit*, or lowland. On the island is a broad avenue of monoliths, and magnificent trees.

"Mere Christianity" Lewis's preferred name for common ground or "great-tradition" Christian orthodoxy, or (as he called it) "Christianity without water". He probably discovered the term in the Puritan writer and preacher Richard Baxter, who writes in his *Church-history of the Government of Bishops* (1680):

> I am a CHRISTIAN, a MEER CHRISTIAN, of no other Religion; and the Church that I am of is the Christian Church, and hath been visible where ever the Christian Religion and Church hath been visible: But must you know what Sect or Party I am of? I am against all Sects and dividing Parties: But if any will call Meer Christians by the name of a Party, because they take up with Meer Chrisitanity, Creed, and Scripture, and will not be of any dividing or contentious Sect, I am of that Party which is so against Parties: If the Name CHRISTIAN be not enough, call me a CATHOLICK CHRISTIAN; not as that word signifieth an hereticating majority of Bishops, but as it signifieth one that hath no Religion, but that which by Christ and the Apostles was left to the Catholick Church, or the Body of Jesus Christ on Earth.

***Mere Christianity* (1952)** One of the most well known of C.S. Lewis's books, *Mere Christianity* is a revised and enlarged edition of three previous books of talks given on BBC* radio, *Broadcast Talks* (called *The Case for Christianity* in the United States) (1942), *Christian Behaviour* (1943), and *Beyond Personality* (1944). It is straightforward and lucid, and its contents are captured in its part titles: "Right and wrong as a clue to the meaning of the universe", "What Christians believe", "Christian behaviour", and "Beyond personality: or first steps in the doctrine of the Trinity". Lewis was invited to give popular talks on BBC radio early in 1941, when war had made people consider ultimate issues more. Lewis had to weigh up two dislikes – the radio, and travelling to London – but his sense of duty won. He regarded England as post-Christian, and felt that many people believed they had tried and rejected Christianity, whereas they had never actually tried it at all. His feelings about the first set of talks were recorded in a letter. The broadcasts were pre-evangelism "rather than evangelism, an attempt to convince people that there is a moral law, that we disobey it, and that the existence of a Lawgiver is at least very probable and also (unless you add the Christian doctrine of the Atonement) that this imparts despair rather than comfort". Some years after the BBC talks, C.S. Lewis recorded a series for radio that was the basis for his book *The Four Loves**. They were only broadcast in the United States. These are some of the few recordings of Lewis's voice available.

Merlin The magician from the time of King Arthur in *That Hideous Strength**, who returns to help to save Logres, the true England. See also: **Atlantis**

Merpeople Inhabitants of the Eastern Sea* near Narnia's* shore, in *The Lion, the Witch and the Wardrobe**, not to be confused with the Sea People* of the Last Sea* encountered in *The Voyage of the "Dawn Treader"**, who can only live in water. "Mer" derives from *mere*, an Early English word for "sea", "lake", or similar.

Mezreel A resort used by the wealthy of Calormen* in the hot summers in *The Horse and His Boy**. It has many attractions, including a lake and notable gardens.

***Miracles: A Preliminary Study* (1947; revised new edition, 1960)** This book, which reveals more than any other C.S. Lewis's view of God* and nature*, was intended for people for whom the question of miracles is real. It is not couched in the specialist language of theology or philosophy, though it has an enormous amount to contribute to both theology and philosophy of religion.

The book was substantially revised and improved after chapter 3 in the first edition, "The Self-Contradiction of the Naturalist", was criticized by philosopher Elizabeth Anscombe* at the Oxford University Socratic Club*. The substance of her critique, and Lewis's response, is found in the essay "Religion without dogma?" in *Undeceptions** (1971).

The first part of the book, consisting of the first seven chapters, describes two basic attitudes of thought about life, the universe, and everything. The first, which Lewis felt was now habitual in the modern person, he called naturalism*. This materialistic view sees the natural universe as all that is; nature is "the whole show". Nothing else exists. Any reality beyond what can be perceived by the five senses lacks plausibility. The possibility of miracles is ruled out in advance; seeking evidence for a miracle is as silly as looking for Father Christmas or the Tooth Fairy.

The second, and opposite, view is supernaturalism*, the theistic view that the universe is a dependent creation of God. Time, space, and geometry are all God's creation, and only exist now because he chose to make them out of nothing. For C.S. Lewis, the naturalist sees nature as a pond of infinite depths made up of nothing but water. The supernaturalist sees nature as a pond with a bottom – mud, earth, rock, and finally the planet itself. The central point is that if naturalism is true, miracles are impossible. If supernaturalism is true, miracles are possible, and, indeed, to be expected.

Lewis points out two insurmountable difficulties with naturalism. It undermines the validity of thought itself, therefore even the claims of naturalism to be true. It also reduces the "oughtness" of things to "isness". If moral obligation turns out only to be caused naturally, then it is no longer an obligation. We can only then be forced or manipulated into behaving as some other people (the Nazis, for example) wish us to. For C.S. Lewis, both conscience and reason provide an analogy for the way a miracle imposes itself upon the natural order. Both conscience and reason are testimonies to the reality of the supernatural world.

The argument in this part of the book owes much to Arthur Balfour's* *Theism and Humanism**, the Gifford Lectures for 1914, which Lewis greatly admired and felt to be unjustly neglected.

After this preparation, C.S. Lewis proceeds to his main theme, the biblical miracles, particularly the incarnation of Jesus Christ. He is particularly concerned with demolishing modern chronological snobbery*, the tendency to treat the past as more primitive than the present, and as therefore superseded. He posits two characteristic ways that this dismissive attitude bars itself from seriously considering the New Testament miracles. One is to see the people of that time as gullible in accepting as miracles events that today would have a natural explanation. The other is to see their imagery as mythological and therefore in need of de- or re-mythologizing in modern terms (the idea of God coming down to earth from up there in heaven* is an example). C.S. Lewis's treatment of both modern fallacies is incisive and gives a fresh perspective. Of particular interest is his treatment of the function of imagery and metaphor in language. He presents some seminal ideas on the relationship between imagination* and thinking, meaning* and truth. Such ideas were at the very foundation of his thinking, scholarship. and fictional work. See also: **theology, C.S. Lewis and**

Miraz, King The prince's wicked, modernizing uncle in *Prince Caspian**, who has stolen the throne from King Caspian* IX. He is aided and abetted by Queen Prunaprismia*, and came to a bad end. Miraz ruthlessly dismisses Caspian's nurse* for telling him stories of Old Narnia* and considers stories of Kings Peter* and Edmund* and the Golden Age* as old wives' tales.

Miraz's castle The stronghold of the usurper, Miraz*, in *Prince Caspian**, to Narnia's* north, not far from the site of the house of the White Witch*, which had existed ages before, and a mile from Beaversdam*. From its lead roofs can be seen on the one side the battlements and on the other a steep roof. Below there is an extensive view of the castle garden. Caspian* and his tutor, Doctor Cornelius*, are able to climb the great central tower of the whole castle, which affords a splendid view of the Narnian sky on a clear night. From there also the distant mountains can be glimpsed, as well as the Great River* nearby.

Monopods Dwarves* in *The Voyage of the "Dawn Treader"** who have been changed into single-footed creatures. See also: **Dufflepuds**

Moonwood In *The Last Battle**, a hare with such exceptional hearing that it is told that he can sit by Caldron Pool* under the waterfall and hear what is whispered at Cair Paravel*.

Moore, Mrs Janie King Askins (1872–1951) C.S. Lewis adopted Mrs Moore as a mother in fulfilment of a promise made to her son, a billet mate of Lewis's during the First World War. According to some, she was Lewis's lover for some years before his commitment to Christian faith. Mrs Moore, along with her surviving child Maureen, set up home in Oxford* during Lewis's undergraduate years, and Lewis began to share her home during this time. With typical generosity, Lewis focused in his letters* and diaries* on her virtues, praising her hospitality. His brother, Warnie*, became less charitable; looking back over the years, he could not understand how Lewis put up with her. As far as Warnie was concerned, "Minto", as she was nicknamed, was Lewis's thorn in the flesh. He sketched out her life and character in a journal entry a few days after her death for posterity in *Brothers and Friends: The Diaries of Major Warren Hamilton Lewis** (entry, 17 January 1951).

Lewis's own diaries (abridged in *All My Road Before Me**) were most likely written for the benefit of Mrs Moore, whom he refers to as "D". There is speculation that "D" in the typescript made by Warnie Lewis (in the Lewis family papers*) may be transcribed from the Greek letter delta and may stand for Diotima, a priestess in Plato's* *Symposium* who introduces Socrates (in a platonic way, of course) to the meaning of love. Mrs Moore, as Diotima, may have introduced love to the young Lewis in a less platonic way, the speculation continues.

Owen Barfield* was acquainted with Mrs Moore in the 1920s: "People have argued that Jack had a relationship with her. It's certainly possible, but unlikely to have been long-enduring; she was quite a lot older than him, and not, I should have thought, physically attractive" (*The Independent*, 7 March 1994).

Mrs Moore, in fact, governed the household in a kind of benign, but often intense, matriarchy that only in later years of her decline seriously rankled with Warnie. With her practical turn of mind, there was something of Mrs Beaver* in her character.

Mother Kirk An allegorical* figure representing the Christian church* in *The Pilgrim's Regress**.

"Mountbracken" Lewis's name, in *Surprised by Joy**, for Glenmachan, home of his mother's cousin, Lady Ewart, and Sir William Quartus Ewart*.

Mount Pire A mountain in Archenland* in *The Horse and His Boy**, created when fair-haired Olvin* fights the two-headed giant*, Pire, and turns him into stone. Shasta* uses the twin-peaked mountain as a landmark for finding Archenland.

Muil In *The Voyage of the "Dawn Treader"**, the westernmost of the Seven Isles*. It is separated from the isle of Brenn* by a choppy strait.

M

Mullugutherum The Warden of the Marches of Underland* in *The Silver Chair*. He is chief of the Earthmen* in the Underland* realm, the Shallow Lands*, of the Green Witch*.

myth C.S. Lewis, like J.R.R. Tolkien*, placed the highest value on the making of myth – or mythopoeia – in imaginative fiction and poetry. Some stories are outright myths – as is the story of Cupid and Psyche* retold by Lewis in *Till We Have Faces*. Other stories have what Lewis called a "mythical quality". Examples he gave were the plots of Robert Louis Stevenson's *The Strange Case of Dr Jekyll and Mr Hyde*, H.G. Wells's *The Door in the Wall*, Franz Kafka's *The Castle*, and the conceptions of Gormenghast in Mervyn Peake's *Titus Groan* and of the Ents and Lothlórien in Tolkien's *The Lord of the Rings*. Both Lewis and Tolkien aspired to myth-making in their fictional creations. They had a theology of myth (see: **theology of romance**).

Recognizing that the term "myth", like "romanticism"*, has many loose meanings (including "untrue"), C.S. Lewis tried to pin down its meaning in his *An Experiment in Criticism*. A story that acheives myth has a number of characteristics. (1) It is independent of the form of words used to tell the story. (2) Narrative features such as suspense or surprise play little part in the distinctive pleasure of myth. (3) Our empathy with the characters of the story is at a minimum; we do not imaginatively transport ourselves into their lives. (4) Myth is always fantasy*, dealing with the impossible and preternatural. (5) Myth is never comic; though the experience may be joyful or sad, it is always grave. (6) The experience in fact is awe-inspiring, containing a numinous* quality. In defining myth in terms of its effect upon us, Lewis was clear that one person's myth may only be a story to another. A story may give enjoyment to a person without being perceived as myth, even though it is myth. Lewis regarded the nineteenth-century writer George MacDonald* as one of the greatest masters of myth making, especially in *Phantastes* and *Lilith*.

Myth has had a central place in modern anthropology, and modern theology. At the time of his conversion, Lewis wrestled with the anthropology of James G. Frazer (1854–1941), as represented in the widely influential *The Golden Bough: A Study in Magic and Religion* (abridged edition 1922). Later in his life, Lewis made known his disquiet with key ideas of myth propounded in the theology of his day, ideas associated for example with Rudolf Bultmann (1884–1976). Lewis saw serious errors in Frazer's view of myth, and in the understanding of myth in the work of leading biblical critics. Frazer explored magic and religions throughout the world in the hope of tracing an important part of the evolution of human thought. As a result *The Golden Bough* (originally in many volumes) is truly encyclopedic. In seeking a unified development, Frazer denied the value of asking whether religions were true or false. Christianity had no uniqueness, he believed, a theme that is increasingly heard in modern theology. Frazer helped to lay the foundation for the relativism that is so familiar today.

James Frazer had documented many myths of dying and rising gods throughout the world. As Lewis grew as a Christian thinker, he continued to reflect on such myths. He argued that "We must not be nervous about 'parallels' and 'pagan Christs': they ought to be there – it would be a stumbling block if they weren't." He explored such "parallel" themes in his powerful "myth retold", *Till We Have Faces**.

At the heart of Christianity, C.S. Lewis believed, is a myth that is also a fact – making the claims of Christianity unique (see: **myth became fact**). But by becoming fact, Lewis points out, it did not cease to be myth, or lose the quality of myth. Lewis praised John Milton for retaining the tangible quality of myth in most of *Paradise Lost*, his great epic, which is one of the most powerful of credal affirmations in Christian literature. Lewis strived to follow Milton's example in his own fiction.

M

Rudolf Bultmann is widely considered to be the most significant and influential New Testament scholar of the twentieth century. Bultmann's key belief was that "faith must not aspire to an objective basis in dogma or in history on pain of losing its character as faith". Bultmann saw the Gospel records as myths, and myths as attempts to portray happenings in the world as having supernatural* causes. In the case of Christ's virgin birth, the event could only have occurred with divine intervention into the world of cause and effect. The modern person, Bultmann believes, cannot accept the idea of supernatural causes of events in the world we see. The Gospels must be stripped of myths to get to the core of what Christ's followers believed in the first century. They were "objectifying" their beliefs in myths appropriate to their day. Lewis's counter to this kind of thinking is found in his study in defence of Christianity, *Miracles**. There he argues that a supernaturalist view is not outmoded, but is essential for proper human thinking and intellectual discovery at any time or place. He also addressed modern biblical critics directly on one occasion (see: **theology, C.S. Lewis and**). Lewis objected to biblical critics who saw the Gospels as legend or romance rather than a factual, historical record. As a literary critic*, and avid reader of myth, Lewis felt that they had little idea of what myth actually is. In several instances, he found them poor readers of the texts they had pored over, perhaps for years.

Like Bultmann, however, C.S. Lewis did recognize the difficulties modern people have in reading the Gospels. Bultmann's procedure was to "demythologize". Lewis, who wanted as an orthodox "mere Christian"* to retain the Gospels as the greatest story but true, chose rather to remythologize central Christian beliefs. He attempted stories that would put over Christian meanings in a modern way, particularly in his Narnia* stories for children (of all ages) and his science-fiction trilogy*. Even his historical novel *Till We Have Faces* is fresh and contemporary as a work of art.

myth became fact An important factor in Lewis's conversion to Christianity was accepting J.R.R. Tolkien's* argument (captured in his poem *Mythopoeia*) that the biblical Gospels have all the best qualities of pagan* myth*, with the unique feature that the events actually happened in documented history. Lewis and Tolkien thus radically differed from views of myth espoused by liberal biblical scholars of the time, which divorced myth from history as a matter of definition.

Lewis, like Tolkien, faced ancient tensions. The tension between realism and fantasy* is one, as myth is a form of fantasy. The use of myth and fantasy in literature and theological fiction didn't denote a lack of confidence until nowadays. Its use in Lewis, and in J.R.R. Tolkien, can be taken as a matter of confidence. When Lewis applied the category of myth when talking about the Gospels, he was not displaying uncertainty about their historicity. So even though there was an awareness of ancient tensions between myth and realism so far as Lewis was concerned, the tension for him was basically reconciled. This is despite the fact that the tension is embedded in the very definition of myth. Myth can be defined in terms of the symbolic* capture or embodiment of a world view of a people or culture, thus having an important believed element. Myth can also be defined as untrue, fictional, and merely imaginative*. The existence of myth writes large the dilemma that the "lies" of the poet and the fiction writer capture profound realities, realities impossible to capture in any other way. Fiction, poetry, and metaphor, though they are "lies", by necessity have a representational element.

Other forms of the inherent tension of myth are evident. The tension between myth and reason (or *logos* *), myth and history, and myth and knowledge, goes back to ancient times. Again, however, it is only in the modern period that this tension has represented a crisis in knowledge. In ancient times, up to what Lewis would have described as the Great Divide (see: **The Old West**) between the Old and Post-Christian West, the tension between myth and fact was creative, as it is in his writings. He has a tangible confidence that the polarity between myth and fact has been reconciled – which reflects a more ancient confidence. In C.S. Lewis's view, heaven* has come down to earth, and our humanity has been taken up to God*.

For C.S. Lewis, myth was also tied with a thousand ties to the ordinary world of nature* and humble fact. In reviewing his friend's *The Lord of the Rings*, Lewis describes just how Tolkien's invented mythology is applicable to the primary, real world. Lewis concentrates on the aspect of recovery*:

> The value of the myth is that it takes all the things we know and restores to them the rich significance which as been hidden by the "veil of familiarity"... As long as the story lingers in our mind, the real things are more themselves. This book applies the treatment not only to bread or apple but to good and evil, to our endless perils, our anguish, and our joys. By dipping them in myth we see them more clearly.

It is clear that, for Lewis, myth plays an important part in how we actually see things. Stories rich in myth provide pairs of spectacles through which we perceive reality in a fresh and restorative way. Myth helps to re-enchant the world.

N

naiads In *The Chronicles of Narnia**, water nymphs*, presiding over brooks, springs, and fountains, taken from classical mythology.

Nain King of Archenland* in the dark time of Miraz* of Narnia* in *Prince Caspian**.

Narnia See: **Narnia: geography; Narnia: history**

Narnia as a secondary world (sub-creation) For many years, it was customary for critics to consider *The Chronicles of Narnia** to have been rush-written in a rather slapdash manner. Whereas Tolkien* spent many years painstakingly writing *The Lord of the Rings,* and over half a century developing the background world of Middle-earth, Lewis wrote the seven Narnia stories in as many years. Yet this dismissive attitude did not fit the actual reading experience of many. Like Tolkien, Lewis was a brilliant medieval scholar. His presence as a thinker and scholar seemed to be tangible in the stories, even though written for the level of a child. What gave the sevenfold stories their unity was a mystery, however. Various attempts were made to account for what held them together so satisfactorily.

While researching the Narnian Chronicles for his doctorate, Michael Ward stumbled across an element in all the stories that Lewis had carefully hidden. He later published his discovery in *Planet Narnia.* It points to Lewis's creation of the world of Narnia as being as skilful in its own way as that of Tolkien's rendering of Middle-earth. Like much of Tolkien's inspiration, Lewis drew upon the imaginative resources of the Middle Ages, allowing the vision of that period to re-enchant the world of the modern reader. Ward shows how medieval astrology, in particular, plays a central shaping role in Lewis's depiction of Narnia and the stories that play out there.

The night sky in Narnia is modelled upon a medieval one, with living stars* and a world that is commonly perceived as flat (even though, in the Middle Ages, scholars were aware that the Earth was a globe). The planets were ruled by intelligences, great lords and ladies (rather like the planets in Lewis's science-fiction trilogy*). There is not a modern separation, therefore, between astronomy* and astrology. Heaven* and the starry skies were one. Signs in the skies are taken with utmost seriousness in Narnia. Centaurs*, for instance, have a remarkable facility in reading the portents.

Michael Ward has argued that the Chronicles playfully embody medieval astronomy, and teases out Lewis's interest in medieval imagery. Each of the stories, Ward argues, represents one of the seven planets of astrology. In this scheme the seven astrological planets (the Moon, Mars, Mercury, Jupiter, Venus, Saturn, and the Sun which remain traditionally rooted in the names of the seven days of the week in many languages, including English) influenced people, events, and the metals in the earth, each in a distinctive way. Ward argues that Lewis uses the astrological planets as master symbols. In *The Voyage of the "Dawn Treader"**, for instance, the voyagers head toward the sunrise, gold (the metal of the sun) tempts Eustace Scrubb* and provides the curse on Deathwater Island*, and light takes on a numinous* quality as the adventurers approach the End of the World and Aslan's Country*. Taking each planet, he shows how its symbolism* is present and embodied throughout one of the Narnian stories, giving a credible account of the influence and appropriateness of that dominant planet. Just as the sun shapes *The Voyage of the "Dawn Treader"*, Jupiter, the planet of kingship, "animates the imaginative vision of *The Lion, the Witch and the*

Wardrobe". Similarly, the characteristic atmosphere or quality of *Prince Caspian** comes from the planet Mars. Venus is the planet Lewis finds appropriate to shape the story and portrayal of Narnia in *The Magician's Nephew**.

Planet Narnia provides a groundbreaking insight into the mysterious process of "sub-creation"*, a feature of the imagination* both Tolkien and Lewis held to be at the centre of storytelling. Sub-creation, in fact, is a concept developed by Lewis's friend J.R.R. Tolkien, and one that deeply influenced him. Lewis was thoroughly familiar with Tolkien's creation of Middle-earth long before the publication of first *The Hobbit* and then *The Lord of the Rings*. The concept is expressed in Tolkien's famous essay "On Fairy Stories". Because of the importance of the concept to Lewis, it is a necessary key to understanding the Narnian Chronicles, as well as further books of his containing other worlds, such as *Out of the Silent Planet** and *Perelandra**.

Tolkien believes that the art of true fantasy* or fairy-story writing is sub-creation: creating another or secondary world with such skill that it has an "inner consistency of reality". Tolkien's key idea is that faerie, the realm or state where faeries have their being, contains a whole cosmos, a microcosm. It contains the moon, the sun, the sky, trees and mountains, rivers, water, and stones, as well as dragons, trolls, dwarves*, goblins, elves, talking animals*, and even a mortal person when enchanted (through giving primary belief to that other world).

Tolkien called the result of sub-creation a secondary world because it is an imagined other world that is thoroughly consistent and plausible on its own inner terms. Narnia, like Middle-earth, is indeed a secondary world. Tolkien brought into focus the storyteller's desire to have a well-imagined world as a context for the story, in which its symbolic geography heightened and illuminated the events.

C.S. Lewis's Narnia is an outstanding example of a successful secondary world, created with Tolkien's views in mind. Ironically,

Tolkien disliked the Narnia stories for containing allegory*. The irony is deep – without the friendship between Lewis and Tolkien, Lewis would not have created Narnia. Tolkien also was indebted to Lewis; he freely admitted that without his friend's encouragement, he never would have completed *The Lord of the Rings*, where his created world of Middle-earth is present, shaping the atmosphere and stories just as Lewis's Narnia is shaped, if Michael Ward is correct, by the ancient planets. See also: **The planets**

Further reading
C.S. Lewis, *Of Other Worlds* (1966); C.S. Lewis (ed.), *Essays Presented to Charles Williams* (1947); Michael Ward, *Planet Narnia* (2008); David C. Downing, *Planets in Peril* (1992).

Narnia: geography In *The Chronicles of Narnia**, Narnia is a small country south of which lies Archenland* and Calormen*, inhabited by both talking* and dumb beasts* and trees, the chief of all its creatures being also its creator, Aslan*, a talking lion. To the far west lies the land of Telmar*, and nearer to Narnia is the Western Wild* – a mountainous region covered with dark forests or with snow and ice. From this region rushes a river that becomes a waterfall, under which is Caldron Pool*. From this flows the River of Narnia, which runs all the way to the Eastern Ocean*. Lantern Waste* lies to the east of the wilderness.

Narnia's capital is Cair Paravel*, the seat of human kings and queens, located at the mouth of the River of Narnia. The Marsh-wiggles* (found only in Narnia) live to the north of Cair Paravel. More northerly lies the River Shribble*, and then the forlorn moorland of Ettinsmoor*. Further north still is a mountainous region and Harfang*, a stronghold of giants*. Near Harfang is the ruins of a once great city, under which lie a number of subterranean lands, including the kingdom of the Green Witch*, destroyed in the time of Prince Rilian*, son of Caspian*, the tenth Telmarine* king. To Narnia's east lies the vast Eastern Ocean*, in which are many islands, and finally the Silver Sea* and World's End*, where Aslan's Country* is.

Narnia is also the name of a small Italian town mentioned by the Roman historian Livy.

In the geography of Narnia, it is likely that Lewis has captured something of the Ulster that he loved from childhood, particularly County Down. Revd Cosslet Quinn, a former rector of St Mark's*, Dundela, recalls vividly the Ulster side of Lewis: "I still remember from one occasion when I met C.S. Lewis, seeing the flash in his eyes as he spoke of the two-thousand-year-old Epic of Cuchulain, and what it ought to mean for an Ulsterman."

Professor Frank Kastor, of Wichita State University, Kansas, finds parallels between the geography and landscapes of Narnia and those of the Ulster that Lewis knew as a boy. He adds his comments in brackets to a quotation from *The Magician's Nephew** to demonstrate some of them.

> All Narnia... lay spread out below them; the river winding through it like a ribbon of quicksilver [THE RIVER LAGAN]. They could already see over the tops of the low hills which lay northward on their right [HILLS OF ANTRIM]; beyond those hills, a great moorland sloped gently up and up to the horizon. On their left (southward) the mountains were much higher [MOUNTAINS OF MOURNE]...

Professor Kastor adds that their destination is the garden, with the magic apple tree, which lies west of Narnia at the blue lake (Lough Neagh), in the mountains of the Western Wild* (north-western Ireland). See also: **Narnia: history**

Narnia: history Because the time of Earth is different from that of Narnia, the children who are drawn into Narnia on a number of occasions find themselves at various parts of its history. Thus, although *The Chronicles of Narnia** cover only about fifty years of our history (from the beginning to the mid-twentieth century), we get a picure of the entire history of Narnia from its creation to its unmaking and the new creation of all worlds, including Narnia and England.

Narnia's creation is recounted in *The Magician's Nephew**. Digory Kirke* and Polly Plummer*, after entering the old and dying world of Charn* through a pool in the Wood Between the Worlds*, find their way by accident into a land of Nothing. Here, gradually, Narnia is created before their eyes by the song of Aslan*. Unfortunately Digory brings evil into that perfect world in the form of Jadis*, destroyer of Charn, whom he had previously awakened in that world. Jadis goes off to the fringes of Narnia, but reappears in later ages as the White Witch*, who puts a spell over Narnia, of always winter but never Christmas. The arrival of the four Pevensie children* through the wardrobe* (told in *The Lion, the Witch and the Wardrobe**) coincides with the return of Aslan and the beginning of the end of her curse. Aslan's death on behalf of Edmund Pevensie, and his return to life by a deeper law than the one by which she operates her magic, leads to her defeat and death. Narnia's Golden Age* follows.

With the return of the children to their world, Narnia slowly falls into disorder. The Telmarines*, led by Caspian* I, occupy the land and silence the talking beasts* and trees. Old Narnia* only survives under cover as Aslan's remnant keeps faith alive that he will return. Prince Caspian* (his story is told in the book of that name), brought up by his wicked Uncle Miraz* and Aunt Prunaprismia*, who have deposed his father Caspian IX, learns of the myth of Old Narnia and longs for it to be true. He escapes a plot to kill him and joins forces with the Old Narnians. In the nick of time, help comes from the four Pevensie children drawn back into Narnia.

He becomes Caspian X after adventures at sea recounted in *The Voyage of the "Dawn Treader"**. His son, Prince Rilian*, is kidnapped and held in servitude in an underworld for ten years by a witch of the line of Jadis. She plots to take over Narnia, using him as a puppet king. As told in the Chronicle of *The Silver Chair**, he is rescued by two cousins of the Pevensie children, Eustace Scrubb* and Jill Pole*, who are brought into Narnia for this task.

After many ages the last king of Narnia, Tirian*, and indeed Narnia itself, are threatened by a devilish plot that uses a counterfeit Aslan and links up with the Calormene* forces (who are a constant threat to Narnia's security). This is Narnia's darkest hour. As told in *The Last Battle**, Tirian prays for help from the Sons of Adam* and Daughters of Eve*, and Aslan brings Eustace and Jill to his aid. Aslan himself finally intervenes and dissolves the whole world. This turns out to be a beginning rather than an end, as the New Narnia* is revealed. See also:

Narnia: geography

Further reading

Walter Hooper, *Past Watchful Dragons* (1980); Martha C. Sammons, *A Guide Through Narnia* (1979); Paul F. Ford, *Companion to Narnia* (1994).

"Narnian Suite" Two poems published in *Poems** (1964) after C.S. Lewis's death. One is a march for "Strings, Kettledrums, and Sixty-three Dwarfs", and the other is a march for "Drum, Trumpet, and Twenty-one Giants". Other poems by Lewis easily fit into a Narnian context because of their medieval or classical subjects – poems such as "The Magician and the Dryad", "The Dragon Speaks" (admired by Tolkien*), or "Dragon-Slayer". Another poem, "Impenitence", in which Lewis refers affectionately to animals and to talking animals* in particular, is almost a defiant defence for the Narnia stories.

Narrative Poems (**1969**) C.S. Lewis wrote both lyrical and narrative verse, and originally hoped to make his name as a poet. This volume contains four stories, including "Dymer"*, "Launcelot", "The Nameless Isle", and "The Queen of Drum" – about the escape of a queen from a dictator into Fairy Land. See also: *The Collected Poems*

Narrowhaven A town on the island of Doorn* in *The Voyage of the "Dawn Treader"**, ruled by Gumpas*. An important feature of the town is its castle, the seat of administration. Under Gumpas's local government, a slave* market is allowed. Caspian* and the other voyagers are appalled by the rundown condition of the castle, reflecting the moral rot that had taken place. See also: **The Lone Islands**

naturalism and supernaturalism In his book *Miracles: A Preliminary Study**, naturalism is the name Lewis gives for the view that nature* is "the whole show", with nothing outside nature existing. He contrasts naturalism with its opposite, supernaturalism. This is the theistic view that nature is contingent, or dependent rather than necessary. God* has created it, but did not have to create it. He could have created other natures, or not created at all. God is complete irrespective of whether or not he created a real nature outside himself.

Two things need to be said about Lewis's formulation of nature and supernature. One is that he is representing an orthodox Judeo–Christian theism, a position that many believe was an essential presupposition for the rise of modern science. The other is that Lewis's view can be formulated in other terms, and, no doubt, in more sophisticated and precise philosophical language. C.S. Lewis was deliberately popularizing. In the process, his thinking (especially as embodied in *Miracles*) is more timeless than a fully fledged philosophical study of its day. He was careful to call *Miracles* a "preliminary study". Nevertheless, after his encounter with philosopher Elizabeth Anscombe*, at a meeting of the Oxford University Socratic Club*, he greatly improved his case for the later paperback edition of *Miracles*.

C.S. Lewis's fundamental distinction between nature and supernature has, surprisingly, been criticized by some fellow believers who seem to take a position difficult to separate from deism (a form of belief in God where the creator of the universe does not intervene in it). Two key elements of this criticism are as follows. One is a dislike of Lewis's metaphors of "interruption" and "invasion" of nature by the supernatural. The critics say that God's creation in every aspect, natural and spiritual, reveals the mark of his personal hand. The other is a rejection of Lewis's analysis of the causation of thinking, in its link to the brain as a mechanism. Lewis's opponents are happy for the brain as a mechanism to have a complete causal story in terms of the laws of physics and chemistry. Thought and human consciousness has a complementary story, perceived by the dimension of faith and ourselves as responsible observers. Thus Lewis's central argument of the self-contradiction of naturalism is undermined.

This criticism, however, ignores the underlying force of Lewis's attack on naturalism, and also is un-selfcritical, by failing to realize the popular character of Lewis's study and apologetics. A number of thinkers have worked on the question of causality on various hierarchical levels, such as the physical and chemical, the biological, and the historical. They have also wrestled with the logical relationship between causal levels – a necessity for any complementarian approach. This work, particularly by Michael Polanyi (who spoke at the Oxford University Socratic Club) and Herman Dooyeweerd, strengthens Lewis's argument, and indeed the traditional theistic position for which he stood. C.S. Lewis's own essay "Transposition" (see: **transposition**) is powerfully suggestive of such an approach.

Lewis's key metaphors, describing the supernatural as invading or interrupting nature, do not imply a dualism in

God's created world. Lewis was not a Platonist in philosophy, even though Plato* was a rich source for and presence in his imagination*, as in *The Chronicles of Narnia**. Lewis uses such metaphors in the context of a nature that is fallen, and hence abnormal. He believed in a real historical fall by disobedient mankind that affected the whole of nature, even though nature still reveals God himself. Supernature, like nature, is marked by both good and evil as a result of primeval disobedience by mankind and some angels*. Lewis's case could include more about the Christian concept of the cultural mandate, where mankind is commanded in Genesis to order and name the natural world. The whole human cultural process could be said to rearrange and act into nature; it transcends the laws of physics and chemistry. He could therefore have extended his analogy between supernatural acts and human thinking to include culture (of which thinking is but a part). Such a broader canvas, however, might not have interested him because of his distrust of overblown systems.

nature

> "In our world," said Eustace, "a star is a huge ball of flaming gas."
>
> "Even in your world, my son [the old man replied], that is not what a star is but only what it is made of."
>
> (*The Voyage of the "Dawn Treader"*)

Like Owen Barfield*, C.S. Lewis believed that, as Elwin Ransom* remarked to Merlin* in *That Hideous Strength**, "the soul has gone out of the wood and water": the world's history is one of mankind's separation from God* on the one hand and nature on the other. This view led to Lewis's opposition to scientism* (but not true science). Our separation from nature came from our wish to exalt ourselves and thus to belittle all else. Christians, Lewis believed, should recognize God's continued activity in the fecundity of natural things such as trees, grass, flowers, and shrubs.

In his atheistic mid-teens C.S. Lewis cared mainly about gods, heroes, and an ideal world of beauty. Many years later he eventually, and reluctantly, accepted a Christian universe. He soon realized the implications of commitment to this "real universe, the divine, magical, terrifying and ecstatic reality in which we all live". What fixed the reality of the natural world forever for him was the incarnation of God himself as a fully human being in a fully real human body: Jesus Christ's resurrection meant that he retains this human body forever. The environment of his resurrected body, and those of his followers in the future, could be called a new Nature, though believers, Lewis included, prefer to call this environment "heaven"*. Lewis was once interviewed by *Time* magazine (8 September 1947). They wondered if his life at Oxford*, a life of writing, walking, teaching, and reading, was monotonous. Lewis's reply baffled them: "I like monotony."

It is upon the humble and common things of life that Lewis's wonderlands of the imagination* are based, "the quiet fulness of ordinary nature". He also saw it (he learned this from George MacDonald*) as the basis of spirituality. In a letter he wrote: "The familiar is in itself a ground for affection. And it is good: because any natural help towards our spiritual duty of loving is good and God seems to build our higher loves round our merely natural impulses – sex, maternity, kinship, old acquaintances…" Conversely, as he demonstrated vividly in his *The Screwtape Letters**, the small things are likely to play more part in the damnation of a person than great acts like murder or betrayal. Because of the link between ordinary reality and imaginative creation, Lewis found himself as much on the defensive about fantasy* as about his lifestyle. A common charge was that literary fantasy is escapism. In his book *Of Other Worlds**, Lewis says of *The Wind in the Willows* (the popular children's story by Kenneth

Grahame): "The happiness which it presents to us is in fact full of the simplest and most attainable things – food, sleep, exercise, friendship, the face of nature, even (in a sense) religion." Such fantasy is the opposite of escapism. It deepens the reality of the real world for us – the terror as well as the beauty.

In making such comments, and holding fervently to such beliefs, C.S. Lewis was in fact struggling with an important problem for any Christian in the modern world: being contented with reality as it is given by God without denying that it is abnormal because of the fall of mankind. Such contentment is by no means synonymous with conservatism in ideas and politics. Lewis did not defend the status quo, carefully dissociated from the political Right, and even strongly believed that soon the time will come when a Christian in the civil service would have a problem about being part of furthering tyranny. In wartime he raised doubts about bombing civilian targets. In his satirical science-fiction story *That Hideous Strength**, the devil's party are officials! His open Christian position made him unpopular with many in the Oxford establishment.

For Lewis, the importance of reality lies in how it impinges upon the individual. No one can experience the humanist's "happiness of the greatest number". Furthermore, what is unbearably painful to one person can be borne by another. Lewis clearly felt life deeply. He does not seem to be exaggerating when he once wrote in a letter, early in 1956: "It seems to me that one can hardly say anything either bad enough or good enough about life." In his "myth retold", *Till We Have Faces**, he goes a long way toward acheiving both at once. C.S. Lewis saw Christianity as carrying the stamp of this same reality upon it. He wrote in 1953: "Christianity is… hard and tender at the same time. It's the blend that does it; neither quality would be any good without the other."

Closely linked to Lewis's zest for ordinary reality, for nature, was his attention to the details of life and experience. This power of observation added detail after detail of exuberant creation to his imaginative writings. He was very aware of nature, seasons, weather, atmosphere, and, of course, animals. In fact, he delighted to put animal characters into his books. In Narnia*, many of the animals can speak. In Perelandra*, the harmony between the new humans of Venus and its native animals beautifully evokes mankind's unfallen state. In *Out of the Silent Planet**, Lewis brilliantly manages to create talking animals* that are acceptable to adult readers. The "proper" bear in *That Hideous Strength**, Mr Bultitude*, was based upon an actual bear in Whipsnade Zoo. The threat to Mr Bultitude by the sinister N.I.C.E.* illustrates Lewis's hatred of vivisection.

Lewis's letters* are also full of references to animals. In a letter to an American lady, he recounted: "We were talking about cats and dogs the other day and decided that both have consciences but the dog, being an honest, humble person, always has a bad one, but the cat is a Pharisee and always has a good one. When he sits and stares you out of countenance he is thanking God that he is not as these dogs, or these humans, or even as these other cats!"

Nature, said Lewis, has the air of a good thing that has been spoiled. It is not only spoiled in and of itself, but also in our human relationship to it. One way this disfiguring comes about is in our way of seeing the natural world. Lewis vividly illustrated this in his short story "The Shoddy Lands". Here he takes us into the mind of a self-centred young woman who lacks a real perception of nature, and thus life. A similiar impoverished view of reality in its full meaning is expressed in his disturbing picture of hell in *The Great Divorce**. He may have been influenced by Charles Williams*, who portrayed hell, and its inroads in our present world, as the absence of meaning*.

For Lewis, the natural world of God's creation imposes a fundamental limit to the human imagination. We cannot, like God, create out of nothing. We can only rearrange elements that God has already made, and which are already brimful of his meanings. Mankind's proper mode of imaginative making is what J.R.R. Tolkien* dubbed sub-creation*. C.S. Lewis believed that evil – whether from human beings or demons* – always results in the disruption or even the destruction of nature. In *The Lion, the Witch and the Wardrobe**, the White Witch* kept Narnia in perpetual winter. In both *The Last Battle** and *That Hideous Strength**, places of natural beauty are despoiled for the sake of economic exploitation, expansion, and so-called progress. In 1947, C.S. Lewis wrote, "The evil reality of lawless applied science… is actually reducing large tracts of Nature to disorder and sterility at this very moment."

Because he normally wrote in a popular manner, Lewis didn't always distinguish between nature as it was originally intended to be from nature as it is now. In his more technical studies, *The Problem of Pain** and *Miracles**, he goes deeper into the meaning of nature as God's creation. In *Miracles* he contrasts this Christian view with what he calls naturalism*, the belief that nature is all that is. He could have used the term materialism*, except that the term "matter" is even harder to pin down than "nature". In his book *Studies in Words**, he devotes a long study to the term "nature". His examination includes its family of words, *phusis* (from which the term "physics" is derived), and "kind". More detail is given on the meaning of the idea of nature in other scholarly works of his, particularly *The Allegory of Love** and *The Discarded Image**. As well as in *Miracles*, he expounds on a biblical view of nature in *Reflections on the Psalms**. Ultimately, there was, for Lewis, an inevitable connection between nature and joy*, as in nature heaven itself is foreshadowed.

Nat Whilk Anglo-Saxon for "I know not whom", used by C.S. Lewis as a pseudonym, usually in the form of the initials "N.W." In the first edition of *A Grief Observed** he called himself "N.W. Clerk". Clerk is Middle English for "scholar". Playing on his

pseudonym, Lewis quotes the medieval authority Natvilcius in
Perelandra* regarding eldila*.

Nesbit, E[dith] (1858–1924) Author of novels and stories for
children, Edith Nesbit created the Bastable family in *The Story
of the Treasure Seekers* (1899) and a sequence of fantasy* tales,
Five Children and It (1902), *The Phoenix and the Carpet* (1904), and
The Story of the Amulet (1906). The tone of her stories influenced
Lewis in writing *The Chronicles of Narnia**, and *The Magician's
Nephew**, set in the period of many of her stories, is a conscious
tribute to her. At the beginning of *The Magician's Nephew*, Lewis
writes: "In those days Mr Sherlock Holmes was still living in
Baker Street and the Bastables were looking for treasure in the
Lewisham Road."

New Narnia See: *The Last Battle*; **Narnia: history; heaven**

N.I.C.E. The National Institute for Co-ordinated Experiments
in Lewis's science-fiction tale *That Hideous Strength**, which
is set up at Belbury*, near Edgestow*, by a group of corrupt
scientists seeking to remake the human race. They wish to purge
it of traditional values of freedom and dignity, and represent
the most satanic inner ring* in history. One N.I.C.E. member,
Filostrato, reveals what he considers to be its inner purpose to
Mark Studdock*: "This Institute… is for something better than
housing and vaccinations and faster trains and curing the people
of cancer. It is for the conquest of death… It is to bring out of
that cocoon of organic life which sheltered the babyhood of
mind the New Man, the man who will not die, the artificial man,
free from Nature. Nature is the ladder we have climbed up by,
now we kick her away." The appliance of science in technology
is allowed to have a totalitarian rule; science is distorted into
technocracy. In the process, new demons take possession. They
are in fact the old demons using a new strategy. This time the

domination of the whole human race appears to be within their grasp. The N.I.C.E. represents all that C.S. Lewis was attacking in his powerful essay *The Abolition of Man**.

Nikabrik the Dwarf A highly cynical member of the resistence to the tyrant Miraz* in *Prince Caspian**. He prefers the old, "realistic" magic of the witches and turns against Aslan*. His position is a comment on pragmatism in twentieth-century thought.

North A key region of the symbolic* landscape of *The Pilgrim's Regress** depicted in the *Mappa Mundi**. It represents the intellectual domain of the human soul, and arid intellectualism.

Northern Frontier In the Chronicles*, the region where troublesome giants* live. The regions to the north of Narnia* represent danger and moral aberration, as do the regions to the south of Archenland*. The White Witch* lives in the north lands, and Miraz's castle* is located in the northern extremity of Narnia. In the south, the Calormenes* represent a constant threat to Narnia's security, even though they have an advanced civilization.

Numinor See: **Atlantis**

numinous An all-pervasive sense of the other is focused in a quality of the numinous, a basic human experience charted by the German thinker Rudolf Otto in his book *The Idea of the Holy ** (1917), which deeply influenced Lewis. The primary numinous experience involves a sense of dependence upon what stands wholly other to mankind. This otherness* is unapproachable and awesome. But it has a fascination. The experience of the numinous is captured better by suggestion and allusion than by a theoretical analysis.

Many realities captured in imaginative fiction could be described as having some quality of the numinous. C.S. Lewis realized this, incorporating the idea into his apologetic for the Christian view of suffering, *The Problem of Pain**, and he cited an event from Kenneth Grahame's fantasy* for children, *The Wind in the Willows*, to illustrate it. This is when Rat and Mole, on a rowing boat on the river in the early hours of the morning, are enraptured by the sound of piping "at the gates of dawn" and experience a shared and uncanny vision of the deity Pan. The final part of *The Voyage of the "Dawn Treader"** particularly embodies the numinous, as the travellers approach Aslan's Country* across the Last Sea* (chapters 15, 16).

Where the numinous is captured, its appeal is first to the imagination*, which also senses it most accurately. It belongs to the area of meaning* that we cannot easily conceptualize. C.S. Lewis found this when he read George MacDonald's* *Phantastes**, describing the effect in *Surprised by Joy** as baptizing his imagination. It was years later that he was able to reconcile this experience with his thinking.

Nurse The nurse in *Prince Caspian**, who tells stories of Old Narnia* to Caspian* and is dismissed. During the liberation of Narnia from Telmarine* rule, Caspian and his nurse meet again. She owes much to C.S. Lewis's nurse, Lizzie Endicott*, who told him myths and folk tales of old Ireland. In Lewis's writings, nurses almost invariably connote the simple goodness of old-time ways.

nymphs Female souls or semi-divine beings in Greek mythology, living in rivers, trees, and mountains. They are young and beautiful, given to music and dancing, elflike in their long lives and other respects. Nymphs of the trees are called dryads* (or hamadryads); those of lakes, rivers, or springs, naiads*; and those of mountains, oreads. In *The Chronicles of Narnia**, they dance with fauns*, arise from the river at Aslan's* roar, and participate in royal weddings. As with elves, there is intermarriage with humans: the sons of Frank* and Helen, the first king and queen of Narnia*, marry nymphs.

O

Octesian One of the seven Telmarine* lords in *The Voyage of the "Dawn Treader"*, sought by the young King Caspian* and his voyagers. Octesian very likely becomes the dragon* found dying by Edmund Pevensie* on Dragon Island*.

***Of Other Worlds* (1966)** A posthumous collection of Lewis's short fiction and essays and brief pieces on narrative fiction edited by Walter Hooper*. The collection was expanded in a 1982 publication entitled *Of This and Other Worlds.*

Old Narnia The Narnia* of the Golden Age* in *Prince Caspian*, remembered in secret under the tyranny of the modernizer Miraz* and the rule of the Telmarines*. The spirits of woods and streams are seldom seen, and talking animals* are in hiding. The schools banish the true history of Narnia from their dreary curriculum. Caspian*, taught about Old Narnia by his nurse* and then his tutor, Doctor Cornelius*, could talk about it for hours.

Old Solar The universal language of rational beings in C.S. Lewis's science-fiction trilogy*, including eldila*, beyond the orbit of the moon and before the fall of mankind and the effects of the Tower of Babel. Earth (or Thulcandra* – the Silent Planet*) is unique in having a diversity of languages. Lewis invented a representative Old Solar vocabulary in providing names and word forms throughout the stories. The idea of inventing languages in fantasy* owes much to J.R.R. Tolkien*, who created several, including Elvish, in which he even wrote lyrics.

O

The Old West Lewis famously defended what he called the Old West in his inaugural lecture upon taking the Chair of Medieval and Renaissance Literature at Cambridge University in 1954, a seat J.R.R. Tolkien* helped him gain. Tolkien was an Elector of the newly established Chair, and described Lewis as "the precise man for the job".

A brief quotation from the lecture will give the flavour:

> Roughly speaking we may say that whereas all history was for our ancestors divided into two periods, the pre-Christian and the Christian, and two only, for us it falls into three - the pre-Christian, the Christian, and what may reasonably be called the post-Christian... Between Jane Austen and us... comes the birth of the machines ... This is parallel to the great changes by which we divide epochs of pre-history. This is on a level with the change from stone to bronze, or from a pastoral to an agricultural economy. It alters Man's place in nature.
> (*"De Descriptione Temporum"* (1955))

Tolkien, along Owen Barfield*, was responsible for helping along the process that led Lewis to become aware of a dramatic shift from the old to the new West, a shift that made the change from Medieval to Renaissance culture insignificant by comparison. Barfield's great achievement, admitted Lewis, was to rid him of his earlier "chronological snobbery"*, an abiding vice of the modern world, according to Barfield. Tolkien, in turn, was responsible for convincing Lewis that the values of pre-Christian paganism* were not merely of aesthetic interest, but were life and death matters reflecting an objective state of affairs.

As a result of Tolkien's arguments, C.S. Lewis came to the conclusion that similarities between Christian teaching and ancient myth* can argue for the truth of Christianity as well as against it. At the heart of Christianity, C.S. Lewis came to believe, is a myth that became fact* – making the claims of Christianity unique.

The continuing popularity of Lewis's premodernism – his sustained rejection of modernism in favour of Old Western values – suggests the existence of a continuity between the Old West and now, despite the Great Divide of which he speaks. It indicates a strong though small stream that has never been eradicated, despite Lewis's fears.

Olvin In *The Horse and His Boy**, the defeater of Pire*, the two-headed giant*, who is turned into the twin-peaked Mount Pire*. Olvin is king of Archenland*, notable for his fair hair. As a result of his victory he wins the Lady Liln*.

Orknies Monsters borrowed from the Early English poem *Beowulf* ("Orcneas"). They participate in the horror of the killing of Aslan* on the Stone Table* in *The Lion, the Witch and the Wardrobe**.

Orual The queen of Glome* in *Till We Have Faces**, and narrator of that story, in which she recounts her life. The physical ugliness of her face (but not her voice) presents a major theme of the novel, shaping many of the events. She is the half-sister of Psyche*, and sister of Redival*. See also: ***Till We Have Faces***

otherness Lewis valued otherness, or other-worldliness. Great stories, he believed, take us outside the prison of our own selves and our presuppositions about reality. Insofar as stories reflect the divine maker in doing this, they help us face the ultimate Other – God* himself, distinct as creator from all else, including ourselves. The very well of fantasy* and imaginative* invention is every person's direct knowledge of the other. Lewis writes that, to make "other worlds" which are convincing and engage your reader, "you must draw on the only real 'other world' we know, that of the spirit." See also: **numinous**

***Out of the Silent Planet* (1938)** The first volume of C.S. Lewis's science-fiction trilogy. Dr Elwin Ransom*, a Tolkien*-like philologist don from Cambridge University, is kidnapped while on a walking holiday in the Midlands and taken to Malacandra* (Mars) by Devine* and Weston*, the latter a famous physicist and materialist (see: **naturalism and supernaturalism**). They are under a misapprehension that the unseen ruler of Malacandra wants a human sacrifice – a fantasy created by their dark minds.

After escaping his captors, Ransom is at first terrified and disoriented by the red planet and its diversity of terrain and inhabitants – various forms of rational life related in a harmonious hierarchy. The inhabitants – sorns* (or, more properly, seroni), hrossa*, and pfifltriggi* – turn out to be civilized and amiable. Ransom, as a linguist, is soon able to pick up the rudiments of their language, Old Solar*. Because of their expectations about the mental level and sensibility of the Malacandrians, however, Weston and Devine only achieve a toehold in the language, leading at times to hilarious effects.

They cannot see the comic contrast between English and the alien language form, which is unable to disguise true meaning*. Weston addresses the Oyarsa* or ruler of Malacandra in the arrogant language of his "scientific" religion of survival, and Ransom interprets for him. However, in translation the effect is not what Weston intended:

> "He says," resumed Ransom, "that these animals learned to do many difficult things, except those who could not; and those ones died and the other animals did not pity them. And he says the best animal now is the kind of man who makes the big huts and carries the heavy weights and does all the other things I told you about; and he is one of these and he says that if the others all knew what he was doing they would be pleased."

Who or what is this Oyarsa that Weston addressed? In *Out of the Silent Planet*, C.S. Lewis imaginatively recreates the medieval picture of the cosmos he later set out in his book *The Discarded Image**. In Deep Heaven, the planets are guided by spiritual intelligences, or Oyarsa, who, with the exception of the one concerned with Earth, are obedient to Maleldil the Young*, their mysterious master. Our planet is the Silent Planet, Thulcandra*, because it is cut off from the courtesy and order of Deep Heaven by a primeval disobedience. See also: **The planets**

Lewis was angry at the science fiction of his time, which invariably portrayed extraterrestrial beings as evil, as the enemies of mankind. The medieval picture was exactly the reverse, and this appealed to him. His reversal of the trend of science fiction had a profound impact that has lasted to this day. Half humorously, Lewis complained in a letter in 1939: "You will be both grieved and amused to hear that out of about 60 reviews only two showed any knowledge that my idea of the fall of the Bent One was anything but an invention of my own… any amount of theology can now be smuggled into people's minds under the cover of romance without their knowing it." This sort of response to *Out of the Silent Planet* was one of the things that made C.S. Lewis realize that he might have something to offer in theological and ethical writing on a broad front.

Oxford City and county town of Oxfordshire, England. It was C.S. Lewis's home from immediately after the First World War until his death in 1963. Oxford is located at the meeting of the rivers Thames and Cherwell, about fifty miles north-west of London. Its importance as early as the tenth century is evident from its mention in the Anglo-Saxon Chronicle for 912.

Before the First World War, Oxford was known as a university city and market town. Then printing was its only major industry. Between the wars, however, the Oxford motor industry grew rapidly. University teaching has been carried on at Oxford since the early years of the twelfth century, perhaps as a result of students migrating from Paris. The university's fame quickly grew, until by the fourteenth century it rivalled any in Europe.

University College, where C.S. Lewis was an undergraduate, is its oldest college, founded in 1249. Erasmus lectured at Oxford, and William Grocyn, John Colet, and Thomas More were some of its great scholars in the fifteenth and sixteenth centuries. Other Oxford scholars beside C.S. Lewis who entered wonderland through fantasy were Charles Dodgson (Lewis Carroll) and J.R.R. Tolkien*.

C.S. Lewis taught philosophy for one year at University College during the absence of its tutor, then, in 1925, he was elected fellow and tutor in English Language and Literature at Magdalen College. He remained there until his appointment to the Chair of Medieval and Renaissance Literature at Cambridge in 1954. During most of C.S. Lewis's life in Oxford he lived at The Kilns*, on the outskirts of Oxford, at Headington. Originally this was isolated, but is now surrounded by a housing estate, where a street is named after him.

Oxford University Socratic Club (1941–1972) A club set up by Estelle "Stella" Aldwinckle* to discuss questions about Christian faith raised by atheists, agnostics, and those disillusioned about religion. C.S. Lewis accepted her invitation to be its first president, a position he held until 1954, when he went to Cambridge. Its committee scoured the pages of *Who's Who* to find notable atheists or other modern thinkers who had the time or the zeal to come and present their creed. Leading Christian thinkers also were main speakers. Lewis himself took this position on eleven occasions. As president, Lewis usually was expected to provide a rejoinder to the speaker. Lead speakers included Charles Williams*, Donald M. MacKinnon, Austin Farrer*, J.Z. Young, C.E.M. Joad, Peter Medawar, H.H. Price, C.H. Waddington, A.J. Ayer, J.D. Bernal, Antony Flew, Jacob

Bronowski, Basil Mitchell, R.M. Hare, Arthur Rendle Short, Ian Ramsey, Iris Murdoch, Gilbert Ryle, Michael Polanyi, J.L. Austin, H.J. Blackham, Michael Dummett, E.E. Evans-Pritchard, Dorothy L. Sayers*, and other outstanding thinkers from different academic disciplines.

Oyarsa See: **eldila**

P

paganism and mysticism in Lewis In one of his letters*
C.S. Lewis speculates that some modern people may need to be
brought to pre-Christian pagan insights in preparation for more
adequately receiving the gospel. He writes:

> It is necessary to recall many to the law of nature *before*
> we talk about God. For Christ promises forgiveness of
> sins: but what is that to those who, since they do not
> know the law of nature, do not know that they have
> sinned? Who will take medicine unless he knows he is
> in the grip of disease?... I would almost dare to say
> "First let us make the younger generation good pagans
> and afterwards let us make them Christians."(*Letters:
> C.S. Lewis and Don Giovanni Calabria: A Study in
> Friendship,* p. 89)

C.S. Lewis explored pre-Christian paganism, the idea of what
he called the *anima naturaliter Christiana* ("a soul that is naturally
Christian"). This, for him, was a kind of natural theology. It
seems that in his apparently foolish preoccupation with myth*
and fantasy*, a Christian voice was in preparation that would still
speak at the beginning of a new millenium to the wider world.
Lewis's success as a contemporary Christian writer reveals that
Christian faith can still strike a deep chord in the world today.
The literary critic George Watson points out that Lewis's literary
critical works (see: **literary critic, C.S.Lewis as a**) largely
belong to the age of modernism, and he was a lifelong anti-
modernist. Paradoxically, Watson remarks, Lewis's "mingling of

formalism and fantasy – a critical and analytical interest in the forms that fantasy takes – was something which, when he died in 1963, was on the point of becoming fashionable".

Lewis's exploration of paganism depends upon a distinction between Christian and theistic mysticism. Theistic mysticism (most notably in the form of Neoplatonism, as shaped by Plotinus) had a profound effect on the medieval West and also on Islam. Christian mysticism (for example, Christian Platonism*) has to struggle to be consonant with orthodox theology.

Lewis's mysticism results in a vision that affects all of his life, thought, and experience. One could therefore start almost anywhere in expounding his mysticism, not just in a theme like, say, a preoccupation with the numinous*. Here is an example from Lewis's characteristic literary criticism*. He speaks of the humble act of reading a book, which in his vision becomes sacramental. In *An Experiment in Criticism*, he posits that good reading has something in common with love, moral action, and the growth of knowledge. Like all these it involves a surrender, in this case by the reader, to the work being read. Good readers are concerned less with altering their opinion than in entering fully into the opinions and worlds of others.

> In reading great literature I become a thousand men and yet remain myself. Like the night sky in the Greek poem, I see with a myriad eyes, but it is still I who see. Here, as in worship, in love, in moral action, and in knowing, I transcend myself; and am never more myself than when I do.

For Lewis (as he learned from Tolkien* particularly) all pagan insights are unfinished and incomplete, anticipating the greatest story, God's* "spell", or the gospel. As a Christian mystic, what he did was grapple with pagan insights, exploring how far the pagan imagination could go without the light of Scripture, which he saw as God's special revelation (see: **The Bible**). In grappling with and affirming pagan insights, his attitude belongs to the thought patterns of the Middle Ages, to a premodernist world.

For Lewis, imagination is the organ of meaning, not truth. Imagination perceives reality. In a sense, reality *is* meaning (see: **meaning and imagination**), in being a dependent creation of God's, referring away from itself to him as its source and meaning.

Pagus A region in *The Pilgrim's Regress** just south of the Main Road*, depicted on the *Mappa Mundi**. The city of Aphroditopolis lies within it.

Papworth, Mr Lewis's black, curly-haired mongrel, mainly a terrier. He was also known as Tykes, Baron Papworth, and Pat. He died in 1937.

Parliament of Owls A meeting of owls in *The Silver Chair**. Jill Pole* and Eustace Scrubb* are carried to it on the back of Glimfeather*. Lewis is probably playing with the title of Chaucer's *The Parliament of Fowls*.

Passarids In *Prince Caspian**, a house of lords under Caspian* IX. When the usurper, Miraz*, takes over, they are sent to their death to fight giants* to the north of Narnia*.

Pattertwig A magnificent talking red squirrel in *Prince Caspian**, the size of a terrier. He is a loyal Old Narnian* met by the runaway Caspian*. Pattertwig also appears in Lewis's abandoned "The Lefay Fragment"*, his original attempt at what eventually became *The Magician's Nephew**.

Pavender A beautiful, rainbow-coloured fish found in Narnia* that provides an excellent meal.

Paxford, Frederick (1898–1979) Handyman and garderner at The Kilns*, Fred Paxford was employed by Lewis and Mrs Janie Moore* in 1930 and remained there until Lewis's death. In his diary, Warnie Lewis* records his occasional irritation with Paxford, but Lewis found his gloomy manner amusing, modelling Puddleglum* the Marsh-wiggle* upon him.

Peepiceek One of Reepicheep's* band of talking mice in *Prince Caspian**, designated as his successor in *The Voyage of the "Dawn Treader"**.

Penelope, Sister (1890–1977) A friend of C.S. Lewis's of the Anglican Community of St Mary the Virgin at Wantage. He corresponded extensively with her, some of which is preserved in *Letters of C.S. Lewis**. *Perelandra** is dedicated to Sister Penelope and her colleagues: "To some ladies at Wantage." There is a story that in one translation this dedication reads: "To some wanton ladies".

Pennyfather, Adela One of a gang of bullying pupils in Experiment House* in *The Silver Chair**, attended by Eustace Scrubb* and Jill Pole*.

Perelandra The planet Venus in C.S. Lewis's science-fiction trilogy. See: *Perelandra (Voyage to Venus)*

Perelandra (Voyage to Venus) (1943) This, the second volume of Lewis's science-fiction trilogy, is set on the planet Perelandra (Venus), a paradisal, oceanic world of floating islands as well as fixed lands. Dr Elwin Ransom* is transported there to rebuff the attacks of the forces of evil incarnate in the human form of his old enemy, Weston*. Perelandra, Ransom discovers, has its own, green-fleshed equivalant of Adam and Eve. The setting is visionary and beautifully realized. The unfallen ecology of

Perelandra, which includes the communion between the Green Lady* and her husband and the animal and fish life of the planet, is intended to contrast with the havoc of sin upon our world. Perelandra presents a forceful and inspiring image of perfection, where natural and spiritual are one.

While the Second World War rages, Ransom is taken in a casket to the planet by the great Oyarsa* or unseen ruler of Malacandra* (Mars), with whom he had become acquainted in his previous adventure in space. He is away for a whole year. On his return he recounts what happened to his friends C.S. Lewis and Dr "Humphrey" Havard*, an account that forms the basis of Lewis's book.

After dropping through the Venusian atmosphere, Ransom finds himself "riding the foamless swell of an ocean, fresh and cool after the fierce temperatures of Heaven, but warm by earthly standards... As he rushed smoothly up the great convex hillside of the next wave he got a mouthful of the water. It was hardly at all flavoured with salt; it was drinkable... Though he had not been aware of thirst till now, his drink gave him a quite astonishing pleasure. It was almost like meeting Pleasure itself for the first time." He is in fact in paradise, brilliantly evoked by Lewis's descriptions.

One fascinating feature of Perelandra is its floating islands, which follow the contours of the sea, with hills becoming valleys in a constant metamorphosis. Many of the dramatic events of the story take place on the islands. In contrast are the fixed lands, upon which the newly created green humans of the planet are as yet forbidden to dwell. This command forms the basis of a re-enactment of the temptation of Eve. There are differences, however, not least as a result of the sacrifice of Maleldil the Young* on Thulcandra* (Earth). Ransom plays a key part, much to his surprise, in frustrating the devilish plans of the bent Oyarsa* of earth to corrupt the unspoiled world. On one of the floating islands Ransom encounters the beautiful Green

Lady and her constant animal companions, including a small dragon with scales of red gold. Her colour is beautiful, like the "green beetle in an English garden". She is like a goddess who seemed to have been fashioned "out of green stone, yet alive". As Ransom often found happening, what was myth* in our world could be fact in others (see: **myth became fact**). When she starts laughing uncontrollably at his strange appearance he realizes that she is fully human.

An unwelcome visitor in a conventional spacecraft arrives in the form of Professor Weston*, who loses no time in engaging the Green Lady in complex and subtle arguments, designed to wear down her resistence to the temptation to disobey the command not to live on the fixed lands. Ransom intervenes with counterargument, but, unlike the possessed scientist, suffers the disadvantage of sleeping from sheer exhaustion. Eventually Ransom realizes, to his dismay, that he must engage Weston in a physical fight to the death. Weston, given over to Satan, is now an "Un-man"*. In the bitter struggle, Ransom receives an unhealable wound to his heel.

The story climaxes in a beautifully poetic vision of the "Great Dance" of the universe, in which all patterns of human and other life interweave. As so often in C.S. Lewis's writings, the theme of joy* is embodied.

The arguments over the nature of obedience and goodness and evil were pursued further by Lewis in his classic study *The Problem of Pain*, published three years earlier. They relate also to Lewis's views on warfare; why he found it impossible to be a pacifist. He continued his exploration of evil in *That Hideous Strength*, set several years later.

Just as his sequel, *That Hideous Strength*, is paralleled by Lewis's study *The Abolition of Man*, *Perelandra* is complemented by *A Preface to Paradise Lost*. This is his study of John Milton's great epic poem, dealing with the fall of humankind, and key themes such as hierarchy. *Perelandra* portrays the imaginative splendour of Milton's themes in a way designed to bewitch the modern reader, bypassing our prejudice against the past – what Lewis called our "chronological snobbery"*.

The poet Ruth Pitter*, a friend of C.S. Lewis, turned some poetic passages from *Perelandra* into verse.

Peridan One of the lords and advisors of Queen Susan* and King Edmund* in Tashbaan*, in *The Horse and His Boy*. Later he leads a charge in battle against the army of Rabadash* the Calormene*.

***The Personal Heresy: A Controversy* (1939)** Jointly authored with E.M.W. Tillyard, a Cambridge literary critic. C.S. Lewis contributed chapters I, III, and V, and a concluding Note, and E.M.W. Tillyard contributed chapters II, IV, and VI, giving an opposing point of view.

C.S. Lewis argues against the view that poetry provides biographical information about the poet, and that it is necessary to know about the poet to understand the poem. He focuses on the inner character of a work of literature, rather than extrinsic factors. For him, in reading poems we look through the poets, rather than at them. We see with their eyes. We can only see if we do not dwell on the particulars of their consciousness. Rather, we indwell them as we attend to a new level of meaning*. The poet's consciousness is a condition of our knowledge, not the knowledge itself. Lewis's analysis bears remarkable similarities to the insights of Michael Polanyi, who was concerned with the nature of consciousness and the way we participate in knowledge.

C.S. Lewis's position here has implications for all the arts (as his later work *An Experiment in Criticism** makes clear). He is saying that art takes us into meanings not normally perceived by us, and perceivable only through the actual arrangement of the artwork. We are reaching meanings that were not accessible to us before the making of the artwork, but which are now available to the artist as well as the reader, viewer, or audience. C.S. Lewis claimed, "If we mean something, we do not mean alone." His Christian view of the world was that it was full of meaning rather than meaningless (or strictly absurd). An artistic arrangement possesses meaning as part of that world. It follows that artistic value has the value that any part of the world has; but its special value for us is that our sense of meaning, our perception, is enlarged. We see with more eyes than merely our own. Lewis would reiterate the poet Shelley's view, in his seminal *A Defence of Poetry*, that imagination* allows us to see quantities as qualities, and to perceive what we know. See also: **literary critic, C.S. Lewis as a**

Peter, High King See: **The Pevensie children**

The Pevensie children (Peter, Susan, Edmund, and Lucy)
The four brothers and sisters, evacuees* from wartime London, who enter Narnia* in *The Lion, the Witch and the Wardrobe** and become kings and queens there. Peter, as eldest, is the High King during Narnia's Golden Age* (echoes of the biblical St Peter). Edmund had for a time been a traitor, but repents and is restored by the sacrifice of Aslan* on the Stone Table*. The children return again to Narnia as told in *Prince Caspian**. After that, however, only the two youngest, Edmund and Lucy, are allowed to return, with their cousin Eustace Scrubb*, in the tale of *The Voyage of the "Dawn Treader"**. While they are enjoying this adventure Peter is being tutored for an exam by Professor Kirke*, and Susan has gone to America with her parents for Mr Pevensie's* lecture tour.

The Pevensie children, with the exception of Susan, who at that time is no longer a friend of Narnia, return to Narnia after a train crash in the apocalyptic final story, *The Last Battle**. Lucy is often the favourite character with young readers of *The Chronicles* *of Narnia**. As Martha C. Sammons puts it: "Lucy is one of the most clearly depicted characters in all the Narnia books... Lucy seems to be spiritually closer to Aslan than anyone else, and they seem to share a special relationship of love!" Lucy's response to Aslan, such as hugging him, is one of the secrets of the lion's success as an imaginative* creation. C.S. Lewis achieves a figure of authority, the creator and true sovereign of Narnia, who is eminently approachable by the innocent and good. Those also, like Edmund and later Eustace, who approach him in fear and repentance find a friend like no other.

C.S. Lewis learned from other writers of children's books the potency of having several characters from one family. Drawing particularly on E. Nesbit's* innovation in creating her Bastable family, Lewis discovered that a story concerning several children of varied characters and ages would grip the attention of a young reader far more than a tale involving simply one character. With children from the same family, the likelihood of spats and angry clashes would increase.

Pevensie, The fate of Susan At the end of all the stories of Narnia*, Susan*, unlike the others who have been in the magical land, is not there. We are told that this is because "She is no longer a friend of Narnia" – she has become too concerned about being "grown-up". As Susan is only twenty-one when she loses her parents and siblings, cousin, and friends in the dreadful railway accident*, it would be premature to conclude that Susan would never again remember Narnia and Aslan*. As Lewis commented in a letter to a young correspondent worried about Susan's fate: "The books don't tell us what happened to Susan. She is left alive in this world at the end, having by then turned into a rather silly, conceited young woman. But there is plenty of time for her to mend, and perhaps she will get to Aslan's Country* in the end – in her own way. I think that whatever she had seen in Narnia she could (if she was the sort that wanted to) persuade herself, as she grew up, that it was 'all nonsense'."

Pevensie, Mr and Mrs Mr Pevensie, in *The Chronicles of Narnia**, is a university lecturer, living in London, who at one stage gives a lecture tour in America, where he and his wife take Susan* with them. Mrs Pevensie is the sister of Alberta Scrubb (see: **Scrubb family**), mother of Eustace*. It is perhaps she who gives the *Dawn Treader** picture to her sister. By coincidence, Mr and Mrs Pevensie are travelling in the same train as the Seven Friends of Narnia* and are thus involved in the fatal accident.

Pfifltriggi One of three intelligent kinds of being on Malacandra*, in *Out of the Silent Planet**. These frog-like creatures are the craftspeople and engineers of the planet. They are expert in digging Malacandra's abundant gold and making artistic objects from it. They also record the history and mythology of their planet onto monoliths at Meldilorn*.

***Phantastes*, George MacDonald (1858)** This is one of ten books Lewis listed as particularly influencing his thinking and vocational attitude (see: **reading of C.S. Lewis**). *Phantastes* was George MacDonald's first prose work of fiction. According to his son and biographer, Greville MacDonald, none of his other writings "has exceeded it in imaginative insight and power of expression. To me it rings with the dominant chord of his life's purpose and work".

It begins:

> I awoke one morning with the usual perplexity of mind which accompanies the return of consciousness. As I lay and looked through the eastern window of my room, a faint streak of peach-colour, dividing a cloud that just rose above the low swell of the horizon, announced the

approach of the sun. As my thoughts, which a deep
and apparently dreamless sleep had dissolved, began
again to assume crystalline forms, the strange events of
the foregoing night presented themselves anew to my
wondering consciousness.

Anodos, the narrator, then recounts how his bedroom had
metamorphosed into a woodland scene. He continues,

After washing as well as I could in the clear stream, I
rose and looked around me. The tree under which I
seemed to have lain all night was one of the advanced
guard of a dense forest, towards which the rivulet ran.
Faint traces of a footpath, much overgrown with grass
and moss, and with here and there a pimpernel even,
were discernible along the right bank. "This," thought
I, "must surely be the path into Fairy Land, which the
lady of last night promised I should so soon find." I
crossed the rivulet, and accompanied it, keeping the
footpath on its right bank, until it led me, as I expected,
into the wood.

Anodos, whose name means "aimless" or "pathless", has many
encounters and adventures, the narrative unfolding with a
dream-like logic rather than the normal pattern of a story. The
effect is to convey a mood and new emotional experience that
instantly captivated Lewis. He first read the book when studying
under W.T. Kirkpatrick*. At that time the teenager was an
atheist. He remembers that

this new world was strange, it was also homely and
humble...What [*Phantastes*] did to me was to convert,
even to baptize... my imagination... The quality which
had enchanted me in his imaginative works turned

241

out to be the quality of the real universe, the divine, magical, terrifying, and ecstatic reality in which we all live. (Preface to *George MacDonald: An Anthology*)

Phars A kingdom neighbouring Glome*, in *Till We Have Faces**. After the marriage of King Trunia* of Phars with Princess Redival* of Glome the two countries enter an alliance, forcing Essur*, to the west of Phars, to stay at peace with the two kingdoms.

phoenix A bird, larger than an eagle, sitting in a tree in the centre of Aslan's* garden, in *The Magician's Nephew**. The phoenix is a traditional symbol*, originating in Greek mythology, of rebirth and immortality because of its resurrection from the ashes.

The Pilgrim's Regress: An Allegorical Apology for Christianity, Reason and Romanticism **(1933; new edition, 1943)** C.S. Lewis was researching the method of allegorical* storytelling for his study *The Allegory of Love** when he wrote this book. In fictional and more general form, it covers the ground of his later account of his life up to his conversion, *Surprised by Joy**. He wrote it during a fortnight's stay with Arthur Greeves*, while on holiday in Ireland.

Twenty years after writing *The Pilgrim's Regress*, Lewis admitted in a letter to a reader: "I don't wonder that you got fogged in *The Pilgrim's Regress*. It was my first religious book and I didn't then know how to make things easy. I was not even trying to very much, because in those days I never dreamed I would become a 'popular' author…"

The Pilgrim's Regress is an intellectual, early twentieth-century version of John Bunyan's great allegory*, *The Pilgrim's Progress*. Instead of Christian, the central figure is John*, loosely based on C.S. Lewis himself. Like in *The Pilgrim's Progress*, the quest* can be mapped. Indeed, Lewis provides his reader with a

*Mappa Mundi**, in which the human soul is divided into North* and South*, the South representing an excess of emotion, and the North arid intellectualism. A straight road travels between them. Needless to say, John's route strays far off the straight and narrow. Like the youthful Lewis, he wavers toward intellectual rather than sensual follies. The story gives a vivid picture of Lewis's intellectual climate of the 1920s and early 1930s.

John's way is a regress rather than a progress because he in fact is travelling away from rather than toward the beautiful Island* that he seeks. The Island is Lewis's equivalent to the Celestial City of Bunyan. When he gains the knowledge of how to acheive his Island, through Mother Kirk*, he has to retrace his steps.

John's quest for the Island is a fine embodiment of the theme of joy*, which is so central in Lewis's autobiography, *Surprised by Joy*. The quest helps John to avoid the various snares and dangers he encounters.

Born in Puritania*, John is taught early to fear the Landlord* of the country. From the first moment, however, that he glimpses the Island in a vision, he is gripped with an intense longing to find it.

On his journey he encounters characters such as Mr Enlightenment* from the city of Claptrap, Mr Vertue, who becomes John's companion, and Media Halfways, from the city of Thrill. Later, John is imprisoned by the Spirit of the Age*, and rescued by the tall, blue-clad figure of Reason. She teaches him many things and directs him back to the Main Road*.

Upon finding the road abruptly cut off by a vast canyon*, John at first refuses the help of Mother Kirk, and has many adventures as he looks for a way down first to the north and then to the south of the main road. After becoming lost, and calling for help, John is aided first by the hermit History and then Reason once more. He finds Mr Vertue in the presence of Mother Kirk, and both follow her guidance and reach the other side of the canyon. From here John can see the sea, and his Island. The two are given a guide to lead them back across the world, for the Island in fact is the other side of the mountains near Puritania, not an Island at all. John's idea of the Landlord has turned out to be false, and the home of the Landlord in those mountains is to be John's as well.

In Lewis's new edition of *The Pilgrim's Regress*, he provided a detailed foreword and notes to the chapters to help his readers with the more obscure points of the allegory. It is in fact best to enjoy the book as a story and not be too concerned with the meaning of every allusion. Read as a quest for joy, and in parallel with *Surprised by Joy*, it yields its main meanings. Clyde S. Kilby's study *Images of Salvation in the Fiction of C.S. Lewis* (1978) provides help with interpretation of the allegory, including its frequent classical references. See also: **chest**

Pire See: **Mount Pire**

Pittencream The only sailor left behind at World's End Island* in *The Voyage of the "Dawn Treader"**, while the ship proceeds on toward World's End*. The cowardly sailor eventually deserts the ship on its return voyage and goes to live in Calormen*, where he tells tall stories about his adventures.

Pitter, Ruth (1897–1992) An important British poet who became a close friend of C.S. Lewis. Her work was admired by W.B. Yeats, Philip Larkin, and other poets, among whom was Elizabeth Jennings, who described her as having "an acute sensibility and deep integrity". In 1955, she was awarded the Queen's Gold Medal for Poetry, the first woman to gain this, and received other awards for her publications. She was largely self-educated, and spent many years employed in painting decorative furniture. Ruth Pitter converted to Christianity largely through the influence of Lewis's wartime BBC* radio broadcasts, which

---

were collected in *Mere Christianity**, and through books such as *The Screwtape Letters**. Later, she came to know him personally, and they visited each other. Lewis confessed to George Sayer* that if he had been the marrying kind, Ruth Pitter was the person he would have wished to marry. With Lewis's agreement, she turned some of his highly poetic prose in *Perelandra** into poetry. See also: **poetry of C.S. Lewis**

Further reading
Don W. King, *Hunting the Unicorn: A Critical Biography of Ruth Pitter* (2008).

The planets In Lewis's science-fiction trilogy (*Out of the Silent Planet**, *Perelandra**, and *That Hideous Strength**), the "true" names of the planets are revealed as part of the story. Lewis reveals that these names are in the tongue of Old Solar*, spoken before the fall of mankind and beyond the moon's orbit.

The sun therefore is properly called *Arbol*, the moon *Sulva*, Mercury *Viritrilbia*, Venus *Perelandra*, Mars *Malacandra*, Jupiter *Glundandra*, and Saturn *Lurga*. Handra in Old Solar means "world". The seven correspond to the astrological planets of the medieval period, which remain the roots of days of the week. Earth is called *Tellus* or *Thulcandra* (the Silent Planet).

According to Michael Ward's study *Planet Narnia*, each of the seven books of Narnia* embody the spirit or quality of a particular planet, shaping both the plot and tone of the book. See also: **Narnia as a secondary world (sub-creation)**

Plato A famous Greek philosopher, born about 427 BC in Athens, who was much admired by C.S. Lewis. He was a founding father of idealism* in philosophy. His work provided much imaginative* inspiration for C.S. Lewis, though, philosophically, Lewis was not a Platonist as such (see: **paganism and mysticism in Lewis**). Some forms of Platonism were deeply influential during the medieval period, which was C.S. Lewis's great love, and which was the object of much of his scholarship. Different aspects of Plato's thought have been emphasized at particular periods of Western history, such as his view of existence or his theory of how we know truth. Belief in the immortality of the soul, as held by C.S. Lewis and the Christian tradition, is not in itself Platonism, nor is imaginative use of the Platonic idea of this world as a copy of a more real one. In his essay "Transposition" (see: **transposition**), C.S. Lewis gives a Christian account of the relationship between spiritual and natural reality (see also: **nature**). Lewis provides a remarkable reworking of Plato's allegory of the Cave in *The Silver Chair**, beautifully providing a Christian defence in answer to the modern claim that God* is a projection of the human being. See also: **God; theology of romance**

Platonism See: **Plato**

Plummer, Polly Digory Kirke's* next-door friend in late Victorian London who is drawn with him into other worlds and eventually Narnia* in *The Magician's Nephew**. Polly lives in a row of terraced houses that have back gardens with tall walls and roof spaces that connect down the row. In later life she is known as Aunt Polly by the Pevensie children* and their friends who have been in Narnia, even though she is no relation. Polly is one of the Seven Friends of Narnia* who witness the end of its world.

Poems **(1964)** This volume contains most of C.S. Lewis's lyrical verse, with the exception of the early cycle of poems entitled *Spirits in Bondage**. They reveal a great variety of themes, and include "Narnian Suite", which is in two parts – a march for "Strings, Kettledrums, and Sixty-three Dwarfs" and a march for "Drum, Trumpet, and Twenty-one Giants" (see: **"Narnian Suite"**). See also: ***The Collected Poems; Narrative Poems***

poesimetres In *The Voyage of the "Dawn Treader"**, Coriakin's* instrument for measuring the metre of poetry.

Poetic Diction, **Owen Barfield** **(1928)** Owen Barfield* believed that, corresponding to steller and biological evolution, there has been an evolution of human consciousness. The evolution of consciousness is reflected precisely in changes in language and perception, from a primitive unity of consciousness, now lost, to a future achievement of a greater human awareness.

Barfield's concept inspired Lewis, especially as it was translated into highly original insights into the nature of poetic language. These insights were embodied in *Poetic Diction*, which concerns the nature of poetic language and a theory of an ancient unity in human awareness that was built into speech.

Poetic Diction offers a theory of knowledge as well as a theory of poetry. At its heart is a philosophy of language. Barfield's's view is that "the individual imagination is the medium of all knowledge from perception upward". The poetic impulse is linked to individual freedom: "the act of the imagination is the individual mind exercising its sovereign unity". The alternative, argues Barfield, is to see knowledge as power, to "mistake efficiency for meaning", leading to a relish for compulsion.

Knowledge as power is contrasted with knowledge by participation (a key word in Barfield). One kind of knowledge "consists of seeing what happens and getting used to it" and the other involves "consciously participating in what is". The proper activity of the imagination* is "concrete thinking" – this is "the perception of resemblance, the demand for unity" (the influence of Samuel Taylor Coleridge on Barfield can be seen here). There is therefore a poetic element in all meaningful language. Lewis elaborates this same point about the poetic condition of meaning in thought in "Bluspels and Flalansferes", available in *Selected Literary Essays*, and in the chapter "Horrid Red Things" in *Miracles** – a chapter that tries to capture in simple language the core of Barfield's ideas in *Poetic Diction*.

poetry of C.S. Lewis C.S. Lewis's early ambition was to be an important poet, and his first book of poetry was published in 1919, when he was twenty and still recovering from war wounds. A long narrative poem, *Dymer**, appeared in 1926. Both reflected his atheism or at least materialistic orientation of this period. Throughout his life he continued to publish verse in periodicals. His shorter poems have been compiled into *The Collected Poems of C.S. Lewis**, and his longer verse into *Narrative Poems**.

Lewis's distinct mark as a writer, however, is his poetic sensibility – he had a poetic way of seeing that was fulfilled by, and central to, his later religious convictions. This sensibility is most present in his prose fiction, but also is part of the attractiveness of his teaching style, whether writing literary history and criticism or philosophical theology. When it is at its best, his poetic way of seeing expresses itself in what he and J.R.R. Tolkien* called mythopoeia, or myth-making. For him great stories and myth* have, like poetry, the ability to make general ideas such as love, courage, and self-sacrifice tangible, specific, and individual. In fact such stories, he felt, can give us as readers actual sensations and feelings that we may never before have experienced (like being in battle, or walking on Mars). Lewis's poetic way of seeing is found, for instance, in *The Chronicles of Narnia**, *The Pilgrim's Regress**, *Till We Have Faces**, *Out of the Silent Planet**, and *Perelandra**. Don W. King argues that it is also to be found in non-fiction books such as *A Grief Observed**.

A poetic sensibility is fundamental to C.S. Lewis's writings, as he once revealed in a letter:

> The imaginative man in me is older, more continuously operative, and in that sense more basic than either the religious writer or the critic… It was he who after my

conversion led me to embody my religious belief in symbolical or mythopoeic forms, ranging from *Screwtape* to a kind of theological science-fiction. And it was, of course, he who has brought me, in the last few years to write the series of Narnian stories for children.

It could be argued that C.S. Lewis also, as much as it is possible for a twentieth-century person, belonged to an older school, an older world, where his heart lay. His concern with, as he put it, "symbolical or mythopoeic forms" in his writing was directly related to his conversion, and his empathy with an older consciousness, the loss of which was highlighted for him by the increasing separation of poetry and prose, and dramatically spotlighted by modernism in poetry. Ruefully he claimed, in his inaugural lecture upon taking up the new Cambridge Chair of Medieval and Renaissance Literature in 1954, "I do not see how anyone can doubt that modern poetry is not only a greater novelty than any other 'new poetry' but new in a new way, almost in a new dimension."

He pointed out elsewhere the unprecedented difficulty of imagining evening, as T.S. Eliot wished his readers to, as a patient on an operating table. Modern poetry sought originality, rejecting what Lewis called "stock responses" to experience. In the old view, goodness and truth are full of light; evil and falsehood are a shadow world. Deity and worship are associated with height. Virtue is linked with loveliness. Love is constant and sweet, death bitter and endurance praiseworthy. "In my opinion," Lewis writes in *A Preface to Paradise Lost**, "such deliberate organisation is one of the first necessities of human life, and one of the main functions of art is to assist it. All that we describe as constancy in love or friendship, as loyalty in political life, or, in general, as perseverance – all solid virtue and stable pleasure – depends on organising chosen attitudes and maintaining them against the eternal flux."

When Lewis's poetry is read, it often seems excessively modelled on older poetry, both in form and content. To describe it, one needs the unfamiliar vocabulary of traditional rhymes and metres, such as rhyme royal, the Spenserian stanza, the alliterative metre, tetrameters, pentameters, iambs, and trochees.

The distinguished poet Ruth Pitter* became a friend of C.S. Lewis, and, though admiring some of his verse, recognized that his true poetry resided in his poetic prose, especially his fiction. It is into prose that Lewis most found expression for his "poetic impulse", as Don W. King calls it. There is also, however, poetic prose embedded in his books of teaching, such as essays and popular theology such as *The Problem of Pain**, *Miracles**, *A Grief Observed*, and *Letters to Malcolm**. King, in a major study of Lewis the poet, believes:

> In *A Grief Observed*, Lewis works through his grief [at losing his wife, Joy Davidman Lewis] to a new understanding and a renewed faith; it is his free verse lament for Joy, himself, and his understanding of God.
>
> *Perelandra* and *A Grief Observed* suggest Lewis's propensity toward poetic prose. Other of Lewis's prose works, including *Mere Christianity*, *The Problem of Pain*, *The Screwtape Letters*, *The Great Divorce*, *The Chronicles of Narnia*, as well as others, demonstrate similar poetic elements, though not as extended nor marked as these.

Don W. King observes that *Perelandra*, the second of the science-fiction trilogy, is the most poetic of all Lewis's prose writings. He demonstrates how the poet Ruth Pitter, with Lewis's approval, turned part of the concluding section of the book into Spenserian stanzas. This concerns the gods, whom Lewis has revealed as ruling angelic beings. Though the gods are difficult for human eyes to see, Ransom* on the planet Perelandra, or Venus as it is known to us, hears their voices and those of the new humans of that planet speaking of the Great Dance of the universe. Ruth Pitter found the prose of this section of the book particularly conducive to poetry, as William Wordsworth before found with his sister Dorothy's journals, or recently Ruth Padel found with Charles Darwin's letters and other prose in her verse biography of the great naturalist.

Further reading
Don W. King, *C.S. Lewis, Poet: The Legacy of His Poetic Impulse* (2001); Ruth Padel, *Darwin: A Life in Poems* (2009).

Poggin An independently minded dwarf* in *The Last Battle*, who sides with King Tirian*, unlike his fellow dwarfs.

Pole, Jill In *The Silver Chair* and *The Last Battle*, a fellow sufferer with Eustace Scrubb* at Experiment House*, a progressive school where they are pupils. She is taken into Narnia* with him on two occasions to help in time of need. Jill, like Lucy*, is an important female character in the Chronicles*. In terms of the theology underlying the stories, her encounter with Aslan* at the stream in *The Silver Chair* is of great significance. She is entrusted with his instructions, analogous perhaps to Moses' receiving of the Law in the Old Testament. *The Silver Chair* in fact focuses on her struggles to remember these signs Aslan has given to her in the quest* to find the lost Prince Rilian*.

The sparky relationship between Jill and Eustace, as they are thrown together for the adventures recounted in *The Silver Chair*, adds reality and depth to the book. They quarrel and make up like real children. Jill grows as a person, from her initial fear in which the idea of adventures was preferable to the reality. By the conclusion of the story, she has developed to the stature of a king or queen of Narnia, even though she is never crowned, preparing her for her mature involvement in the events of *The Last Battle*.

Jill is one of the Seven Friends of Narnia*.

Pomona The Roman goddess of fruit. Peter* remarks in *Prince Caspian** that she placed good spells on the apple orchard at Cair Paravel*.

Potter, Beatrix (1866–1943) The creator of Benjamin Bunny and Peter Rabbit was born in London and introduced to the Lake District (where she eventually lived) on holiday in her teens. Late in life she observed: "It sometimes happens that the town child is more alive to the fresh beauty of the country than a child who is country born. My brother and I were born in London... But our descent, our interest and joy were in the north country." She drew and painted from an early age, and her journals display her literary skill. In childhood she would smuggle animals (such as rabbits, mice, and a hedgehog) into her house. She started sketching her pet animals dressed in clothes and taking part in human activities, whence came the idea of her stories, which began in letters to children. After self-publishing a little book about Peter Rabbit, a London publisher, Frederick Warne & Co., picked it up and produced their own edition in 1902. It quickly became a success, followed by the publications of *The Tailor of Gloucester* and *The Tale of Squirrel Nutkin** in 1903. Copies soon reached the Lewis household on the outskirts of Belfast*. In *Surprised by Joy**, Lewis records that he received an early glimpse of joy* – the inconsolable longing that so features in his writings – through reading the story of Squirrel Nutkin. It confronted him with what he could only describe as "the idea of Autumn". The Beatrix Potter stories also helped Lewis see the potency of talking animals*, so central to *The Chronicles of Narnia**.

prayer See: *Letters to Malcolm: Chiefly on Prayer*

A Preface to Paradise Lost **(1942)** *Paradise Lost* is John Milton's great epic, and C.S. Lewis believed that most recent Milton scholarship had hindered rather than helped a proper reading of the poem. Following the lead given by Charles Williams's* short preface to an edition of Milton's poetical works, Lewis attempted "mainly 'to hinder hindrances' to the appreciation of Paradise Lost". He defended the epic form of literature that Milton chose to use, arguing that it had a right to exist, as does ritual, splendour, and joy* itself. Lewis argued that he differed from the critics of Milton not over the nature of his poetry, but over the nature of mankind and even of joy itself. Qualities that he (and Milton) regard as virtues the critics blame him for. Lewis complains: "It reminds us of Aristotle's question – if water itself sticks in a man's throat, what will you give him to wash it down with? If a man blames port wine for being strong and sweet, or a woman's arms for being white and smooth and round, or the sun for shining, or sleep because it puts thought away, how can we answer him?" See also: **literary critic, C.S. Lewis as a**

The Prelude, William Wordsworth (1850) Lewis listed this as one of the ten foremost books influencing his thinking and vocational attitude (see: **reading of C.S. Lewis**). It was composed by William Wordsworth (1770–1850) the English Romantic poet. *The Prelude, Or, Growth of a Poet's Mind: An Autobiographical Poem* was written by 1805, but not published until 1850. It was written to be preliminary to an autobiographical work, *The Recluse*, which was never finished. This was intended to be a philosophical poem articulating Wordsworth's view of humanity, of nature*, and of society. In *The Prelude* the poet gives an account of his intellectual, imaginative*, and emotional development under the influences of education, nature, and society.

Lewis's autobiography, *Surprised by Joy**, was originally attempted in poetic form and abandoned, and it is possible that *The Prelude* was in his mind as a genre model. In it Lewis traces the symbiotic themes of his intellectual and imaginative development, always set against a strong moral concern. Like *Surprised by Joy*, Wordsworth's *The Prelude* contains friends, books, experiences, and places that shaped the teller.

Preston, Marjorie A friend of Lucy Pevensie* in *The Voyage of the "Dawn Treader"*, who she overhears talking about her to another girl through a spell in Coriakin* the Magician's book.

***Prince Caspian* (1951)** A year after their first adventure in Narnia*, the four Pevensie children* are drawn back to help Caspian*, the true heir to the throne, whose life is in danger from the tyrant Miraz*, who holds control over Narnia. He has suppressed the Old Narnians* who remained loyal to the ancient memory of Aslan* and Narnia's long ago Golden Age*, when the children had been kings and queens at Cair Paravel*.

This story reveals much about the history of Narnia, the rule of humans over the talking animals*, and the Telmarines*, who had stumbled into Narnia long before from our world. See also: **Narnia: history**

Prizzle, Miss The formidable Telmarine* schoolteacher at the girls' school in Beruna*, in *Prince Caspian**. She scolds Gwendolen* for looking out of the window and claiming to see a lion.

***The Problem of Pain* (1940)** C.S. Lewis's purpose in writing this book was to "solve the intellectual problem raised by suffering". He had never felt himself qualified "for the far higher task of teaching fortitude and patience". In this respect, he said that he had nothing to offer his readers "except my conviction that when pain is to be borne, a little courage helps more than much knowledge, a little human sympathy more than much courage, and the least tincture of the love of God more than all". Years later he was able to offer more. After his wife, Joy Davidman

Lewis*, died, he recorded his reactions and reflections in *A Grief Observed**.

For such a small book, Lewis ranged far and wide, discussing God's* control over all human events, including suffering; the goodness of God; human wickedness; the fall of mankind; human pain; hell; animal pain; and heaven*. He took up similar themes in imaginative* form in his science-fiction story *Perelandra**. Austin Farrer* comments that Lewis presents "a world haunted by the supernatural, a conscience haunted by the moral absolute, a history haunted by the divine claim of Christ".

The Problem of Pain, like *Miracles**, is among the best of C.S. Lewis's theological writings, and is a key text in philosophy of religion. It contains fine passages on heaven, joy*, hell, and the sense of the numinous*, which is present in so much of Lewis's fiction. It argues from the starting point of God's relationship to the universe that he has made, and is uncompromising in its supernaturalism*. It also reveals Lewis's position when he was an atheist, and why he finds such a position untenable.

The Dutch title of the book translates as *God's Megaphone*, taken from Lewis's memorable claim: "God whispers to us in our pleasures, speaks in our conscience, but shouts in our pains: it is His megaphone to rouse a deaf world."

Prunaprismia In *Prince Caspian**, the red-haired wife of Caspian's* uncle, the usurper, Miraz*.

Psyche A character, whose name means "the soul" or "butterfly" in Greek, from Apuleius's *The Golden Ass**, upon which C.S. Lewis based his character of the same name in his novel *Till We Have Faces**. In Apuleius's story, Psyche is so beautiful that Venus becomes jealous of her. Cupid, sent by Venus to make Psyche fall in love with an ugly creature, himself falls in love with her. After bringing her to a palace, he only visits her in the dark, and forbids her to see his face. Out of jealousy, Psyche's sisters tell her that her lover is a monster who would devour her. She takes a lamp one night and looks at Cupid's face, but a drop of oil awakes him. In anger, the god leaves her. Psyche seeks her lover throughout the world. Venus sets her various impossible tasks, all of which she accomplishes except the last, when curiosity makes her open a deadly casket from the underworld. At last, however, she is allowed to marry Cupid.

In *Till We Have Faces*, C.S. Lewis essentially follows the classical myth, but retells it through the words of Orual*, Psyche's half-sister, who seeks to defend her actions to the gods as being the result of deep love for Psyche, not jealousy.

Psyche's Palace The palace of the god of the Grey Mountains* in *Till We Have Faces**, in which Princess Psyche* dwells after her marriage. It can't normally be seen by mortal eyes, though her half-sister Orual* glimpses it in the swirling mist. As a child Psyche had dreamed of living in a gold and amber castle and being married to the "greatest king of all". When Orual glimpses the palace, she sees "wall within wall, pillar and arch and architrave, acres of it, a labyrinthine beauty". It was like no house she has ever seen. Pinnacles and buttresses seem to be springing up. They are unimaginably tall and slender, looking as if stone were shooting out into branch and flower.

Puddleglum the Marsh-wiggle The companion of Jill Pole* and Eustace Scrubb* in *The Silver Chair**, in their quest* for the lost Prince Rilian*. He is one of C.S. Lewis's most memorable Narnian* creations. Puddleglum is delightfully pessimistic, though never cynical or disloyal to Aslan*. He is tall and angular, with webbed hands and feet as befits a marshy existence. His character owes something to Lewis's groundsman at The Kilns*, Fred Paxford*. The name is inspired by an old translation Lewis found of Euripides' *Hippolytus*, which included the phrase

"Stygian puddle glum" (John Studley's sixteenth-century translation of "Tacitae Stygis", l. 625). Lewis reproduces the phrase in his *English Literature in the Sixteenth Century**.

Pug A pirate encountered on the island of Felimath* in *The Voyage of the "Dawn Treader"**. He is involved in slave trading*.

Pugrahan The location of the dreaded salt mines in Calormen* in *The Last Battle**.

Puritania The region in *The Pilgrim's Regress** in which John* is brought up, beside the Eastern Mountains* to which he eventually returns. Though not intended as a portrait of Lewis's native Ulster, there are echoes of his childhood in the speech patterns of John's mother and father, the cook, the Steward, and Uncle George, and the book was composed during a holiday to Northern Ireland.

Puzzle the Donkey A simple donkey duped by Shift* the Ape into dressing in a lion skin and pretending to be Aslan* in *The Last Battle**.

Q

The quest The quest often takes the form of a journey in symbolic*
literature. In fiction such as Lewis's, life and experience has the
character of a journey, and this character can be intensified by
art. The Christian possibilities of the quest have been explored
by Thomas Malory (in *Le Morte d'Arthur*) and John Bunyan (in
The Pilgrim's Progress), as well as by J.R.R. Tolkien* and Lewis –
to name a few writers.

The quest motif is a hallmark of Lewis's writings, both fiction
and non-fiction. *The Magician's Nephew** records Digory Kirke's*
double quest for the magic apple and to save his dying mother;
The Voyage of the "Dawn Treader"* also concerns a double quest,
to find the lost Seven Lords* and to discover Aslan's Country*;
Perelandra* features a quest to save the humans of a new world;
The Pilgrim's Regress* documents John's* quest for the island of
his vision; in parallel, Lewis's autobiography *Surprised by Joy**
tells of his personal quest for an elusive joy*; and *Till We Have
Faces** is a tale of Psyche's* quest for her lost lover, and Queen
Orual's* search for the truth about her sister's story about a
palace in the mists and a god who loves her.

R

Rabadash, Prince Also called "The Ridiculous". The vain Calormene* prince in *The Horse and His Boy**, who, after being rejected by Queen Susan*, attempts to conquer Archenland* and Narnia* during the reign of High King Peter* and the other children. After the Battle at Anvard* he is left dangling from a wall hook. Later, Aslan* temporarily turns him into a donkey*.

railway accident The accident in *The Last Battle** that takes the lives of the Seven Friends of Narnia*. The train involved is carrying most of the company on it. Their plan is to meet up with Edmund and Peter Pevensie*, who are waiting at a station en route. Eustace Scrubb* and Jill Pole* are on their way back to Experiment House* and have to change at this particular station for the train to their school. Edmund and Peter are to give them the rings* by which Digory Kirke* and Polly Plummer* had originally arrived in Narnia* half a century before. As the youngest in the company, Eustace and Jill are still able to return to Narnia, and they intend to use the rings to get there to provide help in Narnia's hour of need. The train collides with the station platform (presumably after derailing – Eustace mentions a "frightful jerk and a noise", and Peter remembers seeing it "taking the bend far too fast"). By coincidence, Mr and Mrs Pevensie* are also on the train, on their way to Bristol, leaving Susan* as the only surviving family member.

Ramandu A retired star* in *The Voyage of the "Dawn Treader"**, resplendent in silver clothes, who lives near Aslan's Table* on World's End Island* far across the Eastern Ocean*. The voyagers in the *Dawn Treader** encounter him on their way toward Aslan's Country*. King Caspian* later marries Ramandu's daughter*.

Ramandu is undergoing renewal until he once more can return to the stars. The stars of Narnia* and its world are not made up of flaming gas but of glimmering people with silver clothes and hair. Ramandu has been brought down to World's End Island when old and fading. A bird of morning* would each day bring him a fire-berry from the valleys of the sun. These berries are restoring him. Lewis takes the idea of stars as people (or intelligences) from the imaginative world of the Middle Ages. See also: **The planets**

Ramandu's daughter In *The Voyage of the "Dawn Treader"**, the travellers meet Ramandu* and his daughter on World's End Island*. Later King Caspian* marries her. In the adventure of *The Silver Chair** we learn that one day, many years later, while she is sleeping, she is slain by the Green Witch* in the form of a green serpent. It is while Prince Rilian* is seeking his revenge for his mother's death that he is bewitched by her murderer.

Ramandu's daughter owes much to Tolkien's* conception of elves, which Lewis was familiar with long before the publication of *The Lord of the Rings* (1954–1955). In simplified form, she is like Tolkien's Lúthien or Arwen, immortal yet marrying a human. Her parentage in the stars* is equivalent to Lúthien's mother's status as a Maia, an angelic being.

Ramandu's Island See: **World's End Island**

Ram the Great Becomes king of Archenland* after the events told in *The Horse and His Boy**. He is the son of Cor* and Aravis*, and the most celebrated of all the kings of Archenland.

Ransom, Dr Elwin Hero of C.S. Lewis's science-fiction trilogy*, later renamed the Fisher King, and partially modelled on

J.R.R. Tolkien*. He is a philologist of Cambridge University. Much like C.S. Lewis, he has a war wound, and is a "sedentary scholar". One of his publications is *Dialect and Semantics*. He is a bachelor who finds swimming the only sport he excels at (a skill that proves useful in watery Perelandra*). Ransom is also an anti-vivisectionist. He combines intellectual and heroic qualities, though he tends to put himself down. Clyde S. Kilby points out that Ransom speaks like Lewis himself.

In *Out of the Silent Planet**, Ransom is kidnapped to the planet Malacandra* (Mars), enabling him to learn Old Solar*, the Great Tongue, and discover the nature of life outside quarantined planet Earth. On his return he spends three months in hospital recuperating. (It may have been in this period that Lewis describes him, in "The Dark Tower", as a pale man with grey, distressed-looking eyes.) See: ***The Dark Tower and Other Stories***

In *Perelandra**, he is transported by the Oyarsa* or ruler of Malacandra to the planet Perelandra (Venus) to foil a satanic plot against a new Adam and Eve in that paradisal world. Here he suffers a debilitating wound to the heel.

In *That Hideous Strength** Ransom is revealed as the latest in the succession of Pendragons of Logres. He has been withdrawn from Cambridge to secretly run a community at St Anne's*. This community is what is left of Logres, the true England, and is pitted against the demonic forces of the N.I.C.E.* He may have found The Manor at St Anne's* on one of his walking tours – he originally had a country cottage in Worchester (sic). After the routing of the N.I.C.E., Ransom is permitted the rare honour of returning forever to Perelandra, the Third Heaven, and now dwells with King Arthur and others in Aphallin*.

Elwin Ransom is tall, slightly built, golden-haired, but a little round-shouldered and weak-eyed, aged about thirty-five to forty in the late 1930s when the events of *Out of the Silent Planet* take place. He doesn't have much dress sense, and, at first sight, might have been mistaken for a doctor or schoolteacher. His only relation is a married sister in India.

Lewis tells us that "Ransom" is not his real name, though Ransom is told by the Oyarsa that his name literally means "ransom". Lewis as narrator of the stories tells us he had known Dr Ransom slightly before the events of the first science-fiction tale, corresponding with him on literary and philological subjects, though at that time they seldom met. They become firm friends when Ransom has the idea of asking Lewis to cast his adventures in fictional form. Lewis regards him as sane, wholesome, and honest.

When Ransom returns from Perelandra after his second planetary adventure Lewis finds him glowing with health, rounded with muscle, and seeming ten years younger. He thereafter retains the golden beard that he had grown. This process of rejuvination continues in the story *That Hideous Strength*, where he at first appears to Jane Studdock* to be a boy of twenty, until she notices his strength and his full beard. She is reminded of her mental picture of King Arthur or Solomon.

reading of C.S. Lewis According to the eminent literary critic William Empson, Lewis was "the best read man of his generation, one who read everything and remembered everything he read". Lewis had a bookish background, and spent long, silent hours in the library. What emerged from this background is a richness of thought, imagination*, and writing that has influenced literary criticism, science fiction, children's literature, literary approaches to the Bible*, and Christian apologetics throughout the West. As well as influencing millions of readers of his books, Lewis acknowledged an enormous debt to his own wide reading.

From childhood onward, Lewis read voraciously and eclectically. He typically defended the value of "lowbrow" reading such as Rider Haggard and John Buchan. This bookishness and eclecticism is an important characteristic of

Lewis throughout his life, and is reflected in his diaries* and letters*. He grew up in a house where books were everywhere.

Lewis's capacity for endless reading made him a natural library dweller from his undergraduate studies onwards. Oxford's Bodleian Library has a central place in Lewis's life, work, and affection, as this extract from a letter to his father on 31 March 1928 shows: "I spend all my mornings in the Bodleian… If only one could smoke and if only there were upholstered chairs, this would be one of the most delightful places in the world."

As well as using the Bodleian, Lewis accumulated over the years a considerable personal library, over 2000 volumes of which is now housed in The Marion E. Wade Center at Wheaton College, Illinois, USA. He frequently moved house until becoming established at The Kilns* in 1930, and thereafter his books were divided between his home and his college rooms. Even then shelf space was always insufficient.

Lewis's interest from the beginning, and increasingly so, was in the books of an older period even larger than but including medieval times. For Lewis, all books before the period of modernism, spanning the millennia at least since the ancient Greeks, had important values in common, and thus interrelated in a constantly stimulating way. It was reading, even more so than intellectual debate and friendship (though he hungered for the latter), that fed his mind and imagination and kept him mentally alive. He saw the world through texts, as part of a symbolic* perception of reality. Thus, while experiencing the horrors of wartime trench warfare, he reflected: "This is War. This is what Homer wrote about."

What were some of the texts that helped to provide an intellectual framework for Lewis the scholar and writer? Near the end of his life, Lewis responded to a question from the magazine *The Christian Century*: "What books did most to shape your vocational attitude and your philosophy of life?" This was his list:

Phantastes*, by George MacDonald*
The Everlasting Man*, by G.K. Chesterton*
The Aeneid*, by Virgil
The Temple*, by George Herbert
The Prelude*, by William Wordsworth
The Idea of the Holy*, by Rudolf Otto
The Consolation of Philosophy*, by Boethius
Life of Samuel Johnson*, by James Boswell
Descent into Hell*, by Charles Williams*
Theism and Humanism*, by Arthur James Balfour*

This group of books reflects Lewis's wide interests. There are two works of prose fantasy*, three of poetry (two of them in narrative), one biography, and the remaining four books philosophical theology. Lewis described MacDonald's *Phantastes* as "baptizing his imagination" long before he accepted the claims of Christ, in its account of Anodos's journeys in Fairyland. Charles Williams's horror fantasy *Descent into Hell* traces a process of damnation to which Lewis felt professional scholars are particularly prone, which he seems to have taken as a moral warning to himself. Virgil's *The Aeneid* is an epic poem about the founding of Rome by its Trojan hero, Aeneas, and is one of the greatest Latin literary works. He translated part of it into English verse. Virgil's work epitomizes the adopting of the classical past by Christian Europe in the Middle Ages. *The Temple, Sacred Poems and Private Ejaculations* is a collection of some 160 of Herbert's devotional poems, published for the first time shortly after his death. *The Prelude, or, Growth of a Poet's Mind: An Autobiographical Poem* is a confessional quasi-religious narrative poem in praise of the poetic imagination by Wordsworth, and his greatest work. From another poem Lewis took Wordworth's phrase "surprised by joy" for his own autobiography, which he started composing in verse, perhaps modelled on *The Prelude*. Lewis was a great admirer of Dr Samuel Johnson, and resembled him in the sharpness of his wit. He comes alive in James Boswell's *Life*. Warren Lewis*, looking over his uneven diary, laments that he did not "Boswellise" his brother.

The earliest theology listed by Lewis, Boethius's *The Consolation of Philosophy*, Christianized the wisdom of classical paganism*, and provided a model for philosophy for a thousand years. No other book in the medieval period was more widely read. One-time British prime minister Arthur Balfour wrote up *Theism and Humanism* from the first of his two Gifford Lecture series for Glasgow University. He was concerned with the way naturalistic humanism impoverished reality, in contrast to theism. Rudolf Otto's *The Idea of the Holy* is a study of the sacred, which deeply influenced Lewis's understanding of the numinous* and similar experiences of otherness* such as "joy"*.

G.K. Chesterton was a formative influence on Lewis. The book that he picks out for his top ten, *The Everlasting Man*, is typical of Chesterton's apologetics and characteristically posits the persuasive power of the Gospels. It was the nature of the Gospels in combining apparent history with the quality of great story that was pivotal in Lewis's conversion from naturalism* to Christianity. Lewis remarks in *Surprised by Joy** that in reading *The Everlasting Man* he saw for the first time a complete Christian outline of history presented in a way that made sense to him.

Particularly in his letters*, Lewis frequently refers to other books that made their mark on him. He writes about much of his favourite reading in literary essays (for example, on John Bunyan, Jane Austen, William Morris, and Edmund Spenser). Some of his favourite authors, such as Charles Williams* and Tolkien*, belonged to the Inklings*.

recognition See: **undeception and recognition**

recovery An important feature of fantasy* exploited by Lewis is restoration or recovery, which brings a healing of the wounds caused when we act through the blindness of sin. Lewis rejected what he saw as the restless quest of the modern world to be original. Indeed, meaning* was to be discovered in God's* created world, not somehow to be created by mankind, and in this discovery imagination* working through fantasy was an effective aid. In his book *Orthodoxy*, G.K. Chesterton*, speaks of the way that children normally are not tired of familiar experience. In this sense they share in God's energy and vitality; he never tires of telling the sun to rise each morning. For Lewis, the child's attitude, in fact, is a true view of things, and dipping into the world of story can restore such a sense of freshness. Lewis explains that the child "does not despise real woods because he has read of enchanted woods: the reading makes all real woods a little enchanted". Similarly, for J.R.R. Tolkien*, fairy stories help us to make such a recovery – they bring healing – and "in that sense only a taste for them may make us, or keep us, childish".

Lewis was convinced that through story, the real world becomes a more magical place, full of meaning. We see its pattern and colour in a fresh way. The recovery of a true view of things applies both to individual things such as hills and stones, and to the cosmic – the depths of space and time itself. For in sub-creation*, as Tolkien taught him to believe, there is a "survey" of space and time. Reality is captured in miniature. Through sub-creative stories – the type to which *The Chronicles of Narnia** and his science-fiction trilogy* belong – a renewed view of reality in all its dimensions is given – the homely, the spiritual, the physical, the moral.

red dwarves See: **dwarves; Seven Brothers of the Shuddering Wood**

Redhaven The main settlement on Brenn*, the second of the Seven Isles*. Its hospitable inhabitants sumptuously feast the crew in *The Voyage of the "Dawn Treader"**.

R

Redival The frivolous golden-haired sister of Orual* in *Till We Have Faces**, and half-sister of Psyche*. When Orual becomes queen of Glome* she marries Redival off to Trunia* of the neighbouring kingdom of Phars*, to improve their alliance. Redival's son, Daaran*, becomes heir of Glome's throne on the unmarried Orual's death.

Reepicheep the Mouse A brave and decorous talking mouse of Narnia* who journeys to Aslan's Country* in *The Voyage of the "Dawn Treader"**. Following a wood woman's prophecy (see: **dryad**) when he was in his cradle, Reepicheep embarks on the journey as a personal quest* motivated by longing for Aslan's Country. Mice were granted the privilege of becoming talking animals* after gnawing through Aslan's* cords in *The Lion, the Witch and the Wardrobe**. Reepicheep, the chief of the mice, is around two feet in height, wears a long crimson feather on his head, and carries a long, sharp sword. In *Prince Caspian** he is badly wounded, and his proud tail severed. Lucy* is able to heal him, and Aslan restores his pride. Like King Peter*, Reepicheep represents the chivalric ideal so central to order in Narnia. Mice, and talking mice, are frequent subjects in the tradition of children's literature Lewis draws upon.

Reflections on the Psalms **(1958)** C.S. Lewis disliked the view that the Bible* is seen only as literature, and should be read as such. If it is taken for what it is, those parts of it that are literature can be properly received in this way. The psalms are an important literary part of the Bible, and Lewis felt that he had something he could say about them as a layperson and literary critic*. The psalms, he considered, are great poetry, and some, such as Psalms 18 and 19, are perfect poems. Unless the psalms are read as poetry, "we shall miss what is in them and think we see what is not". *Reflections on the Psalms* is particularly good at bringing out how the Hebrews had an appetite and longing for God*, how they appreciated his Law (which they saw as rooted into nature* as the very structure of reality), and how they viewed nature. There are three key chapters that deal with the inspiration of Scripture and "second meanings" within it. See also: **theology, C.S. Lewis and; The Bible; literary critic, C.S. Lewis as a;**

***Rehabilitations and Other Essays* (1939)** In his preface, C.S. Lewis tells us that all the pieces in this collection are written in defence of things that he loves that have been the objects of attack. The first two essays defend Romantic poets such as Shelley and William Morris against "popular hatred or neglect of Romanticism"*. The third and fourth defend the present (1939) Oxford* University English syllabus. The fifth supports the reading of many popular books that have, he believes, greatly increased his power of enjoying more serious literature as well as what is called "real life". The sixth essay champions Anglo-Saxon poetry. The contents are as follows.

Shelley, Dryden, and Mr. Eliot. A reasoned and powerful defence of the greatness of Percy Bysshe Shelley (1792–1822) as a poet, even judged by classical criteria. C.S. Lewis's deep sympathy for the unbeliever is strikingly evident. Lewis's title refers to two very different poets, John Dryden (1631–1700) and T.S. Eliot (1888–1965), and to Eliot's preference for Dryden's poetry over Shelley's, which he discusses.

William Morris. This essay is of particular interest for a study of C.S. Lewis's fiction, for he owed a debt to William Morris.

The Idea of an "English School". This piece is of historical interest, because C.S. Lewis, along with J.R.R. Tolkien*, helped to shape the Oxford University English syllabus for many years.

Our English Syllabus. C.S. Lewis reveals his thoughts on the purpose of education*.

High and Low Brows. This defence of some popular reading as being acceptable as "good literature" anticipates the ideas that reached mature form in C.S. Lewis's *An Experiment in Criticism**.

The Alliterative Metre. Along with this defence of an Anglo-Saxon and Old Norse metre, C.S. Lewis includes an example of his own poem employing it, "The Planets". In *Narrative Poems**, a longer example, "The Nameless Isle" is included.

Bluspels and Flalansferes: A Semantic Nightmare. This is a seminal essay on the relationship between thinking and imagining, truth and meaning*, metaphor and concept.

Variation in Shakespeare and Others. An essay on Shakespeare's poetic method. He saw Shakespeare's greatness as having "combined two species of excellence… the imaginative splendour of the highest type of lyric and the realistic presentation of human life and character".

Christianity and Literature*. An early attempt by C.S. Lewis to relate his faith to literature.

See also: **literary critic, C.S. Lewis as a**

Restimar One of the seven Telmarine* lords of Caspian* IX in *The Voyage of the "Dawn Treader"**. The usurper, Miraz*, has sent them away to search for new lands across the vast Eastern Ocean*. He is found by the voyagers, turned to gold in a bewitched pool on Deathwater Island*.

Revilian One of the seven Telmarine* lords of Caspian* IX in *The Voyage of the "Dawn Treader"**. Sent away by Miraz* with Restimar*, the travellers discover him sleeping at Aslan's Table* on World's End Island*, along with two other lords, Argoz* and Mavramorn*.

Rhince Drinian's* ship's mate in the tale of *The Voyage of the "Dawn Treader"**.

Rhindon The name of the sword given to Peter Pevensie* by Father Christmas* in *The Lion, the Witch and the Wardrobe**.

Rhoop One of the seven Telmarine* lords, in *The Voyage of the "Dawn Treader"**, of Caspian* IX, sent away by the usurper, Miraz*, to search for new lands across the vast Eastern Ocean*. He is discovered trapped on the nightmarish Dark Island*. Later in the voyage he is granted restful sleep at Aslan's Table* on World's End Island*.

Rilian, Prince The son of King Caspian* X (formerly Prince Caspian). The Green Witch* kidnaps Rilian for ten years. The tale of his daring rescue by Eustace Scrubb*, Jill Pole*, and Puddleglum* the Marsh-wiggle* is told in *The Silver Chair**.

rings In *The Magician's Nephew**, yellow-coloured and green-coloured rings made from magical Atlantian* dust by the minor magician and scientist Andrew Ketterley*, uncle of Digory Kirke*. Digory's friend, Polly Plummer*, is whisked into another world after being tricked by Uncle Andrew into touching a ring, and Digory uses one ring to follow her and the other to bring her back. This leads to the beginning of all the adventures in other worlds and in Narnia* particularly. Nearly fifty years later, the rings are retrieved from the London garden where Polly and Digory have buried them, with the aim of using them once again to travel to Narnia in its hour of greatest need.

Rishda Tarkaan A Calormene* captain in *The Last Battle**, who assists Shift* the Ape and Ginger* the Cat against King Tirian*. His fate is to be carried away by the demon god of Calormen*, Tash*.

River Rush In *Prince Caspian**, we are told that the Rush joins the Great River* at Beruna*. See also **Narnia: geography**

River Shribble An important Narnian* river in *The Silver Chair**,

R

flowing from west to east and marking the boundary between the northern marshes and Ettinsmoor*.

river-god Called from the Great River* by Aslan* in *Prince Caspian*. The modern Telmarine* bridge at Beruna* chains him, and Aslan frees him by destroying it through Bacchus*.

romance, theology of See: **theology of romance**

romanticism C.S. Lewis wished for the word "romantic" to be banned as it now had so many usages as to be virtually useless. He failed to find another term however to characterize the central preoccupation he shared with his friends J.R.R. Tolkien*, Owen Barfield*, and Charles Williams*, or kindred spirits such as G.K. Chesterton* and Lewis's mentor, George MacDonald*.

He tells us in his preface to the third edition of *The Pilgrim's Regress** that when he wrote that book in the early 1930s, he meant "romanticism" to mean the special experience of inconsolable longing, or joy*. He certainly was not in revolt against reason or classicism, which romanticism is sometimes taken to mean. He was not a subjectivist, seeing art as the expression of its maker's soul (see: **subjectivism**).

In English literature, the Romantic movement is often taken to begin with the publication of *Lyrical Ballads* in 1798 by William Wordsworth and Samuel Taylor Coleridge. This was part of a wide reaction in Europe against deism and a mechanistic view of nature* and mankind. Romanticism gave rise to the Gothic genre, and its offspring, Mary Shelley's remarkable *Frankenstein* (1818) and the eventual rise of science fiction. It also created a vogue for historical romance, as in the novels of Sir Walter Scott. In Germany Romanticism was connected with the rise of modernist theology, in reaction to rationalism. George MacDonald's* rejection of his native Calvinism was part of the same trend.

The underlying link between different aspects of romanticism, as far as C.S. Lewis was concerned, is a preoccupation with the imagination* and creative fantasy*. This linking thread can be seen in all the main influences upon C.S. Lewis. Indeed, a brief outline of these influences is the best way of characterizing the romanticism of C.S. Lewis. "Romantic" influences upon him can, for convenience, be divided into four areas: (1) ancient mythologies; (2) older writers; (3) nineteenth-century authors; and (4) contemporary sources. These influences are mentioned by C.S. Lewis, or came through friends and acquaintances such as J.R.R. Tolkien*, Charles Williams*, Dorothy L. Sayers*, or from his mentor, George MacDonald.

(1) Ancient mythologies. Old Norse mythology affects some features of Lewis's Narnia* stories and deeply influenced J.R.R. Tolkien's fantasies. Lewis drew more upon classical mythology, most notably in *Till We Have Faces** and in characters such as Mr Tumnus* in Narnia. Lewis mentions his great love of Irish mythology. Welsh and British mythology – especially "The Matter of Britain" and Merlin* (see: **Atlantis**) – is found in *That Hideous Strength**. Lewis believed that scattered among pagan myths there are certain "good stories" that prefigure Christian truth (see: **paganism and mysticism in Lewis**). They anticipate and give form to adequate vehicles of truth.

(2) Older writers. Some main sources seem to be Boethius (see: ***The Consolation of Philosophy***), Spenser, Malory, Bunyan, and Milton, whose influence on *Perelandra** is marked. Milton is probably an important root of the science fiction genre, of which, according to Brian Aldiss, C.S. Lewis is an important part. John Bunyan and earlier medieval allegorists deeply influenced C.S. Lewis also. Edmund Spenser was one of Lewis's favourite authors.

(3) Nineteenth-century authors. Most important of the writers from this period influencing C.S. Lewis was George MacDonald. MacDonald in turn confesses a debt to the German

Romanticism of Novalis and others. C.S. Lewis's concept of joy* or *sehnsucht* is found in German Romanticism. He mentions that William Morris (1834–1896) influenced his work. While an undergraduate at Oxford*, Lewis gave a paper on Morris to The Martlets, a university society. Here he compared Morris to Homer and Thomas Malory, but, the minute book records, "The general sense of the Society was that too high a position had been claimed" for the writer. Lewis later wrote (the piece, "William Morris", can be found in *Selected Literary Essays*) that Morris "seems to retire far from the real world and to build a world out of his wishes; but when he has finished the result stands out as a picture of experience ineluctably true".

(4) Contemporary sources. A number of influences on his work are mentioned by Lewis, including James Stephens, G.K. Chesterton* (his thought, not so much his fiction), E.R. Eddison, and David Lindsay*. He also discusses the ideas of Rudolf Otto on the numinous* (see: *The Idea of the Holy*) in *The Problem of Pain**, and seeks to embody that quality in his fantasies, for example in Aslan's Country*.

Both C.S. Lewis and J.R.R. Tolkien considered E.R. Eddison (1882–1945) an important writer, and he was much discussed by the Inklings*. Tolkien disliked his invented names; he felt that they lacked colour and conviction. Eddison's geography of his imaginary three kingdoms – Rerek, Meszria, and Fingiswold – bears a superficial resemblance to the geography of Tolkien's Middle-earth. Eddison was appreciated for his attempts at sub-creation*.

The Inklings themselves influenced C.S. Lewis, particularly Tolkien, Charles Williams, and Owen Barfield.

See also: **theology of romance; literary critic, C.S. Lewis as a; myth; meaning and imagination**

Roonwit A great and golden-bearded centaur* in *The Last Battle**. He reads of danger in the stars* over Narnia* and warns

King Tirian*. He is killed by a Calormene* arrow. Centaurs originate in Greek mythology, where they are much fiercer and less friendly than in Narnia. Roonwit's name may be derived from the word *runwita*, "knower of secrets", found in the Early English poem *Beowulf* (l. 1325).

Rumblebuffin The giant* in *The Lion, the Witch and the Wardrobe** who assists in the fight against the White Witch*. In attempting to borrow a handkerchief from Lucy*, he picks her up by mistake. The giant is a member of the respected Buffin* family, a not very clever family, but old and with traditions.

Rush River See: **River Rush**

Rynelf A wise and experienced sailor on the galleon in *The Voyage of the "Dawn Treader"**.

S

St Anne's The country house in *That Hideous Strength** in which Elwin Ransom* forms a community in opposition to the sinister N.I.C.E.*, and which represents the spiritual England (Logres), the remnant of Atlantis*.

St Mark's, Dundela The Church* of Ireland place of worship attended by the Lewis family in his childhood Ulster. Dundela is on the outskirts of east Belfast*, the church a short walk from Little Lea*. Lewis was baptized here on 29 January 1899 and confirmed on 6 December 1914 to please his father. Lewis's grandfather, Thomas Hamilton (1826–1905), was St Mark's first rector. In 1932, the Lewis brothers gave a stained glass window to the church in memory of Albert* and Flora Lewis*, their parents. The traditional symbol of St Mark is the Lion, which is also the title of the church magazine, so it is fitting that Aslan* of Narnia* is a lion.

salamanders Salamanders dwell in Bism* in the great fire-river in *The Silver Chair**. They are witty and eloquent small dragons. In medieval lore, salamanders were the one creature able to live in fire, as birds live in air and fish in water.

Sallowpad An old, wise raven who is advisor to King Edmund*, Queen Susan*, and Queen Lucy* in *The Horse and His Boy**.

satyrs Fertility gods of the woods and hills in Greek mythology. They are grotesque creatures, combining human and bestial features, such as a horse's tail or goat's legs. Satyrs appear

275

throughout *The Chronicles of Narnia**. The satyr Wraggle* fights against Tirian* in the final battle of Narnia*. Another (Silenus*, from classical mythology) accompanies Bacchus*.

Sayer, George (1914–2005) A pupil and friend of C.S. Lewis's who published an acclaimed major biography in 1988 of his one-time tutor, *Jack: C.S. Lewis and His Times*. Lewis sometimes stayed in his home in Malvern. George Sayer was head of the English department at Malvern College* from 1949 to 1974. When Sayer first met his tutor he was told by J.R.R. Tolkien*, "You'll never get to the bottom of him." Sayer's biography particularly dwells on Lewis's early life, his early poetry, his relationship with Mrs Janie Moore*, his life as a university lecturer, and his domestic life.

Sayers, Dorothy Leigh (1893–1957) Dorothy L. Sayers, best known for her detective stories about Lord Peter Wimsey, was a friend of C.S. Lewis's and later met his wife, Joy Davidman Lewis*. She also was acquainted with Charles Williams*, and contributed to *Essays Presented to Charles Williams**, the posthumous tribute from the Inklings*. Her robust popular theological writings, including *The Mind of the Maker* (1941), reveal a sharp and brilliant mind that, like those of Lewis and G.K. Chesterton*, delighted in dogma and orthodoxy. Her series of BBC* radio plays, *The Man Born to Be King*, was immensely popular in wartime Britain. Toward the end of her life she discovered Dante's *The Divine Comedy*, and translated it into fresh, contemporary English (a task completed after her death by Barbara Reynolds).

C.S. Lewis wrote a panegyric to Dorothy L. Sayers that was read out at her memorial service and concludes, "Let us thank the Author who invented her."

science-fiction trilogy See: ***Out of the Silent Planet**; **Perelandra**; **That Hideous Strength***

scientism Science is one of the most significant communal endeavours of mankind, the historical origins of which lie in the Judeo–Christian idea of the Two Books, the Word of God and the Book of Nature, from a single author. Scientism is the idolatry of science, where it becomes the sole authority, the model and arbiter of truth, as under modernism. Lewis attacks scienticism particularly in his science-fiction trilogy*. Professor Weston* embodies all that Lewis dislikes in the attitude of scientism. Its inevitable consequence, technocracy – the tyranny of technique, the subjugation of nature* by technology – is satirized by Lewis in *That Hideous Strength**, where it is epitomized in the N.I.C.E.*. Under technocracy, he tried to demonstrate, scientific technology becomes the characteristically modern form of magic, truth by power. Lewis sought to rehabilitate an older view of nature in order to help his contemporaries to become aware of what he saw as the grotesque shortcomings of scientism. Such a rehabilitation can be seen in his exposition of the medieval model of the cosmos, *The Discarded Image**; in the world of Narnia*; in the figure of Merlin* in *That Hideous Strength*; and in the philologist-hero Dr Elwin Ransom*, who later becomes the Fisher King of Arthurian legend.

Screwtape In *The Screwtape Letters** and its brief sequel, *Screwtape Proposes a Toast**, an eminent Under-Secretary to the High Command of hell and uncle of the junior tempter, Wormwood*. Lewis deliberately gives Screwtape a certain, twisted eminence, in his belief that greater beings are capable of greater evil. Interestingly, Screwtape admits hell's lack of power against its Enemy, but continues to trust optimistically in its bureaucracy. Screwtape ceased to be a practising tempter long before, when he was rewarded with his important administrative post.

The Screwtape Letters (1942) The most direct of several books about devilry that C.S. Lewis wrote, and, of all his books, the one he found most unpleasant to compose. It gave him, he says, a sort of spiritual cramp, because of the inverse perspective of hell that it employs. The book is a comic, satirical look at perhaps the most serious subject possible, damnation. The letters first appeared in a religious journal called *The Guardian*. One reader, a country clergyman, wrote in to cancel his subscription on the grounds that "much of the advice given in these letters seemed to him not only erroneous but positively diabolical".

The Screwtape Letters consists of letters of advice and warning from a senior devil prominent in the Lowerarchy of hell to his nephew, Wormwood*, a trainee tempter. Screwtape writes them just before and during the Second World War. Wormwood, fresh from the Tempters' Training College*, has been assigned a young man. His task is to secure his damnation. Unfortunately for Wormwood, his client becomes a Christian. Screwtape passes on a number of useful suggestions for reclaiming the young man. These come both from his centuries of experience and from information from hell's Intelligence Department. Screwtape is also in touch with other tempters assigned to the patient's friends, acquaintances, and relations. Wormwood particularly sees great possibilities in the person of the young man's mother, who is very trying. The young man successfully avoids the pull of the inner ring* of a smart set of people. Wormwood faces hell when, first, his patient falls in love with a Christian girl, and, second, when he fails to keep the young man out of the danger of death and he is killed in an air raid, and is forever out of the reach of hell's clutches. Screwtape's only consolation lies in devouring his incompetent nephew.

The Screwtape Letters is one of C.S. Lewis's most popular books. His view of a personal devil comes over clearly, despite the satirical genre that he employs. Though considered by Lewis not to be among the best of his books, it stands in a long line of books concerned with angels*, demons, heaven*, and hell, such as Dante's *The Divine Comedy*, Milton's *Paradise Lost*, and John Macgowan's* *Dialogues of Devils*. The novels of Lewis's

pupil Harry Blamires*, including *Highway to Heaven*, continue
the same tradition.

***Screwtape Proposes a Toast* (1959)** A collection of literary
and theological pieces, including several reprinted from
Transposition and Other Addresses* and *They Asked for a Paper**. It
contains "Screwtape Proposes a Toast", "The Inner Ring"*, "Is
Theology Poetry?", "Transposition" (see: **transposition**), "On
Obstinacy in Belief", "The Weight of Glory", "Good Work
and Good Works", and "A Slip of the Tongue". See also: *The
Screwtape Letters*

Scrubb, Eustace Clarence A cousin of the Pevensie children*,
he is drawn into Narnia*, along with Lucy* and Edmund*, in
The Voyage of the "Dawn Treader"*. He returns to Narnia on two
other occasions with Jill Pole*, a school friend, as recounted in
The Silver Chair* and *The Last Battle**. When we first meet him,
he is self-centred and spoiled by the modern education he is
receiving at Experiment House*. He exemplifies a vice Lewis said
he suffered from as a young man, what he called "chronological
snobbery"*. In *The Voyage of the "Dawn Treader"**, the focus falls
on Eustace for a time when the third-person narrative alternates
with quotations from his diaries. Eustace's adventures with the
voyagers on the *Dawn Treader** give him a wider view of life,
particularly after his experience of turning into a dragon* on
Dragon Island*. This experience, and his undragoning by Aslan*,
provide a powerful image of sin, repentance, and Christian
salvation. Unlike his cousins, Eustace is never a monarch in
Narnia, though he is given regal dress (with the other Seven
Friends of Narnia*) as the New Narnia* unfolds.

Scrubb family The Scrubb family – the parents Alberta and
Harold, and their son, Eustace – are "modern" people. Their
values are satirized by Lewis (Eustace's preference for books of

facts; Alberta's vegetarianism; their use of alternative medicine), but he does not treat them as sinister. Characteristically, the parents send Eustace to boarding school at Experiment House*, representing the worst in modern education*. The Scrubbs live in Cambridge. Alberta is the sister of Mrs Pevensie*.

Sea Girl A girl seen herding fish by Lucy* in *The Voyage of the "Dawn Treader"**, as the ship passes over the clear waters of the Last Sea* before Aslan's Country*. She and Lucy become friends simply by seeing each other, even though their worlds can never touch. See also: **Sea People**

Sea People Undersea people seen by Lucy* in *The Voyage of the "Dawn Treader"**. They ride sea horses, wear no clothes, and have bodies the colour of old ivory, with dark purple hair. Their beautiful submarine land is made up of mountains, hills, forests, and parkland. The Sea People enjoy hunting, and use small fierce fish as falcons are used in our world.

Sea Serpent This attacks the ship in *The Voyage of the "Dawn Treader"**, after the travellers have visited Burnt Island*.

Sensible, Mr An allegorical* figure in *The Pilgrim's Regress** representing cultured worldliness.

Seven Brothers of the Shuddering Wood Red dwarves* living in the rocks and trees of the mountains of Narnia's* southern border with Archenland*, in *Prince Caspian**. They work in a forge underground, their heavy blows making the ground above tremble. They aid Caspian* in the fight to oust the tyrant Miraz*, providing dwarf-wrought armour and fighters.

Seven Friends of Narnia In *The Last Battle**, seven of those who have entered Narnia* from our world decide to meet up regularly to discuss that magical world and their memories of it. Prince Tirian*, in a dream, sees them assembled, and they see him as a spectre (beings from Narnia cannot physically enter our world, with the exception of Aslan*, who appears under a different name and form). The friends are: Digory Kirke*; Polly Plummer*; Peter, Edmund, and Lucy Pevensie*; Eustace Scrubb*; and Jill Pole*. Susan Pevensie* is not part of the company as, at that time, she is no longer a friend of Narnia, because of her immaturity in striving to be "grown-up" (see: **Pevensie, The fate of Susan**).

Seven Isles A group of seven small islands a few days' sailing from the coast of Narnia*, described in *The Voyage of the "Dawn Treader"*. Muil* is the westernmost island, separated from Brenn* by a choppy stretch of water. On Brenn, the town of Redhaven* provides supplies for shipping in the area.

The Seven Lords Telmarine* lords of Caspian* IX. The usurper, Miraz*, had sent them away to search for new lands in the Eastern Ocean* during his reign, as recounted in *Prince Caspian*. In its sequel, the tale of *The Voyage of the "Dawn Treader"*, Caspian seeks the seven missing lords. The seven are: Argoz*, Bern*, Mavramorn*, Octesian*, Restimar*, Revilian*, and Rhoop*.

A Severe Mercy **(1977)** This is an account of love, courtship, marriage, and grief in which C.S. Lewis played an important pastoral part, mainly through letters to its author, Sheldon Vanauken (1914–1996). The American movingly records his romance with Jean Davis, whom he calls "Davy", their conversion to Christian faith, and her subsequent early death. A key discovery of the young couple's is that God's* love is stronger than their own deeply romantic love of each other. The "shining barrier" they had erected around their love was invaded by Jesus Christ, who replaced each other as the centre of their lives. At Oxford* University, where they studied, C.S. Lewis and Christian friends influenced their conversion.

Thereafter Lewis is both mentor and friend. After Davy's death, and though Sheldon is in America, Lewis stays close to his suffering by letter. Vanauken's book is particularly important to those for whom C.S. Lewis inspires a sacramental view of Christian faith. Such a view is exemplified well in Leanne Payne's study, *Real Presence: The Holy Spirit in the Works of C.S. Lewis* (1989).

Shadowbrute See: **god of the Grey Mountains**

Shadow Lands The name given to this world by Aslan* in *The Last Battle**, to mark its contrast to the real, new world of his country. In this contrast Lewis makes powerful use of Plato*, particularly his famous allegory* of the Cave in *The Republic*.

Shallow Lands See: **Underland**

Shar A lord of Archenland* in *The Horse and His Boy**, who fights valiantly in the Battle of Anvard*.

Shasta A twin son of King Lune* of Archenland* in *The Horse and His Boy**. This son is lost in Calormen*, to the south, for many years. There he has the name Shasta. *The Horse and His Boy** is the tale of how he returns to Archenland, learns his true identity and name (Cor), and gains his Calormene* wife, Aravis*. To them is born Ram the Great*, the most notable of all the kings of Archenland. Cor's identical twin is named Corin*. Shasta, in a moment of profound recognition*, realizes that Aslan* is behind all stories, including his own and that of Aravis.

Shift the Ape A Narnian* talking animal* in *The Last Battle**, who deceives many loyal beasts and trees into believing that Aslan* has returned, and that Puzzle the Donkey*, draped in an ill-fitting lion skin, is he. Shift's treachery knows no boundaries, and he forms an alliance with Narnia's traditional enemy, Calormen*.

Shribble River See: **River Shribble**

signs, four Signs entrusted to Jill Pole* by Aslan* in *The Silver Chair**, to lead her and her friend Eustace Scrubb* in their appointed quest* for the lost Prince Rilian*, son of their old friend Caspian*. Jill is instructed to remember and believe the signs, but she has frequent difficulties in doing so.

The Silent Planet See: **The planets**

Silenus An elderly drunken satyr* and companion of Bacchus* in Greek mythology*. He accompanies Bacchus on a donkey in *The Lion, the Witch and the Wardrobe** and *Prince Caspian**, and is an expert musician. Enormously overweight, he keeps falling off his horse and constantly calls out for refreshment, which stimulates grapevines to produce lots of fruit. On Mr Tumnus's* bookshelf is a learned volume called *The Life and Letters of Silenus*.

Silver Chair The chair in Underland* in *The Silver Chair**, to which Prince Rilian* is bound each night for the period when his mind starts to clear from the Green Witch's* enchantment that grips him. His freedom from the chair marks the end of his enslavement to the spell.

***The Silver Chair* (1953)** The sequel to *The Voyage of the "Dawn Treader"**. It concerns Eustace Scrubb* and another pupil of Experiment House* (a "modern school") a girl named Jill Pole*. They are brought to Narnia* by Aslan* to search for the long-lost Prince Rilian*, son of Caspian* X, the Caspian of the previous adventure, now in his old age. Their search takes them into the wild lands north of Narnia, and eventually into a realm under the earth called Underland*. The two children are accompanied by one of C.S. Lewis's most memorable creations, Puddleglum* the Marsh-wiggle*. They encounter and destroy the Green Witch*, murderer of Rilian's mother. Before that, they narrowly escape being eaten by the giants* of the city of Harfang*, for whom man is a delicacy, and even Marsh-wiggle is in their cookery book.

Silver Sea The reach of ocean covered with lily-like white flowers found by the travellers in *The Voyage of the "Dawn Treader"**. As they penetrate the dazzlingly bright sea, the voyagers discover its waters becoming gradually more shallow as World's End* is approached. It proves necessary to leave the *Dawn Treader** and use a rowing boat instead. Beyond World's End lies Aslan's Country*.

slave trade In *The Voyage of the "Dawn Treader"**, slave trading is a strong indicator of the blight that seized Narnia* under the tyranny of Miraz* the Telmarine*. Pirates such as Pug* ply their trade in the Lone Islands* and sell their captives to Calormen*, where slavery is an accepted part of the economic structure. Slavery returns to Narnia in *The Last Battle**, with the alliance between Shift* the Ape and the Calormenes*.

Slinkey A renegade fox who sides with the Calormenes* in *The Last Battle**, and is killed by Eustace Scrubb*.

Slubgob Dr Slubgob is the principal of the Tempters' Training College* of hell in *The Screwtape Letters**.

Slumtrimpet The tempter assigned to the fiancée of Wormwood's* charge in *The Screwtape Letters**.

Smith, Sarah One of the inhabitants of heaven*, the Solid People*, who travel to its hinterlands to meet bus trippers from hell in the dream story *The Great Divorce**. One tripper, a dwarf named Frank (see: **The Dwarf**), was her husband in Golders Green, London, in the previous life. There is a magnificent procession in her honour, which is observed by Lewis, who has accompanied the trippers, and the solid spirit of George MacDonald*, his mentor. The encounter between Sarah Smith and Frank, which fails to persuade Frank to stay, leads Lewis to ask some searching questions of MacDonald.

Socratic Club See: **Oxford University Socratic Club**

The Solid People The inhabitants of heaven* in *The Great Divorce** whose reality contrasts with the insubstantiality of the bus trippers from hell. Lewis was particularly drawn to the biblical image of "the weight of glory", the title of a published sermon of his. He felt that there was a correspondence between particularity in people, places, and things and in substance. See also: **nature; God**

Son of Adam The name by which male humans are formally addressed in the Narnian Chronicles*. The Narnian* throne may only properly be occupied by Sons of Adam and Daughters of Eve. See also: **Daughter of Eve**

Sopespian A lord of the usurper, King Miraz*, in *Prince Caspian**, who turns traitor and plans his death.

Sorlois A city of the long-dead world of Charn* in *The Magician's Nephew**.

sorn Sorns (or, properly, seroni) are one of three intelligent kinds of being living on the planet Malacandra*. As befits the

285

stereotype of the sedentary intelligentsia, the scholarly sorns have long thin legs, top-heavy bodies, and thin faces with long, drooping noses and mouths. They are three times as tall as the earthman Elwin Ransom*. Sorns have scientific interests, including cosmology and astronomy, and enjoy metaphysical speculation. Ransom finds, in response to their eager probing, that his knowledge of Earth geography, history, and science is extremely sketchy.

South A key region in the symbolic* landscape of *The Pilgrim's Regress*, depicted on the *Mappa Mundi*. It represents the emotional and visceral side of the human soul (see: **chest**).

Spear-head Narnia's* north star in *The Voyage of the "Dawn Treader"*, brighter than our own pole star.

***Spenser's Images of Life* (1967)** C.S. Lewis's longest piece of literary criticism*, as opposed to literary history. It is based upon his Cambridge lectures on Edmund Spenser's great poem *The Faerie Queene*. He intended to turn his material into a book, but did not live to do so. Lewis's holograph notes were expanded and edited into this book by Alastair Fowler of Brasenose College, Oxford* University. Fowler expressed his hope "that if Lewis himself had lived to write the book it might have stood out among his works as a critical new departure".

C.S. Lewis approaches *The Faerie Queene* as a splendid and majestic pageant of the universe and nature*, which celebrates God*, in Lewis's own phrase, as "the glad creator". He argues that if the poem is to be fully enjoyed and understood by the modern reader, conventional views of epic and allegory* need to be modified. He suggests in his introduction: "We should expect, then, from Spenser's poem, a simple fairy-tale pleasure sophisticated by polyphonic technique, a simple 'moral' sophisticated by a learned iconography. Moreover, we should expect to find all of these reacting on one another, to produce a work very different from what we are used to." Lewis considers *The Faerie Queene* to be perhaps the most difficult poem in English, above the demand of great literature for both a simple and a sophisticated response.

His final chapter analyses the story of King Arthur in Spenser's poem. See also: **literary critic, C.S. Lewis as a**

Spirit of the Age An allegorical* figure in *The Pilgrim's Regress**
portrayed as a Giant* who imprisons John* the modern pilgrim.

Spirits in Bondage: A Cycle of Lyrics (**1919**) Written while C.S. Lewis was an atheist, and when he had a strong ambition to be a poet, this collection of poetry was published under the pseudonym of Clive Hamilton (Hamilton was his mother's maiden name, and his brother's middle name). According to Lewis, the poems are "mainly strung around the idea... that nature is wholly diabolical and malevolent and that God*, if he exists, is outside of and in opposition to the cosmic arrangements".

The volume has similarities of outlook with his early, long narrative poem, *Dymer**. See also: **Narrative Poems; The Collected Poems; Poems**

Spivvins A pupil at Experiment House* in *The Silver Chair**. who is bullied by a gang and whose secret Eustace Scrubb* keeps, despite being tortured.

Splendour Hyaline A swan-shaped galleon used by the kings and queens of Narnia* in *The Horse and His Boy** and *Prince Caspian**. Though richly furnished, she is also able to fight in battle. She has a swan's head at her prow and carved wings going back nearly to her waist. The sails are of silk and great lanterns hang to her stern.

"Spotty" Sorner A member of the gang of bullying pupils in Experiment House*, in *The Silver Chair**.

Stable Hill In *The Last Battle**, there is a stable here in which Shift* keeps Puzzle* the Donkey, as he pretends to be Aslan*. Later Tash*, the Calormene* demon god, enters the stable, followed by Aslan himself. When the great lion takes it over, its inside turns out to be larger than its outside.

stars In *The Chronicles of Narnia**, stars are living beings, as in the medieval imagination* Lewis draws upon. They are sung into being by Aslan* at the creation of Narnia*. Stars featured include Ramandu* and Coriakin*. In his portayal of stars Lewis may have been influenced by J.R.R. Tolkien*, for whom living stars were central to his imagined world in which Middle-earth lay, particularly Eärendil. See: **The planets**

Sterk Sterk lay between Stratford and Edgestow* on the railway line to London in *That Hideous Strength**. In *Out of the Silent Planet**, the deserted country home of Professor Weston* lies on the far side of the hills a good four miles from Sterk. Elwin Ransom* comes across Weston's home while on a walking tour, heading for Sterk. The town has industrial areas beyond it, in contrast to the featureless, desolate countryside in which Ransom is kidnapped.

Stevens, Courtenay E. ("Tom Brown") (1905–1976) A member of the Inklings*, and a fellow and tutor in Ancient History at Magdalen College, Oxford* University, from 1934. He acquired the nickname "Tom Brown Stevens" while a schoolboy at Winchester College.

Stonefoot A giant* that Roonwit* summons to battle in *The Last Battle**, at the command of King Tirian*.

stone knife This was used by the White Witch* to slay Aslan*, as recounted in *The Lion, the Witch and the Wardrobe**. Later in the history of Narnia*, the travellers discover it kept by Ramandu* at Aslan's Table* in *The Voyage of the "Dawn Treader"**.

The Stone Table A table of ancient magic in *The Lion, the Witch and the Wardrobe**, upon which Aslan*, the great lion, is slain by the White Witch*, and which is split forever when he returns to life. It is a slab of grey stone supported by four upright stones. The table is obviously ancient, and covered with engraved lines and figures. A mound called Aslan's How* is eventually built over it and plays a significant part in the actions recorded in *Prince Caspian**. The table has similarities with ancient Celtic flat stones (cromlechs), and represents a transfiguration of the pagan* by the Christian.

Stormness Head A distinctive peak in Narnia's* southern mountains in *The Horse and His Boy**. Clouds assembling around the peak signify bad weather, hence the peak's name. The main pass into Narnia from Archenland* runs through Stormness Gap nearby.

Strawberry The horse of London cabby*, Frank*, in *The Magician's Nephew**, who is turned into a talking and flying horse by Aslan* and renamed Fledge*.

Studdock, Jane The wife of Mark Studdock* in *That Hideous Strength**. Like Damaris Tighe in Charles Williams's* novel *The Place of the Lion* (much admired by Lewis and other Inklings), Jane is a postgraduate student. Six months after her marriage, alone during the day in their tiny flat, she is experiencing a crisis over the meaning of romantic love* even while she works on John Donne's love poetry.

As a child Jane had given up any belief in the supernatural along with Father Christmas. She is, however, gifted with unwelcomed second sight, by which the devilish activities of the N.I.C.E.* are opened to her. She is the innocent agent who alone can reveal the hidden whereabouts of the sleeping Merlin*, in a trance since the Dark Ages. As such she is sought both by the N.I.C.E. and the opposing forces of humanity, led by Dr Elwin Ransom*.

As Jane is slowly drawn into the community surrounding Ransom, there is no violation of her personhood like that of her husband Mark as he moves closer to the inner ring* of the N.I.C.E. at Belbury*. Gradually her sense of reality, and her committment to the marriage of love, return until she is able to receive back again the undeceived and restored Mark (see: **undeception and recognition**).

Studdock, Mark Gainsby A junior fellow of Bracton College* of the Midlands university of Edgestow* in *That Hideous Strength**. His subject is sociology. Six months before the story opens, he marries Jane*, a postgraduate student of English literature. Mark is drawn into involvement with the sinister N.I.C.E.*, whose headquarters are within a few miles at Belbury*. There his very soul is endangered by the lure of the N.I.C.E.'s "inner ring"* of members. We learn that the temptation of the inner ring has beset Mark throughout his young life.

With daunting self-honesty, C.S. Lewis modelled Mark on aspects of himself as a new lecturer at Magdalen College, Oxford* University. Mark finds himself constantly denying his spontaneous like and dislike of people in order to go deeper into Belbury's inner circle. In fact, his natural reaction was to dislike all the core people.

Jane, his wife, provides his connection with reality. Whenever he thinks about her, she is a mirror. He imagines her disliking his pretty heavy drinking at Belbury. She would be scathing about its leading lights. He knows that she wouldn't fit in there, despite efforts to persuade him to get her to join Belbury. Her real self would be a living criticism of all that the N.I.C.E. stands for. From Jane's point of view, Mark is a person easily taken in. He likes to be liked, opening him to manipulation.

According to the story's narrator, revealed as Lewis himself, Mark's mind holds virtually no remnant of noble thought, either Christian or pagan*, that could lodge. He hasn't had either a properly scientific or a classical education*, merely a modern one. He has bypassed the disciplines of abstract thought and of the traditions of civilization, the "literatures of freedom and dignity". These lacks make him a man of straw. He has done well in academic subjects that require no exact knowledge, being good at essays and general papers. He has typically once written an article on vagrancy though he had no knowledge of the tramp's life of the roads.

Mark experiences "undeception"* after being falsely arrested for the murder of Hingest, a fellow of Bracton disillusioned after a brief flirtation with the N.I.C.E. Painful self-knowledge suddenly enlightens him. He sees himself as being always drawn toward odious inner rings*, even at school losing his only real friend in his efforts to get into an unpleasant society called Grip. Later, he leaves behind his undergraduate friends, such as Arthur Denniston*. In this new state of being undeceived, his public self or face falls off him, leaving himself as the person responsible for all his follies. Jane is the only real person he has left, and he has nearly discarded her for the N.I.C.E. and the sinister forces behind it.

Mark's undeception is part of the story of his faltering steps toward Christian conversion. At Belbury, Mark is Wither's* chosen pupil for initiation into the satanic inner circle. At the point when he is expected to despoil a figure of a crucified man, he suddenly realizes for the first time that there might be something in Christianity. Whereas his wife Jane had abandoned belief in Christianity, Mark had never believed.

Studies in Words (1960; 1967 expanded second edition)
C.S. Lewis became Professor of Renaissance and Medieval Literature at Cambridge University at the end of 1954, setting the pattern of his work with his inaugural address, "*De Descriptione Temporum*"*. His book *Studies in Words*, enlarged for the second edition after his death, is based on lectures he gave at Cambridge, and is mainly addressed to undergraduates studying literature. He warns in his preface that the book is not an essay in linguistics; his purpose is merely lexical and historical. His approach, however, differs greatly from that of a dictionary, with a number of advantages. His studies provide an aid to more accurate reading, and the words studied are selected for the light they shed on ideas and sentiments. The history of ideas, Lewis believes, is intimately recorded in the shifts of meaning* in words. There is value in considering the relationship between words in a family of meaning, rather than considering words and their roots individually.

The modern reader's natural tendency is to assume that they know the meaning of words in old texts. Lewis confesses that he early cultivated the habit of following up the slightest "semantic discomfort" he felt with a word, a habit now second nature. Any such discomfort rouses him, like a terrier, to the game of discovering the history of thought and sentiment that underlies the semantic biography of a word. Owen Barfield* displayed a similar instinct. See also: **literary critic, C.S. Lewis as a**

sub-creation See: **Narnia as a secondary world**

subjectivism C.S. Lewis was deeply concerned about an increasing loss of objective values in his day. He explained, in an essay, "The Poison of Subjectivism" (1943):

> Until modern times no thinker of the first rank ever doubted that our judgments of value were rational

judgments or that what they discovered was objective... The modern view is very different. It does not believe that value judgments are really judgments at all. They are sentiments, or complexes, or attitudes... To say that a thing is good is merely to express our feeling about it; and our feeling about it is the feeling we have been socially conditioned to have.

Seventy years after that article was published, this kind of subjectivism has deepened. Values that were once seen as objective, absolute, or universal are sometimes today even perceived as tools used by interest groups to exert power and authority over others. Lewis argued the reverse of this. Rather than qualities such as goodness, love, and similar values being power structures – tools of oppression – they are in reality common to humanity and definitive to what makes us human. They indeed limit, check, and subvert the self-interested and self-absorbed powers that seek to subjugate human beings.

Looking at his own time, Lewis believed that the Nazis with their "Thousand Year" Reich exerted their malign power because of their subjectivism – they were not self-regulated by objective principles such as justice and the view that racism and anti-Semitism are terribly wrong. Lewis believed that if we only see morality as a changeable sentiment, we have no grounds for saying the Nazis were wrong. No one ideology then can be better or worse than another. See also: ***The Abolition of Man***

Further reading

Jerry Root, *C.S. Lewis and a Problem of Evil: An Investigation of a Persuasive Theme* (2009).

Sunless Sea In *The Silver Chair**, the sea crossed by Eustace Scrubb*, Jill Pole*, and Puddleglum*, in order to reach Underland* in their quest* for the lost Prince Rilian*.

supernatural, supernaturalism See: **naturalism and supernaturalism**

Surprised by Joy: The Shape of My Early Life (**1955**) C.S. Lewis's autobiography, this records his life from early days, up to his conversion to Christianity at the age of thirty-three. "Joy"* is a technical term he used to help to define a distinct tone of feeling that he discovered in early childhood, and which stayed with him on and off throughout his adolescence and early manhood. This inconsolable longing contradicted the atheism and materialism* that his intellect embraced. In first theism and then Christianity, both his intellect and his imagination* were fulfilled. A key moment in his journey to faith was the discovery of George MacDonald's* *Phantastes*.*

Prior to that reconciliation, Lewis portrays the "two hemispheres" of his mind in turbulent conflict. One side was made up of a deep ocean of myth* and poetry; the other was occupied by the shallow waters of a superficial rationalism. What he considered to be real mostly lacked beauty and meaning*. Most of what he loved he was convinced was only a product of wistful imagination.

In writing, Lewis may have had in mind, as a genre model, William Wordsworth's powerful autobiographical poem, *The Prelude*.*

Susan, Queen See: **The Pevensie children**

Swanwhite A queen of such beauty in *The Last Battle*,* that if she looked into any pool, her reflected face shone out for a year and a day afterward just like a star in the night sky.

symbolism C.S. Lewis belongs to the tradition of romanticism*, but with important differences, one being that the imagination* is not the organ of truth. As with the Romantics, but not to the extent of J.R.R. Tolkien's* fantasy*, symbols play an integrating part in his fiction. His symbolism helps to make his work a lamp as well as a mirror; depicting reality, but also illuminating it. In this *A–Z*, a number of his characteristic symbols or symbolic themes are included, such as angels*, cosmic war*, joy*, the *Mappa Mundi**, recovery*, North* and South*, the numinous*, and the quest*.

The geography and history of Narnia* is also symbolic, enriching the stories scattered across Narnian history. Further enrichment is obtained from invented beings such as Puddleglum* the Marsh-wiggle*. There are also the powerful symbolic landscapes of Malacandra* and Perelandra*, inhabited with creatures such as the sorns*, pfifltriggi*, and eldila*.

The process of invention that Tolkien called sub-creation* allows the imagination to employ both subconscious and conscious resources of the mind. This is particularly so with regard to language, which is intimately connected to the whole self, and not just theoretical thought. Sub-creation allows powerful archetypes to become an effective part of an artwork. This helps to account for the universal appeal of deeply imaginative writing like Lewis's.

Archetypes are recurrent symbols, plot structures, and character types that make up much of the material of literature. In symbolic literature like Lewis's, the archetypes are focused and definite, but so-called realistic fiction is also replete with hidden archetypes. Lewis takes many archetypes from the Bible* (such as the End of the World in *The Last Battle**), which the influencial literary theorest Northrop Frye called "a grammar of literary archetypes", and Leland Ryken, a leading analyist of the influence of the Bible on literature, described as "the great repository of archetypes in Western literature". See also: **Narnia as a secondary world**

T

Talapal The name for Ungit* (or Aphrodite) in *Till We Have Faces**, used in the kingdom of Essur*.

***The Tale of Squirrel Nutkin*, Beatrix Potter (1903)** This tale belongs to the nursery tradition of talking animal* stories, a genre that inspired the child Lewis's Boxen*. *The Tale of Squirrel Nutkin* provided Lewis with his second recorded glimpse of joy* (the first being a flowering current bush), as recounted in his autobiography, *Surprised by Joy**.

talking animals (talking beasts) C.S. Lewis was constantly fascinated by the gap between humanity and the sub-humanity of beasts. The title of his tale of Narnia* *The Horse and His Boy** tells it all. The pronoun "his" bridges the gap between animal and human; the boy, Shasta* (Cor*), belongs as much to the talking Narnian horse, Bree*, as Bree belongs to Shasta. Lewis's fascination with this gap is evident, also, in his description of the warm inner life of the bear, Mr Bultitude*, in *That Hideous Strength**, and in his magnificent concept of Narnia as a land of talking beasts created by the great talking lion, Aslan*. Talking animals are normally found only in children's books, such as *The Wind in the Willows*, by Kenneth Grahame, a book much admired and quoted by C.S. Lewis. In his science-fiction tale *Out of the Silent Planet**, however, Lewis smuggles in talking animals that are palatable to its adult readers. Most notably this is the case with the hrossa*, who, though personal beings, also retain the qualities of animals.

Lewis regarded the invention of talking beasts as a feature of what J.R.R. Tolkien* called "sub-creation"*. Lewis once wrote: "We do not want merely to see beauty... we want something else which can hardly be put into words – to be united with the beauty we see, to pass into it, to receive it into ourselves, to bathe in it, to become part of it. That is why we have peopled air and earth and water with gods and goddesses and nymphs and elves." And, we could add, the talking beasts of Narnia and Malacandra*. See also: **nature**

The Tao Lewis's adopted name for The Way, which holds to values and virtues found universally and which are based on nature* as structured by a divine creator. Lewis's most eloquent defence of the objectivity of values and virtues is his essay *The Abolition of Man*, the themes of which are treated fictionally in *That Hideous Strength*. Lewis believed that a cosmic war* is raging between goodness and evil, and he memorably depicted the battle for the human soul in the allegorical* *Mappa Mundi*, found in his *The Pilgrim's Regress*. Lewis also sketches The Tao in his case for Christian belief, *Mere Christianity*.

Tarin A young officer of the king's guard in *Till We Have Faces*, at the royal palace in Glome*. After King Trom* discovers that he has been flirting with Redival*, his daughter, Tarin is castrated and sold as a slave in Ringal. This is one of Trom's many mistakes, as Tarin's father seeks revenge. Tarin becomes great in the south and east of Glome and later visits Queen Orual*. From him, Orual learns of her selfish neglect of Redival, a factor that helps in the queen's painful undeception*.

Tarkaan In Calormen*, a great lord, or noble. Its feminine form is "Tarkheena".

Tarva A splendid planet visible in Narnia's* night sky in *Prince Caspian*. Every 200 years it passes close to another bright planet, Alambil*. Glenstorm*, the centaur*, interprets this rare event as a sign to begin the revolt against Telmarine* rule, which has suppressed Old Narnia*.

Tash The demon god of Calormen*, who appears in terrifying form in *The Last Battle*. He has a head of a gigantic vulture, four arms, and twenty razor-sharp, long talons. A dreadful smoke surrounding him at times keeps its shape – his shape. The Calormene* nobility considers itself descended from Tash. In the last days, part of the deception of Calormene spin-doctors, led by Shift*, is to syncretize Tash and Aslan* into a mixture they called "Tashlan"*.

Tashbaan The capital of Calormen* in *The Horse and His Boy*, named after the country's deity, Tash*. The city is one of the wonders of the world. It is situated on a river island, with a many-arched bridge leading to it from the southern riverbank. The city is gated, with high walls. Within them, buildings are crowded together and climb to the top of a hill. At its summit is displayed the magnificent House of the Tisroc* and the great temple of Tash, with its silver-plated dome. From the city hill, it is possible for visitors to see the masts of ships at anchor at the river's mouth. To the south of Tashbaan a range of low wooded hills is visible. See also: **Calormen**

Tashlan A merging of Tash* and Aslan* in *The Last Battle*, to deny the latter's uniqueness as creator of Narnia* and the other lands. This "new theology" is spearheaded by Shift* the talking ape (a satire by C.S. Lewis on modernist theology of his time).

Tehishbaan A Calormene* town in *The Last Battle*, lying west of the Great Desert*. Emeth* comes from here.

Telmar, Land of This lies to the far west of Narnia*. Pirates who accidentally stumble into the region from our world populate it. See also: **Telmarines**

Telmarines Descendants of pirates who accidently stumble into the land of Telmar* after entering a magical cave in a South Sea island. They become a proud and fierce nation. After a famine, the Telmarines, led by King Caspian* I, cross the Western Mountains and conquer the peaceful land of Narnia*, long after the reign of High King Peter and the other Pevensie children*. They silence the talking animals* and trees, drive away dwarves* and fauns*, and even try to cover up the memory of such things. Prince Caspian learns of the "Old Narnia"*, as it is then called, in secret, from his nurse* and then his tutor, Doctor Cornelius*, as told in *Prince Caspian**. See also: **Narnia: history**

Tempters' Training College The college in *The Screwtape Letters**, and its brief sequel, *Screwtape Proposes a Toast**, where junior devils* learn their skills in damning human beings or in attempting to reclaim those who have gone over to the Enemy. After graduation, novices appear to have practical experience under the guidance of an experienced devil. Wormwood* is a recent graduate, advised by letter by his eminent uncle, Screwtape*. Every year, the Tempters' Training College holds a dinner. One year, Screwtape is the guest of honour, and his speech is recorded in *Screwtape Proposes a Toast**. The college's principal is Dr Slubgob*.

Tegnér's Drapa A poem by Esaias Tegnér, translated in verse from the Swedish by Henry Wadsworth Longfellow, which provided the young Lewis's third recalled glimpse of joy* when it spoke of the death of Balder*.

The Temple: Sacred Poems and Private Ejaculations, George Herbert (1633) A collection of 160 poems first published shortly after the death of George Herbert (1593–1633). He is an outstanding poet from an age of great writers, a fame he never knew. It was when he realized he was dying of tuberculosis that he sent the collection of poems in manuscript to his friend Nicholas Ferrar to judge whether to burn them or to publish them. Isaak Walton's biography of him appeared in 1670. He ministered in the Church* of England, obtaining the living of Bemerton in Wiltshire in 1630. Lewis listed *The Temple* as one of the ten books that most influenced his thinking and vocational attitude (see: **reading of C.S. Lewis**). Herbert's notable poems include "The Church Porch", a doctrinal poem, and "The Altar" and "Easter Wings", pattern poems where the lines form the shape of the subject. Other poets considered "metaphysical" include John Donne, Henry Vaughan, and Andrew Marvell. Lewis felt that George Herbert was superior to any other author he had read in capturing life in its very essence as we experience it in real time.

Terebinthia An island in *The Voyage of the "Dawn Treader"**, visited by the ship before Eustace Scrubb*, Edmund*, and Lucy* joined the voyage. It lies off the coast of Narnia*, beyond Galma*. The island, a haunt of pirates, has been plagued by a terrible illness, and its main town is in quarantine. In *The Silver Chair**, King Caspian* seeks Aslan* there. A terebinth is a type of tree found in Europe and the Middle East.

***That Hideous Strength* (1945; abridged paperback version 1955)** The final volume of the science-fiction trilogy, begun in *Out of the Silent Planet** and *Perelandra** (*Voyage to Venus*). It continues C.S. Lewis's presentation of the problem of good and evil. In this "modern fairy tale for grown-ups", Dr Elwin Ransom* stays on Earth. The setting is the small Midlands university town of Edgestow*, just after the Second World War. The "progressive element" among the fellows of Bracton College* engineer the sale of a piece of property called Bragdon Wood* to the N.I.C.E.*, the National Institute for Co-ordinated Experiments. According to Arthurian legend, the magician Merlin* lay secretly in a trance within the wood, his "sleeping" body preserved from aging.

The N.I.C.E. is a sinister, totalitarian organization of technocrats: scientists given over to the pragmatic use of technology for social and individual control. Deeply involved in the Institute is Dick Devine*, now Lord Feverstone, first encountered by Ransom before the war as his kidnapper, along with Professor Weston*, stealing him off to Mars.

Mark Studdock*, a fellow in sociology at Bracton, is duped into working for the N.I.C.E., whereas his wife, Jane*, a research student, finds herself helping the other side, led by Ransom, now revealed as the great Pendragon of Logres. Her gift of second sight helps to locate Merlin* and to provide vital intelligence. Merlin's ancient magic, linked into the power of the eldila* of Deep Heaven, overcomes the evil of the N.I.C.E. In a satirical climax, Merlin revives the curse of Babel, confused speech, as a fitting judgment on people who have despised ordinary humanity.

This book, as a sequel to the previous stories, set on other planets, brings matters "down to earth", under the influence of Lewis's friend, Charles Williams*. It is set on Thulcandra*, the silent planet Earth, so called because it is cut off by evil from the beatific language and worlds of Deep Heaven. In another sense, matters are brought "down to earth" because Lewis takes pains in characterizing the marriage and personalities of Mark and Jane Studdock*. In the style of Charles Williams, the supernatural* world impinges upon the everyday world of ordinary people. There are other Williams-like touches also. Jane, like Damaris Tighe in Williams's *The Place of the Lion,* is engaged upon literary research. More notably, C.S. Lewis makes use of the mythical geography of Logres, the spiritual and true England, which draws on the Arthurian matter that is the focus of Williams's unfinished cycle of poems.

As Lewis makes clear in his preface, his story illustrates the point that he made in one of his most forceful studies of ethics, *The Abolition of Man** (1943). This is that a world that rejects objective principles of right and wrong, beauty and ugliness, also rejects what constitutes mankind's very nature, and creates an unhumanity. The new society projected by the N.I.C.E. is the corruption of the Un-man* of Perelandra writ large.

As a study of evil, *That Hideous Strength* shows how wickedness sows the seeds of its own destruction. Professor Weston's forays into space with evil intent had allowed the ending of an ancient prohibition. This was that no inhabitants of Deep Heaven would ever come to the quarantined planet Earth until the very end of things. Now that bent mankind had tried to contaminate unfallen worlds such as Mars and Venus, however, the eldila of Deep Heaven could unleash their good powers through a suitable human agent – Merlin*.

The novel has been criticized for being overly complex in structure. It has, for example, an uneasy mixture of satire and serious study of damnation, a mixture that worked in *The Screwtape Letters**. Nevertheless, it is one of Lewis's fictions that makes the most impact upon its reader, revealing a power to portray ordinary human beings in a "realistic" setting. It is plausible as an anti-utopian parable of our times, like Aldous Huxley's *Brave New World* (1932) and George Orwell's *Nineteen Eighty-Four* (1949). Furthermore, it was a necessary preparation for probably his best novel, *Till We Have Faces**.

Theism and Humanism, Arthur James Balfour (1915) This is one of ten books that Lewis claimed particularly shaped his thinking and vocational attitude (see: **reading of C.S. Lewis**).

Balfour* was an intellectually brilliant British prime minister who authored several works of philosophy. This book was based upon the prestigious Gifford Lectures, given at Glasgow University in 1913–1914. Balfour fervently believed, and argued in this book, that God*, personal and infinite, was the origin of what was "most assured in knowledge, all that is, or seems, most beautiful in art or nature, and all this is, or seems, most noble in morality". God must be central in a system of belief. Like the French philosopher Descartes, he saw God as the guarantor of knowledge. Indeed, wrote Balfour, he is

> the condition of scientific knowledge. If He be excluded
> from the causal series which produces beliefs, the
> cognitive series which justifies them is corrupted at
> the root. And it is only in a theistic setting that beauty
> can retain its deepest meaning, and love its brightest
> lustre, so these great truths of aesthetics and ethics
> are but half-truths, isolated and imperfect, unless we
> add to them yet a third. We must hold that reason and
> the works of reason have their source in God; that
> from Him they draw their inspiration; and that if they
> repudiate their origin, by this very act they proclaim
> their own insufficiency.

Such ideas anticipate Lewis's arguments in the early chapters of *Miracles*, particularly chapter 3.

An earlier Balfour work, *Defence of Philosophic Doubt* (1879), was read appreciatively by Andrew Seth (later known as Professor Pringle Pattison), who invited the young Balfour to address his philosophy class at Edinburgh University. The second half of the Gifford Lectures, delayed by the onset of war, was published as *Theism and Thought* in 1923. A lecture given in Oxford* in 1909, "Beauty: and the Criticism of Beauty", contains insights that anticipate Lewis's thinking on aesthetics, in for instance

An Experiment in Criticism*. Balfour asks: "Why should we be impatient because we can give no account of the characteristics common to all that is beautiful, when we can give no account of the characteristics common to all that is lovable?" He concludes: "Let us, then, be content, since we can do no better, that our admirations should be even as our loves" (*Essays Speculative and Political* (1921)). Like Lewis also, he distrusts the aesthete's distinction between high and low art.

Balfour had the astonishing ability to lecture, whether on philosophy or a political issue, virtually without notes. He would simply jot down several bare headings on the back of a long envelope. Such a method could sustain him for an hour of closely argued discourse. See also: **idealism, C.S. Lewis and**

theology, C.S. Lewis and C.S. Lewis, by profession, was a literary critic* who also had philosophical interests. Anything that he wrote on theology, such as *Miracles**, *The Problem of Pain**, *Reflections on the Psalms**, or *Mere Christianity**, he regarded as the offerings of a lay person. Some of his opinions he presented explicitly as speculation. He tried to set forward an orthodox theology, what he called "mere Christianity"*. A few of the views he held (such as on the inspiration of Scripture), evangelicals could not be entirely happy with. However, many of the views he held could be searingly painful to a liberal theologian – such as his supernaturalism*, his literal belief in heaven*, hell, and the devil*, and his unflinching emphasis on the demands of truth (he had no concept of a merely religious truth, separate from reason and historical fact). His many years as an atheist gave him a deep sympathy for the unbeliever's position.

An important contribution that Lewis made to theology was on the nature of language, and how language pictures reality, including the deep reality of the world that we do not normally see. His work on the relationship between meaning* and theoretical truth-claims reveals how it was possible for him to hold that the Bible* has the character of a revelation from God* that involves statements of knowledge. If Lewis is correct in his view of meaning and truth, this biblical revelation, that is, claims knowledge of facts, and of the very nature of the real world. This is even though most of the Bible is made up of historical narrative, with other sections of poetry, allegory*, parable, and apocalyptic, and only a relatively small proportion of didactic material. It follows from Lewis's view that biblical history provides the meaning of the terms of the biblical statements about the nature of God, sin, salvation, the atonement, and the like. Biblical history, epitomized in the Gospels, combined the qualities of a good story with being factual (see: **myth became fact**). This kind of approach has brought more joy to evangelicals, Roman Catholics, and other orthodox groups than to the theologically liberal.

C.S. Lewis's great dislike of liberal theology is expressed in an essay admired by his close friend at Oxford*, the outstanding theologian Austin Farrer*. The essay is "Fern-Seeds and Elephants" (also called "Modern Theology and Biblical Criticism"), first published in *Christian Reflections**. His orthodoxy was a traditional Anglican kind, and like Dorothy L. Sayers* and G.K. Chesterton*, he delighted in dogma. See also: **theology of romance**

theology of romance Like J.R.R. Tolkien* and Charles Williams*, C.S. Lewis composed his fiction according to a theology of romanticism* which owed much to the nineteenth-century writer who was Lewis's mentor, George MacDonald*. The term "romantic theologian", Lewis tells us, was invented by Charles Williams. What Lewis says about Williams in his introduction to *Essays Presented to Charles Williams** applies also to himself.

"A romantic theologian," C.S. Lewis says, "does not mean one who is romantic about theology but one who is theological about romance, one who considers the theological implications of those experiences which are called romantic. The belief that the most serious and ecstatic experiences either of human love or of imaginative literature have such theological implications and that they can be healthy and fruitful only if the implications are diligently thought out and severely lived, is the root principle of all his [Williams's] work."

"The imaginative man in me is older, more continuously operative, and in that sense more basic than either the religious writer or the critic," Lewis confessed in a letter written in 1954. His imagination* had made him try to be a poet and, after his conversion, "to embody my religious belief in symbolical or mythopoeic forms". These included *The Screwtape Letters** and the science-fiction trilogy*, written for adults, and *The Chronicles of Narnia**, which he wrote for children – not to give them what they wanted, "but because the fairy-tale was the genre best fitted for what I wanted to say".

Whereas a key preoccupation of Charles Williams was romantic love, C.S. Lewis was "theological" about romantic longing or joy*, and Tolkien reflected deeply on the theological implications of fairy tale and myth*, particularly the aspect of sub-creation*.

R.J. Reilly, who has written on C.S. Lewis as part of a new literary movement, saw him as an advocate of "romantic religion". This was the "attempt to reach religious truths by means and techniques traditionally called romantic" C.S. Lewis, however, was not doing anything new in this. Rather, he was presenting in modern terms what seemed to be a normal attitude of mind a few centuries before. It was perhaps beginning to be lost even in the seventeenth century, when John Bunyan was forced to defend what now could be called "romantic religion" in his author's apology at the beginning of *The Pilgrim's Progress*. Bunyan's reasoning in that prologue follows along lines somewhat similar to Lewis's defence of the imagination.

In *Surprised by Joy**, C.S. Lewis reported some of his "romantic" sensations – responses to natural beauty, and literary and artistic responses – in the hope that others would recognize similar experiences of their own.

Several structural features of fairy tales and other stories that embodied myths fascinated J.R.R. Tolkien. These features are all related to a sense of imaginative decorum, a sense that imagining can, in itself, be good or bad, as rules or norms apply strictly in fantasy*, as they do in thought. Meaning* can only be created by skill or art, and play an essential part in human thought and language. As Tolkien said, "The incarnate mind, the tongue, and the tale are in our world coeval." As Owen Barfield* has shown in his introduction to the second edition of *Poetic Diction**, the ideal in logical positivism and related types of modern linguistic philosophy is, strictly, absurd; it systematically eliminates meanings from the framing of truths, expecting thereby to guarantee their validity. In Tolkien's view, the opposite is the case. The richer the meanings involved in the framing of truths, the more guarantee is there of their validity.

G.K. Chesterton once wrote that we should sometimes take our tea in the top of a tree, as our perceptions tend to get dulled. One of the essential features of the fairy tale or mythopoeic fantasy is the sense of recovery* – the regaining of health or a clear view of things. Tolkien pointed out that we too often get caught in the specific corridor of daily, mundane life, and lose a view of "things as we are (or were) meant to see them". Entry into an imaginary world "shocks us more fully awake than we are for most of our lives". C.S. Lewis said the latter of myth, but it applies to this feature of recovery. Part of this recovery is a sense of imaginative unity, a survey of the depths of space and time. The essential patterns of reality are seen in a fresh way.

Lewis suggests that imaginative literature creates a symbolic* perception of reality. A story is like a pair of spectacles that we look through. He gave a very simple illustration of this kind of perception in his essay "On Stories", in explaining the logic of the fairy story, which "is as strict as that of a realistic novel, though different". Referring to *The Wind in the Willows*, he asked:

> Does anyone believe that Kenneth Grahame made an arbitrary choice when he gave his principal character the form of a toad, or that a stag, a pigeon, a lion, would have done as well? The choice is based on the fact that the real toad's face has a grotesque resemblance to a certain kind of human face – a rather apoplectic face with a fatuous grin on it... Looking at the creature we thus see, isolated and fixed, an aspect of human vanity in its funniest and most pardonable form.

The Encyclopedia of Fantasy points out the subversive nature of fantasy in encouraging a shift in our perception of things: "It could be argued that, if fantasy (and debatably the literature of the fantastic as a whole) has a purpose other than to entertain, it is to show readers *how to perceive*; an extension of the argument is that fantasy may try to alter readers' perception of reality." This point is explained more, as follows: "The best fantasy introduces its readers into a playground of rethought perception, where there are no restrictions other than those of the human imagination... Most full-fantasy texts have at their core the urge to *change* the reader; that is, full fantasy is by definition a subversive literary form."

Lewis is a key twentieth-century example of a writer of Christian fantasy, along with J.R.R. Tolkien and Charles Williams. These writers stand in a rich tradition, dating back to early stories of King Arthur. Such writers give a high place to the imagination as an organ of meaning*.

In the light of a theological perspective on romance like Lewis's, the definition of fantasy in *The Encyclopedia of Fantasy* is helpful: "A fantasy text is a self-coherent narrative. When set in this world, it tells a story which is impossible in the world as we perceive it; when set in an other world, that other world will be impossible, though stories set there may be possible in its terms." This self-coherence requires belief in some kind of overarching story. Thus the fantasy text might well differ in its use of the fantastic from modernism and postmodernism, both of which, according to the *Encyclopedia*, question the very nature of story in their different ways.

The imagination for C.S. Lewis is concerned with apprehending realities (even if they belong to the unseen world), rather than with grasping concepts. Imaginative invention is justifiable in its own right – it does not have the burden of carrying didactic truths.

This is why good works of imagination cannot be reduced to "morals" and lessons, although lessons can be derived from them, and the truer the work the greater the lessons that can be drawn from it. In a review of Tolkien's *The Lord of the Rings*, Lewis noted that "What shows that we are reading myth, not allegory, is that there are no pointers to a specifically theological, or political, or psychological application. A myth points, for each reader, to the realm he lives in most. It is a master key; use it on what door you like." He continued, "The value of the myth is that it takes all the things we know and restores to them the rich significance which has been hidden by 'the veil of familiarity'." Perhaps remembering his childhood, Lewis gives as an example a boy enjoying some otherwise unattractive cold meat by supposing he has killed a buffalo with his bow and arrow, and that the meat is from that buffalo. The uninviting meat becomes savoury by being "dipped in a story".

Similarly, he wrote elsewhere (in the essay "Sometimes Fairy Stories May Say Best What Needs to Be Said") that although this sort of writing works with some readers but not with others, when it works fantasy can "generalize while remaining concrete" and "at its best it can do more: it can give us experiences we have never had and thus, instead of 'commenting on life', can add to it". This had a special importance for Lewis as a Christian communicator, because fantasy can "steal past" the religious associations and demands that destroy one's ability to feel the truth of the Christian revelation as one should. He argued that by "casting all these things into an imaginary world, stripping them of their stained-glass and Sunday school associations, one could make them for the first time appear in their potency". The writer could, then, "steal past those watchful dragons".

Out of this belief about the nature* and necessity of the imagination, the features of Lewis's theology of romance emerge: a sense of otherness*, a recognition of the numinous*, a longing for joy*, the understanding of art as sub-creation*, and a yearning for recovery* and healing. Central to Lewis's theology of romance are several theological themes including: God*, cosmic war*, myth became fact*, transposition*, and undeception and recognition*.

***They Asked for a Paper* (1962)** A collection of literary and theological pieces, including several reprinted from *Transposition and Other Addresses**. It contains "*De Descriptione Temporum*"*, "The Literary Impact of the Authorized Version", "Hamlet: The Prince or the Poem?", "Kipling's World", "Sir Walter Scott", "Lilies that Fester", "Psycho-analysis and Literary Criticism", "The Inner Ring"*, "Is Theology Poetry?", "Transposition" (see: **transposition**), "On Obstinacy in Belief", and "The Weight of Glory".

***They Stand Together: The Letters of C.S. Lewis to Arthur Greeves (1914–1963)* (1979)** Walter Hooper* had the opportunity to assist C.S. Lewis with his correspondence near the end of his life, and spent ten years editing Lewis's letters* before *They Stand Together* appeared in 1979. In an interview shortly after publication, Walter Hooper told the author that this correspondence would easily run into many volumes. From this vast output, he decided to select letters to one man, Arthur Greeves*, a close friend of Lewis's over a period of almost fifty years; that is, from his atheistic mid-teens to literally days before Lewis died. These letters give rich insight to Lewis's life and to the development of his Christian thought and imagination*.

As Walter Hooper pointed out to the author, this selection makes up a more complete autobiography than *Surprised by Joy**, where he tells his life from a particular point of view – his awareness of joy*, the longing that no earthly philosophy or bodily pleasure could satisfy, and how only Christian theism made sense of it. Also, that story finishes at C.S. Lewis's conversion in his early thirties. Walter Hooper's collection contains 296 letters.

A factor that fascinated Walter Hooper in compiling the letters was the sheer detective work involved. He told the author, "I like detective work very much. I like details and I like mysteries. I knew that I was up against something extremely difficult in dating these letters. But they do not make sense, perfect sense, unless they are in the right order." At the end of his life, Arthur Greeves had tried to put the correct dates on the letters from Lewis, but was often confused. "Greeves notices, say, that Lewis had taken a holiday in Cornwall, so that he assumes that a letter also from Cornwall was written at the same time. There are really two visits, and the letters are years apart. When you put them together you have to stretch the sense in them. Once you put them in their right place the sense comes through – you get so much more out of them."

The biggest mystery was why there were originally so few letters toward the end of the correspondence. It was solved by accident. Walter Hooper says that in 1974, "I wrote on other business to the head-master of Campbell College, Belfast, about one of Lewis's friends. He wrote back and told me that Greeves' cousin, Lisbeth Greeves, had put in her keeping by Arthur a number of letters that dealt with his brother's alcoholism." As Major W.H. Lewis* was dead, and his alcoholism was now well known, Walter Hooper felt that these letters, with their first-hand accounts, should be included. His brother's alcoholism "was a very great problem for C.S. Lewis", and one of the many that he shared with Arthur Greeves in the letters. This is why, in one place, C.S. Lewis speaks of him as "my father confessor". One letter vividly recounts his conversion to Christianity. We also learn much about the Ulsterman Arthur Greeves from these letters, though Lewis kept few of Arthur's side of the correspondence. The foundation of their friendship*, it is clear, was a common way of seeing the world. See also: **letters of C.S. Lewis**

three sleepers Three of the missing Seven Lords in *The Voyage of the "Dawn Treader"**, sought by Caspian*: Argoz*, Revilian*, and Mavramorn*. The voyagers find them sleeping an enchanted sleep at Aslan's Table* on World's End Island*.

Thulcandra The name for planet Earth in the language of Old Solar* in *Out of the Silent Planet** and the others of C.S. Lewis's science-fiction trilogy. It means "silent planet". See also: **The planets**

Till We Have Faces: A Myth Retold **(1956)** At different times, C.S. Lewis regarded either *Till We Have Faces* or *Perelandra** as his best fictional book. In the former he retells an old classical myth, that of Cupid and Psyche*, in the realistic setting of a historical novel. It is set several hundred years BC in the imaginary and barbaric country of Glome* somewhere to the north of the Greeklands. The story is told through the eyes of Queen Orual* of Glome. Having heard a legend in the nearby land of Essur* similar to the myth of Cupid and Psyche, she seeks to set the record straight. The gods, she claims, have distorted the story in certain key respects. She recognizes herself and her half-sister Psyche in the newly sprung-up legend.

The gods, Orual said, had called her deep love for Psyche jealousy. They had also said that she saw Psyche's Palace*, whereas Orual had only seen shapes in a mist, a fantasy that momentarily resembled a palace. There had been no evidence that Psyche had married a god and dwelled in his palace. Orual therefore recounts her version of the story, being as truthful as possible. She had a reader in mind from the Grecklands, and agreed with the Greek demand for truth and rational honesty. She has to tell her lifestory to do this properly.

Orual is a princess, the daughter of a barbarian and callous king, Trom*, and has a sister, Redival*. Orual's mother dies young; Trom marries again and the stepmother dies giving birth to the beautiful Psyche. Psyche's outstanding beauty contrasts with Orual's ugliness (in later life she wore a veil). The king engages a Greek slave, named The Fox*, to teach his daughters. The Fox is able to pass on his Greek Stoicism and rationalism to Psyche and Orual, though the daughters never reject the paganism* of their land.

In Glome the goddess Ungit*, a deformed version of Venus, is worshipped. After a drought and other disasters, a lot is drawn that falls on the innocent Psyche to be sacrified on the Grey Mountains to the Shadowbrute or Westwind*, the god of the mountain.

Sometime afterward, Orual, accompanied by a faithful member of the king's guard, Bardia*, seeks the bones of Psyche to bury her. Finding no trace of Psyche, Bardia and Orual explore further and find the beautiful and sheltered valley of the god*. Here Psyche is living, wearing rags but full of health. She claims to be married to the god of the mountain, whose face she has never seen. Orual, afraid that the "god" is a monster or outlaw, persuades Psyche, against her will, to shine a light on her husband's face, while sleeping. As in the Greek myth, Psyche as a result is condemned to wander the earth, doing impossible tasks. During a terrible storm, which follows and disfigures the valley, Orual seems to see a beautiful god who tells her, "You also shall be Psyche."

Orual's account goes on to record the bitter years of her suffering and grief at the loss of Psyche, haunted by the fantasy that she can hear Psyche's weeping. Succeeding King Trom, she reforms the kingdom, and does her best to rule justly, applying civilized principles learned via The Fox from the Greeks. She becomes a great queen and a renowned warrior. Late in life she decides to travel the wider world and it is then she hears what she believes to be the warped story of Orual, Psyche, and the god, causing her to write her account. Most of *Till We Have Faces* is made up of this narration.

The short second part of the novel – still in Orual's voice – continues a few days later. Orual has undergone a devastating undeception*, whereby, in painful self-knowledge, she discovers how her affection for Psyche had become poisoned by possessiveness. Her clinging and impossible love for Bardia had also blighted his life. In this discovery, which allowed the restoration of a true love for Psyche, was the consolation that she had also been Psyche, as the god had said. She had suffered on Psyche's behalf, in a substitutionary manner, bearing her burdens and thus easing her tasks. By what Charles Williams* called "the Way of Exchange", Orual had thus helped Psyche to be reunited with her divine husband. With the curing of her poisoned love, Orual in a vision sees that she has become beautiful. She has gained a face in becoming a full person. After this reconciliation, the aged Queen Orual dies, her narration ending with her.

This novel is unlike Lewis's other fiction and is consequently less easy to interpret. It in fact repays several readings. One key to *Till We Have Faces* is the theme of love. It is helpful to see Lewis's study *The Four Loves** as parallel to it, in the way that *The*

Abolition of Man* is parallel to *That Hideous Strength**. The loves of affection and eros* are particularly explored. Another key is that of substitution and atonement. Psyche is prepared to die for the sake of the people of Glome. Orual is a substitute for much of Psyche's suffering and pain.

Psyche herself represents a Christlikeness, though she is not intended as a figure of Christ. Lewis wrote in explanation to Clyde S. Kilby: "Psyche is an instance of the *anima naturaliter Christiana* making the best of the pagan religion she is brought up in and thus being guided (but always 'under the cloud,' always in terms of her own imagination or that of her people) toward the true God. She is in some ways like Christ not because she is a symbol of Him but because every good man or woman is like Christ."

This limitation of the imagination of paganism* comes out in the ugly figures of Ungit and the Shadowbrute*, deformed images of the brighter Greek deities of Venus (Aphrodite) and Cupid. The truth that these poor images are trying to glimpse is even more beautiful, free of the vindictiveness of the Greek deities. Psyche is able to see a glimpse of the true God* himself, in all his beauty, and in his legitimate demand for a perfect sacrifice.

A further key to this novel lies in the theme of the conflict of imagination* and reason, so important to Lewis himself throughout his life, and vividly portrayed in *Surprised by Joy**. The final identification of the half-sisters Orual and Psyche in the story represents the harmony and satisfaction of both reason and imagination made fully possible, Lewis believed, only within Christianity. See also: **The Four Loves**

Time, Father In *The Silver Chair** a giant* sleeping man with a noble face and a flowing beard is discovered by Eustace Scrubb*, Jill Pole* and Puddleglum*. They are told that he is old Father Time, once a king in Overland. He has sunk into the Deep Realm* and there dreams of the happenings in the upper world. He will not wake until the end of the world. Father Time appears again in *The Last Battle**, having been awakened by Aslan's* roar and given a new name. He helps to bring on the end of the existing world of Narnia* by blowing a last trump on his horn after which the stars* fall from the sky.

Tirian, King The final king of Narnia* in *The Last Battle**, who, along with his dear friend, Jewel* the Unicorn, makes a heroic last stand against the Calormene* and other forces of darkness. Eustace Scrubb* and Jill Pole* come to help him in answer to his prayer to Aslan*. See also: **Narnia: history**

The Tisroc The Calormene* sovereign in *The Horse and His Boy** and *The Last Battle**.

Toadpipe Secretary to Screwtape* in *The Screwtape Letters**.

Tolkien, J.R.R. (1892–1973) John Ronald Reuel Tolkien was one of C.S. Lewis's closest friends, and like him valued friendship* highly. Until the beginning of the 1960s, Professor Tolkien was known mainly to a few learned scholars, a small but enthusiastic readership of the hardback three volumes of *The Lord of the Rings*, and a substantial child readership of *The Hobbit*. Now, in the post-Hobbit era, he has been read by a colossal number of people around the world. BBC* radio successfully dramatized *The Lord of the Rings* over thirteen hours in the 1980s, and the beginning of the new millennium saw the appearance of Peter Jackson's films of *The Lord of the Rings*. Since his death in 1973, *The Silmarillion* has been published, followed by many volumes of material from ages of Middle-earth long before the period of the adventures of the Bagginses.

Tolkien was born in South Africa in 1892, but his family soon moved to England. He attended King Edward's School, in the heart of Birmingham, and was familiar with Worcestershire and the Vale of Evesham. It is said that the Malvern Hills helped to inspire the mountains of Gondor in Middle-earth. After graduating from Exeter College, Oxford* University, he saw bitter action in the First World War, losing all but one of his best friends.

It was during the First World War that Tolkien began working on *The Silmarillion*, writing "The Fall of Gondolin" in 1917 while convalescent. In fact, in general plot, and in several major episodes, most of the legendary cycle of *The Silmarillion* was already constructed before 1930 – before the writing and publication of *The Hobbit*, the forerunner of *The Lord of the Rings*. In the latter books there are numerous references to matters covered by *The Silmarillion*; ruins of once-great places, sites of battles long ago, strange and beautiful names from the deep past, and Elvish swords made in Gondolin, before its fall, for the Goblin Wars.

Tolkien's lifelong study and teaching of languages was the spring and nourishment of his imaginative* creations. Just as science-fiction writers generally make use of plausible technological inventions and possibilities, Tolkien used his deep and expert knowledge of language in his fantasies. He created in his youth two forms of the Elvish tongue, starting a process that led to a history and geography to surround these languages, and peoples to speak them (and other tongues). He explains: "I had to posit a basic and phonetic structure of Primitive Elvish, and then modify this by series of changes (such as actually do occur in known languages) so that the two end results would have a consistent structure and character, but be quite different."

The imaginative possibilities of an invented language were also explored by C.S. Lewis, under his influence. Lewis acknowledges a great debt, especially to his idea of sub-creation (see: **Narnia as a secondary world**). Lewis makes use of the possibilities of his own imagined language, Old Solar*, in *Out of the Silent Planet**, and its sequels. The debt was mutual: it is unlikely that Tolkien would have completed *The Lord of the Rings* for publication without Lewis's fervent encouragement.

After the First World War, Tolkien began university teaching. After a few years at Leeds University, he moved to Oxford to become Rawlinson and Bosworth Professor of Anglo-Saxon; this was in 1925. In the next year he met C.S. Lewis. Their long friendship was soon to begin (see: **friendship of J.R.R. Tolkien and C.S. Lewis**). Lewis had then been an English don at Magdalen College for one year. They met at the English Faculty Meeting on 11 May 1926.

They began meeting in each other's rooms and talking far into the night. These conversations proved crucial both for the two men's writings, and for Lewis's conversion to Christianity. The friendship exorcized two prejudices that had been deeply inculcated in Lewis. One, he said, was not to put trust in a Roman Catholic. The other was to distrust a philologist. Tolkien was both.

A typical note of the time occurs in a letter from C.S. Lewis to his Ulster friend Arthur Greeves* in December 1929: "Tolkien... came back with me to college... and sat discoursing of the gods and giants and Asgard for three hours."

Tolkien himself recalled sharing with Lewis his work on *The Silmarillion*, influencing the latter's science-fiction trilogy*. The pattern of their future lives, including the later Inklings*, was being formed. Tolkien remembered: "In the early days of our association Jack used to come to my house and I read aloud to him The Silmarillion so far as it had then gone, including a very long poem: Beren and Lúthien."

The gist of one of the long conversations between Lewis and Tolkien was fortunately recorded by Lewis in another letter to Arthur Greeves in October 1931. It was a crucial factor in his conversion, as he moved from mere theism to Christianity. Tolkien argued that human stories tend to fall into certain patterns, and can embody myth. In the Christian Gospels, he believed, there are all the best elements of good stories, including fairy stories, with the astounding additional factor that everything is also true in the actual, primary world. For him, it combines mythic and historical, factual truth, with no divorce between the two. C.S. Lewis's conversion deepened the friendship (See: **myth became fact**.)

Tolkien's academic writings were sparing and rare. In 1936 he gave a lecture to the British Academy entitled "Beowulf: The Monsters and the Critics", which, according to literary scholar Donald K. Fry, "completely altered the course of Beowulf studies". It was a defence of the artistic unity of that Old English tale. In 1939 he gave the Andrew Lang Lecture at St Andrews University, "On Fairy Stories", which was later published in *Essays Presented to Charles Williams** – the Inklings' tribute to the writer who had a great deal in common with Tolkien and Lewis. It sets out Tolkien's basic ideas concerning imagination*, fantasy*, and sub-creation.

The professor's famous *The Hobbit*, which started as stories told to his young children, came out in 1937. He continued with its adult sequel, *The Lord of the Rings*, more and more leaving aside his first love, *The Silmarillion*. It was a long, painstaking task, partly undertaken in the converted garage of his Oxford home. At one point, he did not touch the manuscript for a whole year. He wrote it in the evenings, for he was fully engaged in his university work. During the Second World War, and afterwards, he read portions to the Inklings, or simply to Lewis alone. He attended almost all the Inklings meetings during that period, even though he was busy. In 1945 Tolkien was honoured by a new Chair at Oxford, Merton Professor of English Language and Literature, reflecting his by now wider interests. Tolkien retained the Chair until his retirement in 1959.

With C.S. Lewis's marriage to Joy Davidman*, and other cooling factors, the relationship between the two friends was not sustained so deeply, and Tolkien grieved over the estrangement.

The scholarly storyteller's retirement years were spent revising *The Lord of the Rings*, brushing up and publishing some shorter pieces of story and poetry, and working on various drafts of *The Silmarillion*. Tolkien also spent much time dodging reporters and youthful Americans, as the 1960s marked the exploding popularity of his fantasies, when his readership went from thousands to many millions. An interviewer at the time, Daphne Castell, tried to capture his personal manner: "He talks very quickly, striding up and down the converted garage which serves as his study, waving his pipe, making little jabs with it to mark important points; and now and then jamming it back in, and talking round it… He has the habits of speech of the true story-teller… Every sentence is important, and lively, and striking…"

Further reading
Humphrey Carpenter, *J.R.R. Tolkien: A Biography* (1977); Humphrey Carpenter, *The Inklings: C.S. Lewis, J.R.R. Tolkien, Charles Williams and Their Friends* (1978); Humphrey Carpenter (ed.), *The Letters of J.R.R. Tolkien* (1981); Daphne Castell, "The Realms of Tolkien", *New Worlds SF*, Vol. 50, No. 168, 1966; Colin Duriez, *J.R.R. Tolkien and C.S. Lewis: The Story of Their Friendship* (in USA, *Tolkien and C.S. Lewis: The Gift of Friendship*) (2003); Colin Duriez, *J.R.R. Tolkien: The Making of a Legend* (2012).

tombs of the ancient kings Tombs north of the great city of Tashbaan*, capital of Calormen*, in *The Horse and His Boy*. They are reputed to be haunted, and look like giant beehives. Shasta* (Cor*) spends the night there. He has agreed to rendezvous at the tombs with Aravis*, and the two Narnian* talking horses, Bree* and Hwin*.

transposition This is C.S. Lewis's name for a concept he explained in one of the most important addresses he gave, published in *Transposition and Other Addresses*. The talk was preached originally as a sermon on Whit Sunday in Mansfield College, Oxford* University, 28 May 1944.

C.S. Lewis's theory of transposition has affinities with the ideas of another Oxford thinker, Michael Polanyi (1891–1976). Transposition, says Lewis, is an "adaptation of a richer to a poorer medium". No denigration of the poorer medium is implied, only an assessment of its necessary limits. In a Christian universe, as understood by C.S. Lewis, all parts have value in themselves.

To explain the idea of transposition, C.S. Lewis begins his address considering the phenomenon of speaking in tongues at Pentecost, recorded in the New Testament. Looking from below, in a purely naturalist way, one would say that the phenomenon was "merely" or "nothing but" an affair of the nerves and sensations, resulting in gibberish. Seen from above, however, he said, both the fact and the meaning* are clear – this event is a supernatural* act of the Holy Spirit. The spiritual is transposed into physical language.

In a similar way, in our emotional life, we can reduce emotion to mere sensation if we refuse to see its meaning on a higher level. An identical sensation can stand for a variety of emotions, as the emotions are a richer medium translating into a poorer one.

This point about the danger of reduction came home vividly to C.S. Lewis during his conversion to Christianity. In his quest for joy* he suddenly realized that he had made the basic mistake of identifying the quality of joy, or inconsolable longing, with the sensation that it aroused. When his attention focused on the sensation, joy itself vanished, leaving only its traces. He had to focus outside himself on the object of the joy. This dramatically changed the nature of his quest, which helped to lead him eventually to God* himself.

C.S. Lewis illustrated the principle of transposition in language and music. He points out,

> If you are to translate from a language which has a
> large vocabulary into a language which has a small

vocabulary, then you must be allowed to use several words in more than one sense. If you are to write a language with twenty-two vowel sounds in an alphabet with only five vowel characters then you must be allowed to give each of those five characters more than one value. If you are making a piano version of a piece originally scored for an orchestra, then the same piano notes which represent flutes in one passage must also represent violins in another.

Lewis found the concept of transposition very helpful in understanding the incarnation of Jesus Christ. The insight of one of the creeds is that the incarnation worked "not by conversion of the Godhead into flesh, but by taking of the Manhood into God". The idea of humanity being veritably drawn into deity seemed to C.S. Lewis a kind of transposition. It was like what happened, for example, "when a sensation (not in itself a pleasure) is drawn into the joy it accompanies".

The idea of transposition also helped him understand the bodily resurrection. It underpins his discussion of nature* and supernature in *Miracles**. He didn't conceive of the natural and spiritual, or think of the mind and the body, in a kind of Platonic* hierarchy, where the natural and the bodily is less real than the spiritual and the mental. Rather, he saw the relationship as transpositional, with the spiritual and natural worlds as equally parts of God's creation. In this passage, Lewis speculates that there may be many natures in a transpositional relationship with each other:

> There cannot, from the nature of the case, be evidence that God never created and never will create, more than one system. Each [system] would be at least extra-natural in relation to all the others; and if any one of them is more concrete, more permanent, more excellent, and

richer than another it will be to that other *super*-natural. Nor will a partial contact between any two obliterate their distinctiveness. In that way there might be natures piled upon natures to any height God pleased, each Supernatural to that below it and Subnatural to that which surpassed it. (*Miracles*, chapter XVI)

Michael Polanyi develops ideas rather similar to Lewis's transposition into a theory of how we know and what we know. His theory has the value of avoiding subjectivism* (as in postmodernist thinking) and objectivism (as in positivism). We know, and grow in knowledge, by indwelling and being committed to what we know, not by artificially trying to stand outside our knowledge and to neutrally observe it. It is from a vantage point that we see truth. If our attention becomes focused on our vantage point, we are no longer attending to the truth. For Polanyi, the meaning of the particulars of a lower level resides in a higher level. We could say that the higher level has been transposed into the lower level. If we take the genetic code, the meaning of biological life cannot be reduced to the physics and chemistry of that code. It would be like saying that the meaning of a recording of Beethoven's Fifth Symphony could be reduced to a description of the patterns written onto the recording medium.

That Lewis was aware of the consequences of his view of transposition for knowledge is clear from his ideas on meaning and imagination*. Like Owen Barfield*, he believed that mankind has moved away from a unified consciousness into a seemingly unbridgable division of subject and object. Theoretical reasoning abstracts from real things, real emotions, real events. In his theory of transposition, Lewis is revealing his tangible vision of how all things – especially the natural and the supernatural* – cohere. He saw this desirable unity, for example, in the Gospel story, where he felt that the quality of myth* is not lost in historical facticity of the events. See also: **myth became fact**

Transposition and Other Addresses **(1949)** A selection of addresses given by C.S. Lewis during the war years and immediately afterward, including a famous sermon, one of the outstanding documents in the history of Christianity. The contents are "Transposition" (see: **transposition**), "Learning in War-Time"*, "Membership", "The Inner Ring"*, and the sermon "The Weight of Glory".

tree people Tree spirits, or dryads*, in the Narnian Chronicles*, taken from classical mythology. The life of a tree person is tied up with the life of the tree with which it is associated. If the tree dies, they die. The spirits are embodied in trees a little like the Ents in Tolkien's* *The Lord of the Rings*.

Trom The bullying and insensitive king of Glome* in *Till We Have Faces**; the father of Orual*, Redival*, and Psyche*. His savage temper leads him on impulse to beat his daughters (usually Orual, whose ugly face he despises), send a faithful servant to certain death in the silver mines, and castrate Tarin*, a young officer who has flirted with Redival. When the lot falls on Psyche to be the atoning sacrifice, his feeling is of relief that he is spared rather than sorrow for his daughter. Later his conscience troubles him as he is dying, and he mistakes the veiled Orual for Psyche, come back to haunt him.

Trufflehunter A badger and loyal Old Narnian* in *Prince Caspian**, who helps Caspian* against the tyrant King Miraz*. See also: **talking animals**

Trumpkin the Dwarf In *Prince Caspian** the Pevensie children* rescue Trumpkin, a red dwarf*, from some of the men of

King Miraz*. He is a loyal Old Narnian*, and leads them to the hideout of Prince Caspian* in Aslan's How*. Trumpkin is referred to as the D.L.F.* (the "Dear Little Friend"). By the time of the events in *The Voyage of the "Dawn Treader"** he is Caspian's regent, and is later, in *The Silver Chair**, an aged lord chancellor. He is the most fully drawn dwarf in the Chronicles* and has an important narrative role, filling out the back story about Caspian. He is also an affectionate allusion to the "Great Knock", C.S. Lewis's nickname for his old tutor, W.T. Kirkpatrick*. He is an honest sceptic.

Trunia A prince of Phars*, neighbouring Glome*, in *Till We Have Faces**. He is at war with his surly brother, Argan*, and the old king, their father. After Orual* kills Argan in single combat, Trunia is proclaimed king of Phars, and marries Redival*. Their son, Daaran*, is proclaimed heir to the throne by the virgin queen, Orual.

Tumnus, Mr Lucy Pevensie* meets this faun* as she steps through the wardrobe* into the land of Narnia*, in *The Lion, the Witch and the Wardrobe**. For not handing Lucy over to the White Witch*, Tumnus is punished by being turned to stone. He is later restored by Aslan*, the great lion. In the tale of *The Horse and His Boy**, set in the same period, Mr Tumnus is with the visiting Narnian party in Tashbaan*, the capital of Calormen*.

C.S. Lewis tells that the story of *The Lion, the Witch and the Wardrobe*, and thus the entire *Chronicles of Narnia**, began with Mr Tumnus. "The *Lion* all began with a picture of a Faun carrying an umbrella and parcels in a snowy wood. This picture had been in my mind since I was about sixteen. Then one day, when I was about forty, I said to myself: 'Let's try to make a story about it'" (*Radio Times*, 15 July 1960).

Mr Tumnus represents a pagan* element in Narnia, a wildness in nature*. His name may also be intended to suggest a shortened form of the word "autumn", the idea of which evoked "sweet desire" in Lewis as a child. Mr Tumnus is near the portal between our world and Narnia when Lucy comes across him, and he functions initially as a guide.

Tumnus's Cave In *The Lion, the Witch and the Wardrobe**, a cave in an unusually large, reddish rock, in which a cheerful wood fire burns. Further light is provided by an oil lamp. It is dry and clean, with a carpet on the floor and two chairs, one for Mr Tumnus* "and one for a friend". There is a table, a dresser, and a mantelpiece over the fire, with a portrait of an old faun* hanging above it. In a corner is a door, probably leading to a bedroom, and, on another wall, a shelf of books, one of which is called *Is Man a Myth?* The cave is later ransacked and despoiled by Maugrim* after he arrests Mr Tumnus.

Turkish delight A favourite confection of Edmund Pevensie* in *The Lion, the Witch and the Wardrobe**. The White Witch* uses Turkish delight to take Edmund into her power.

Tynan, Kenneth (1927–1980) Drama critic Kenneth Tynan was one of C.S. Lewis's most famous pupils at Magdalen College, Oxford* University. He was there from 1945–1949. In an interview given shortly before he died, he confessed: "Lewis was undoubtedly the most powerful and formative influence of my whole life up to that point... I found Lewis the most impressive mind I had ever seen in action." Like others, he compared Lewis to Dr Samuel Johnson: "He had the breadth and clarity of mind... he had the same swiftness to grasp the heart of a problem and the same sort of pouncing intelligence to follow it through to its conclusion. I found him immensely invigorating, stimulating and inspiring."

As a teacher Tynan found Lewis "incomparable". Lewis's study *English Literature in the Sixteenth Century** was regarded by

Tynan as "the most brilliant book of any literary criticism to have been published in my adult lifetime". Most of the opinions in it he heard expressed when Lewis was his tutor. His greatest quality was his ability as a teacher to "take you into the medieval mind and the mind of a classical writer... and make you understand" that they "were really vivid and alive". No other teacher could do this. Tynan felt that he had been in Chaucer's mind after talking to C.S. Lewis about the poet. See also: ***Life of Samuel Johnson***

Further reading

Stephen Schofield (ed.), *In Search of C.S. Lewis* (1983).

U

Ulster novel, C.S. Lewis's See: **"The Easley Fragment"**

undeception and recognition Undeception was a frequent theme of C.S. Lewis's, for whom a characteristic of the human condition is the state of being deceived by others, by sin, or by oneself. He refers to the concept of undeception in his essay "A Note on Jane Austen" in *Selected Literary Essays*. He finds the theme in her novels, which were favourite reading for him. Many of Lewis's fictional characters experience undeception, usually associated with redemption. Such characters include Mark Studdock*, in *That Hideous Strength**, Prince Rilian* in *The Silver Chair**, and Queen Orual* in *Till We Have Faces**. In *The Pilgrim's Regress**, John* undergoes many undeceptions about the nature of joy* (as Lewis himself did, as recounted in *Surprised by Joy**). John, for instance, confuses a desire for The Island* with sexual lust. "Regress", in fact, in the book's title, is its dynamic term for the state of being deceived. Lewis regarded the purpose of his fiction as helping to undeceive modern people, who are separated from the past, with its knowledge of perenniel human values, and from an acquaintance with even basic Christian teaching about the realities of sin, redemption, immortality, divine judgment, and grace.

Undeception is an instance of the category of recognition in Lewis's fiction – a quality that has theological implications. According to *The Encyclopedia of Fantasy*, recognition affirms a story-shaped world. For Aristotle, "Recognition marks a fundamental shift in the process of a story from increasing ignorance to knowledge" (John Clute). Protagonists, in a sense, recognize that they are in an unfolding story – a narrative precedes the event they are in, and will reach a conclusion subsequent to that event. In C.S. Lewis's fiction, recognition is perhaps best illustrated by the moment in *The Last Battle** when the children and others realize that they are in a new Narnia*, a Narnia that is also linked to England transfigured, the beginning of a new chapter in the great story.

This sense of story, of beginnings and endings, and new beginnings, is also evident in Lewis's science fiction. In the second volume of his science-fiction trilogy*, the King of Perelandra* is explaining future events to Elwin Ransom*, the unlikely visitor from Earth:

> "... Our bodies will be changed, but not all changed... And so will all our sons and daughters be changed in the time of their ripeness, until the number is made up which Maleldil read in His Father's mind before times flowed."
>
> "And that," said Ransom, "will be the end?"
>
> Tor the King stared at him.
>
> "The end?" he said."Who spoke of an end?"
>
> "The end of your world, I mean," said Ransom.
>
> "Splendour of Heaven!" said Tor. "Your thoughts are unlike ours. About that time we shall be not far from the beginning of all things..." (*Perelandra*, chapter 17.)

For Lewis, a key moment of recognition in the Gospels is Jesus Christ's resurrection – the sudden turn that denies final defeat. Lewis memorably captures this turn in the restoration of Aslan* after his cruel death on the Stone Table*.

Undeceptions: Essays on Theology and Ethics (1971)
Published in the United States under the title *God in the Dock*, a large collection of C.S. Lewis's pieces written over a period of

many years. Subsequently, much of the contents of *Undeceptions* has been republished in two small paperback collections, *God in the Dock* (1979) and *Timeless at Heart* (1987).

Undeceptions includes a number of articles of interest, including Lewis's account of the founding of the Oxford University Socratic Club*, "Vivisection", "Cross-Examination" (an interview for *Decision* magazine), and "The Humanitarian Theory of Punishment".

Underland The realm of the Green Witch* in *The Silver Chair*, where she keeps Prince Rilian* in enchanted imprisonment. Underland is known by the even deeper world of Bism* as the Shallow Lands. Gnomes*, or Earthmen*, under the Green Witch's rule are forced to dig tunnels to be used in an invasion of Narnia*. Eustace Scrubb* and Jill Pole*, with the lugubrious help of Puddleglum* the Marsh-wiggle*, enter Underland and rescue Prince Rilian after his undeception*. With the death of the Green Witch, Underland is destroyed, but not before the party escapes and the gnomes joyfully return to Bism.

Ungit The deity worshipped in Glome*, in *Till We Have Faces*, a crudely paganized* form of Aphrodite or Venus. She is the mother of the god of the Grey Mountains* (or a debased image of Cupid* in Greek myth).

Un-man See: **Weston, Professor Edward Rolles**

Uvilas A great Telmarine* lord in the reign of Caspian* IX, who with Belisar is murdered at Miraz's* instigation during a hunting party. The event, recorded in *Prince Caspian*, is made to seem like an accident with arrows.

V

valley of the god The secret and beautiful valley beyond the Grey Mountains in *Till We Have Faces**, where Psyche* dwelled in the palace of the god. See also: **Psyche's Palace; god of the Grey Mountains**

Vanauken, Sheldon See: *A Severe Mercy*

Virgil See: *The Aeneid* **of Virgil**

***The Voyage of the "Dawn Treader"* (1952)** The sequel to *Prince Caspian**, this is the story of a double quest*, for the Seven Lords* of Narnia* who disappeared during the reign of the wicked King Miraz*, and for Aslan's Country* at the End of the World over the Eastern Ocean*. Reepicheep* the Mouse is particularly seeking Aslan's Country, and his quest embodies Lewis's characteristic theme of joy*. During the sea journey of the *Dawn Treader** various islands are encountered, each with its own kind of adventure. Of the original Pevensie children*, only Edmund and Lucy return to Narnia in this story. Their spoilt cousin, a "modern boy" called Eustace Scrubb*, is also drawn into Narnia. At one stage he turns into a dragon*, and he is sorry for his behaviour. Only Aslan*, the great lion, is able to peel off his dragon skin and restore him.

The children join the ship on its journey between Narnia and the Lone Islands*. Here they fall into the hands of slave traders*. Beyond the Lone Islands they encounter a great storm, and the bedraggled *Dawn Treader** limps into the haven of Dragon Island*, where Eustace becomes a better boy. Pursuing their quest eastward, and beyond Burnt Island*, they are endangered by a great Sea Serpent*. Nearby, at Deathwater Island*, they find a missing lord turned to gold, and narrowly miss the same fate. Yet further east they come across the mysterious Island of Voices*, where Lucy reads a great magician's book of magic, in one of the most delightful episodes in *The Chronicles of Narnia**. Further on, after the nightmare adventure at Dark Island*, they find refreshment at World's End Island*. Here they meet Ramandu* and his beautiful daughter, who later becomes Caspian's* queen. After sailing across the final Silver Sea*, they approach the vicinity of Aslan's Country, the end of Reepicheep's quest.

Voyage to Venus* (1943)** See: ***Perelandra (Voyage to Venus)

W

Wain, John (1925–1994) A famous pupil of C.S. Lewis's, and for a time member of the Inklings*. His autobiographical *Sprightly Running* (1962) records his experiences of wartime Oxford*: "Once a week, I trod the broad, shallow stairs up to C.S. Lewis's study in the 'new building' at Magdalen. And there, with the deer-haunted grove on one side of us, and the tower and bridge on the other, we talked about English literature as armies grappled and bombs exploded." In 1947 John Wain became a lecturer in English at Reading University, staying there until 1955. His novel *Hurry on Down* (1953) was followed by further novels, as well as books of criticism and poetry. From 1973 to 1978 he was Professor of Poetry at Oxford University.

war See: **cosmic war**

Warden of the Marches of Underland, the Mullugutherum, the watcher of the borders of Underland* in *The Silver Chair*, who accosts Eustace Scrubb*, Jill Pole*, and Puddleglum* the Marsh-wiggle* when they tumble down into the dark world below Narnia*. The Warden is accompanied by a hundred armed Earthmen*, all dull with the spell cast upon underland creatures by the Green Witch*.

wardrobe A wardrobe in *The Lion, the Witch and the Wardrobe*, made out of a tree that grew from a magic apple brought from Narnia* by Digory Kirke*. It stands in an empty room in his rambling country house. The wardrobe provides a portal into Narnia. Lewis was inspired by wardrobes in stories of two authors he admired, George MacDonald* and E. Nesbit*. In *Phantastes**, Anodos enters a mysterious wardrobe in a spare chamber; from there he is transported into Fairy Land, where he is inflicted with a baleful shadow he cannot lose. In E. Nesbit's* short story "The Aunt and Amabel", Amabel finds her way into a magical world through a "Bigwardrobeinaspareroom".

"Warnie" See **Lewis, Warren Hamilton "Warnie"**

War of Deliverance A name used in *The Last Battle** for the liberating battle against the tyrant Miraz* by the Old Narnians*, led by Caspian*, the proper monarch. In *Prince Caspian**, he calls on help from outside the world by sounding the horn* given to Susan Pevensie long before by Father Christmas*. In answer, the Pevensie children* are called into Narnia* and aid Caspian. While the brothers fight, Susan and Lucy* accompany Aslan* on a joyful and wild romp of dance and celebration that is as essential as fighting to restore the Old Narnia.

water rat Tirian* and Jewel* come across a water rat on a raft on the river carrying logs destined for Calormen*, in *The Last Battle**. Thus Tirian learns that something is gravely wrong in Narnia*.

werewolf A human being who can turn into a wolf (possibly from Early English *wer*, man). C.S. Lewis does not explain how such changeling humans arrived in Narnia*. In *The Lion, the Witch and the Wardrobe** the White Witch* calls werewolves into battle, and in *Prince Caspian** Nikabrik* has a sinister friend with a dull, grey voice who turns out to be a werewolf.

Western Wild A region of high hills and broken mountain ranges to the far west of Narnia* in *The Magician's Nephew**. Digory Kirke* and Polly Plummer* travel there on the back of Fledge*, the flying horse, in their quest* for the magic apple. See also: **Narnia: geography**

Weston, Professor Edward Rolles A scientist who represents all that C.S. Lewis dislikes about the modern world in *Out of the Silent Planet** and *Perelandra**. He embodies the destruction of universal human values as set out in Lewis's book *The Abolition of Man**. Rather than true science, of which Lewis approved, Weston represented scientism*, the idolatry of science. With him, science becomes totalitarian, as a means of guaranteeing the survival of mankind, even if all human qualities are eliminated. In the first story, Weston has invented a spacecraft capable of reaching Mars (Malacandra*). He and Devine* kidnap Elwin Ransom*. In the later story, Ransom again encounters him, this time on the planet Venus (Perelandra*). Weston is increasingly demonized as he allows a satanic possession of his faculties, and eventually becomes an Un-man.

Westwind See: **god of the Grey Mountains**

white stag A creature of extraordinary beauty in *The Lion, the Witch and the Wardrobe**. While being pursued in a hunt, it leads the Pevensie children*, now long-established kings and queens in Narnia*, back to the Lantern Waste*, where they return to England via the back of the wardrobe*. It is said that the stag granted wishes if caught.

The White Witch Another name for Jadis, the destroyer of the exhausted world of Charn*, visited by Digory Kirke* and Polly Plummer* in *The Magician's Nephew**. Through foolish curiosity, and despite Polly's reservations, Digory rings a bell, which awakens her. Jadis is drawn with them first back to late Victorian London and then to Narnia*, just as it is being created. As the Narnian ages flow on, she grows in power and puts the land under a curse of perpetual winter but never Christmas. Finally, as told in *The Lion, the Witch and the Wardrobe**, she is slain by Aslan*. Jadis is the progenitor of a line of witches, including the Green Witch*, who tries to dominate Narnia during the time of King Caspian* X, as recounted in the tale of *The Silver Chair**. The White Witch owes something to "The Snow Queen", the short story by Hans Christian Andersen, particularly where little Kay meets the Snow Queen on her sledge.

In *The Magician's Nephew*, there are many parallels between Jadis and Andrew Ketterley*. Jadis, for instance, also has a superior attitude to ordinary people, thinking she is above all moral rules. In *Prince Caspian** the Hag* calls her the "White Lady", and Nikabrik* also sees her positively, because of her alliance with dwarves*.

wild fresney A wild herb in *The Last Battle**, which looks like wood sorrel but has a better flavour, especially if seasoned with a little butter and pepper.

Williams, Charles (1886–1945) Equally enigmatic as an author and a person, Charles Williams became a firm friend of C.S. Lewis's in the 1930s, after Lewis read his novel *The Place of the Lion* (1931). This coincided with his delighted reading of the proofs of Lewis's *The Allegory of Love** for Oxford University Press. Lewis wrote to Williams on 11 March 1936:

> A book sometimes crosses one's path which is so like
> the sound of one's native language in a strange country
> that it feels almost uncivil not to wave some kind of flag
> in answer. I have just read your *Place of the Lion* and it
> is to me one of the major literary events of my life –
> comparable to my first discovery of George MacDonald,
> G. K. Chesterton, or Wm. Morris.

W

He was admitted into the literary circle surrounding Lewis, the Inklings*, and exerted a deep and lasting influence on him. J.R.R. Tolkien* describes Lewis as being under Williams's "spell", and did not entirely approve of this, feeling that Lewis was too impressionable a man.

Charles Williams's writings – encompassing fiction, poetry, drama, theology, church* history, biography, and literary criticism – become more accessible in the light of the writings of C.S. Lewis influenced by him. There are many elements consciously drawn from Williams in Lewis's *That Hideous Strength*, *The Great Divorce*, *Till We Have Faces*, and *The Four Loves*. Lewis was particularly influenced by Williams's novel *The Place of the Lion*, his Arthurian cycle of poetry (including *Taliessin Through Logres*), and his theological understanding of romanticism*, especially the experience of falling in love*, romantic love.

The poet Anne Ridler captured the essence of Charles Williams when she wrote: "In Williams' universe there is a clear logic, a sense of terrible justice which is not our justice and yet is not divorced from love." George MacDonald* similarly spoke of God's* "inexorable love". For Anne Ridler "the whole man… was greater even than the sum of his works". Similarly T.S. Eliot – who greatly admired Charles Williams – said, in a broadcast talk: "It is the whole work, not any one or several masterpieces, that we have to take into account in estimating the importance of the man. I think he was a man of unusual genius, and I regard his work as important. But it has an importance of a kind not easy to explain." The poet and literary critic Geoffrey Hill said, in 2005: "Williams was a good theologian and, at his best, a great critic both formally and informally of English poetry," and singled out for praise *The English Poetic Mind* (1932), which he called his "critical masterpiece".

Like C.S. Lewis, Williams's thought and writings centred around the three themes of reason, romanticism, and

Christianity. Also like Lewis, he was an Anglican, but much higher, an Anglo-Catholic. His interest in romanticism comes out, in a literary way, in his interest in and use of symbols* – or "Images", as he preferred to call them. In the business of living, he was interested in the experience of romantic and other forms of love, and the theological implications of human love. As regards reason, he rejected the equation of rational abstraction with reality, and helped to introduce the writings of Søren Kierkegaard to English readers. Yet he felt passionately that the whole human personality must be ordered by reason to have integrity and spiritual health. In this regard, his least satisfactory novel, *Shadows of Ecstasy* (1933), concerns a conflict between the over-intellectualized European races and the deeply emotional, intuitive approach to life of the Africans. Charles Williams constantly sought the balance between the abstract and the "feeling" mind, between intellect and emotion, between reason and imagination*.

Charles Williams was in his early forties when his novel *War in Heaven* was published in 1930. Prior to this he had brought out five minor books, four of which were verse, and one of which was a play. His important work begins with the novels; his noteworthy works appear after 1930, packed into the last fifteen years of his life. During these final years, twenty-eight books were published (an average of almost two a year) as well as numerous articles and reviews. The last third or so of these years of maturity as a thinker and writer were spent in Oxford*. They involved Williams's normal editorial duties with Oxford University Press, lecturing and tutorials for the university, constant meetings with C.S. Lewis and the Inklings, and frequent weekends in his London home. His wife stayed behind to look after the flat when Williams was evacuated to Oxford with the OUP.

Charles Williams was born in Islington, London, on 20 September 1886. His father was a foreign correspondence clerk in French and German to a firm of importers until his failing eyesight forced the family to move out of London to the countryside at St Albans. There they set up a shop selling artists' materials, and his father contributed short stories to various periodicals. He guided his son's reading, and they went on long walks together. Charles Williams dedicated his third book of poems to "My father and my other teachers". The talented boy gained a county council scholarship to St Albans Grammar School. Here he formed a friendship that lasted many years with George Robinson, who shared his tastes, pursuits, and literary inventions. With Williams, and his sister Edith, the friend sometimes acted plays to the family circle. The two friends gained places at University College London, beginning their studies at the age of fifteen. The family unfortunately were not able to keep up paying the fees, and Charles Williams managed to get a job in a Methodist bookshop.

His fortunes changed through meeting an editor from the London office of the Oxford University Press who was looking for someone to help him with the proofs of the complete works of the Victorian novelist William Makepeace Thackeray, which, in 1908, was going through the press. Williams stayed on the staff until his death, creating a distinctive atmosphere affectionately remembered by those who worked with him, particularly women. He married, was considered medically unfit for the wartime army, and lost two of his closest friends in the First World War. In 1922 his only son, Michael, was born.

In the autumn of that year Charles Williams began what was to become a habitual event – giving adult evening classes in literature for the London County Council to supplement the modest family income. He wrote his series of seven supernatural thrillers, including *The Place of the Lion*, for the same reason.

When Williams was evacuated with the OUP to Oxford he brought a distinctive atmosphere there, vividly captured in John Wain's* autobiography, *Sprightly Running*. Wain comments: "he gave himself to Oxford as unreservedly as Oxford gave itself to him".

Oxford University recognized Charles Williams in 1943 with an honorary MA. In his *A Preface to Paradise Lost**, C.S. Lewis publicly acknowledged his debt to Williams's interpretation of Milton. T.S. Eliot praised his work on Dante, as did Dorothy L. Sayers* (who made a vivid translation of *The Divine Comedy*). After his unexpected death, Lewis published a commentary on Williams's unfinished cycle of Arthurian poetry, *Arthurian Torso**. Several of the Inklings – including Lewis, Tolkien, Owen Barfield*, and W.H. "Warnie" Lewis* – contributed to a posthumous tribute, *Essays Presented to Charles Williams**. See also: **theology of romance**

Further reading
John Wain, *Sprightly Running: Part of an Autobiography* (1962); Humphrey Carpenter, *The Inklings: C.S. Lewis, J.R.R. Tolkien, Charles Williams and Their Friends* (1978); Alice Mary Hadfield, *Charles Williams: An Exploration of His Life and Work* (1983); Glen Cavaliero, *Charles Williams: Poet of Theology* (1983); Colin Duriez and David Porter, *The Inklings Handbook: The Lives, Thought and Writings of C.S. Lewis, J.R.R. Tolkien, Charles Williams, Owen Barfield and Their Friends* (2001); Suzanne Bray and Richard Sturch, *Charles Williams and His Contemporaries* (2009).

Wimbleweather A giant*, and one of the loyal Old Narnians* in the tale of *Prince Caspian**. He is a marshal in the combat between Peter Pevensie* and the usurper, King Miraz*. Like most giants he is not at all clever, at one stage muffing a strategic battle move. His tears of misery after that occasion soaked some sleeping talking mice in the hideout of Prince Caspian* in Aslan's How*.

Winding Arrow A river in *The Horse and His Boy**, marking the northern fringe of the Great Desert* and border of Calormen*. It flows eastward to the sea.

W

Winterblott, Edith One of the gang of bullying pupils in Experiment House* in *The Silver Chair*.

Wisdom An allegorical* figure in *The Pilgrim's Regress*, from whom John* learns the shortcomings of ideologies he had hitherto held dear, such as idealism* in philosophy, Hegelianism, and naturalism*.

Wither, John Deputy Director of the N.I.C.E.*, in *That Hideous Strength*. He is an old man with white hair and an effusively polite manner that is contradicted by a distracted air that is betrayed by his inattentive eyes. In fact, the story reveals, he is fast losing his humanity as he falls deeper and deeper into what is effectively a demonic possession. Wither's bumbling manner coexists with a ruthless power over those who have the misfortune to be under him in any way. In Wither, Lewis illustrates a theme, found also in *The Screwtape Letters*, of insatiable hunger bonding those on devilish intent. In the abandonment of their humanity, Lewis is implying, there is no other bond.

Another leading member of the N.I.C.E. is Professor Augustus Frost, apparently a psychologist, who represents the same sign of loss of humanity. He and the Deputy Director are pictured at one point drawing close like lovers in their unspoken hunger to assimilate each other, just as Screwtape* desires his bungling nephew. One of them gradually draws his chair closer to the other as they discuss the fate of Jane Studdock*, whom they seek to capture via her husband, Mark Studdock*, because of her gift of second sight, which they need in order to find the ancient wizard, Merlin*. Lewis writes, "They were now sitting so close together that their faces almost touched, as if they had been lovers about to kiss... With sudden swift convulsive movement, the two old men lurched forward towards each other and sat swaying to and fro, locked in an embrace from which each seemed to be struggling to escape." This bond of insatiable

hunger contrasts with the humane community at St Anne's* led
by Elwin Ransom*.

The Wood Between the Worlds A quiet and rich woodland in
The Magician's Nephew, where the trees seem alive and nothing
can unrule its peace. It contains many pools, which lead to
other worlds. First Polly Plummer* and then Digory Kirke*
arrive here after touching a ring* made by Uncle Andrew* from
magical dust. After the dissolution of Charn*, its particular
pool disappears. There is a pool, however, to enter a world of
Nothing in which Narnia* is created by the song of Aslan*.

Wooses Haunting spirits in *The Lion, the Witch and the Wardrobe*,
summoned to the execution of Aslan* by the White Witch*.
Lewis probably derived their name from wodwos in *Sir Gawain
and the Green Knight*, perhaps via Tolkien's* woses (wild men of
the woods).

Word, Deplorable See: **Deplorable Word**

World's End A vast, flat plain of short green grass in *The Voyage
of the "Dawn Treader"*, that at its horizon seems to intersect
with a bright blue sky, almost as with a glass-like wall. Here, on
the boundary of all worlds near Aslan's Country*, Edmund*,
Lucy*, and Eustace Scrubb* meet a lamb*, or rather they meet
Aslan* as a lamb rather than a lion.

World's End Island An island encountered by the travellers
in *The Voyage of the "Dawn Treader"*. It is so far to the east of
Narnia*, across the Eastern Ocean*, that it is close to Aslan's
Country*. The island is carpeted with a fine, springy turf,
sprinkled with a plant like heather. On it there is a roofless wide
space paved with smooth stones and surrounded by grey pillars.
A long table is to be found on this space, covered with a crimson

cloth, and known as Aslan's Table*, as he placed it there. The table is stocked with food each day by flocks of great white birds. As they swoop toward the island, the birds sing an unknown human language.

Ramandu*, an elderly star*, and his beautiful daughter, live here, as told in *The Voyage of the "Dawn Treader"**. Three of the missing Seven Lords* lie asleep at Aslan's Table.

The island is also known as Ramandu's Island, Island of the Three Sleepers, and Island of the Star.

Wormwood An incompetent junior tempter, and nephew of the eminent Screwtape*, high in hell's bureaucracy, in *The Screwtape Letters**. Wormwood is a recent graduate of the Tempters' Training College*, and fails to make the grade on his first assignment, despite guidance by letter from Screwtape, and the frequent progress reports demanded by him. Wormwood's charge successfully stays in the clutches of the Enemy.

Wraggle A satyr* in *The Last Battle**, who traitorously fights against Tirian's* loyal Narnians* and who is fatally wounded by one of Jill Pole's* arrows.

Wynyard School See: **"Belsen"**

"Wyvern" See: **Malvern College**

Z

Zalindreh The location of a Calormene* battle in *The Horse and His Boy**, in which Bree* had valiantly fought as a warhorse.

Zardeenah A Calormene* moon goddess in *The Horse and His Boy**, known as Lady of the Night, to whose service all maidens are pledged until they marry.

Bibliography of C.S. Lewis

Writings of C.S. Lewis

Spirits in Bondage: A Cycle of Lyrics (London: William Heinemann, 1919).

Dymer (London: J. M. Dent, 1926; new edition 1950).

The Pilgrim's Regress: An Allegorical Apology for Christianity, Reason and Romanticism (London: J. M. Dent, 1933; new edition 1943).

The Allegory of Love: A Study in Medieval Tradition (Oxford: Clarendon Press, 1936).

Out of the Silent Planet (London: John Lane, 1938).

Rehabilitations and Other Essays (London: Oxford University Press, 1939).

The Personal Heresy: A Controversy, with E.M.W. Tillyard (London: Oxford University Press, 1939).

The Problem of Pain (London: Geoffrey Bles, 1940).

Broadcast Talks (London: Geoffrey Bles, 1942).

A Preface to Paradise Lost (London: Oxford University Press, 1942).

The Screwtape Letters (London: Geoffrey Bles, 1942). Reprinted with an additional letter as *The Screwtape Letters and Screwtape Proposes a Toast* (London: Geoffrey Bles, 1961). Further new material in *The Screwtape Letters with Screwtape Proposes a Toast* (New York: Macmillan, 1982).

The Weight of Glory (London: SPCK, Little Books on Religion No. 189, 1942).

Christian Behaviour: A Further Series of Broadcast Talks (London: Geoffrey Bles, 1943).

Perelandra (London: John Lane, 1943). Reprinted in paperback as *Voyage to Venus* (Pan Books: London, 1953).

The Abolition of Man: Reflections on Education with Special Reference to the Teaching of English in the Upper Forms of Schools, Riddell Memorial Lectures, fifteenth series (London: Oxford University Press, 1943).

Beyond Personality: The Christian Idea of God (London: Geoffrey Bles, 1944).

That Hideous Strength: A Modern Fairy-Tale for Grown-Ups (London: John Lane, 1945). A version abridged by the author was published as *The Tortured Planet* (New York: Avon Books, 1946) and as *That Hideous Strength* (London: Pan Books, 1955).

The Great Divorce: A Dream (London: Geoffrey Bles, 1946). Originally published as a series in *The Guardian*. Bles inaccurately dated the book as 1945.

George MacDonald: Anthology, compiled by, and with an introduction by, C.S. Lewis (London: Geoffrey Bles, 1946).

Essays Presented to Charles Williams, edited by, and with an introduction by, C.S. Lewis (London: Oxford University Press, 1947).

Miracles: A Preliminary Study (London: Geoffrey Bles, 1947; reprinted, with an expanded version of chapter 3, London: Collins Fontana Books, 1960).

Arthurian Torso: Containing the Posthumous Fragment of the Figure of Arthur by Charles Williams and A Commentary on the Arthurian Poems of Charles Williams by C.S. Lewis (London: Oxford University Press, 1948).

Transposition and Other Addresses (London: Geoffrey Bles, 1949), published in the United States as *The Weight of Glory and Other Addresses* (New York: Macmillan, 1949).

The Lion, the Witch and the Wardrobe (London: Geoffrey Bles, 1950).

Prince Caspian: The Return to Narnia (London: Geoffrey Bles, 1951).

Mere Christianity (London: Geoffrey Bles, 1952). A revised and expanded version of *Broadcast Talks, Christian Behaviour and Beyond Personality.*

The Voyage of the "Dawn Treader" (London: Geoffrey Bles, 1952).

The Silver Chair (London: Geoffrey Bles, 1953).

The Horse and His Boy (London: Geoffrey Bles, 1954).

English Literature in the Sixteenth Century, Excluding Drama, Volume III of The Oxford History of English Literature (Oxford: Clarendon Press, 1954). In 1990 the series was renumbered and Lewis's volume was reissued as Volume IV, *Poetry and Prose in the Sixteenth Century.*

The Magician's Nephew (London: Bodley Head, 1955).

Surprised by Joy: The Shape of My Early Life (London: Geoffrey Bles, 1955).

The Last Battle (London: Bodley Head, 1956).

Till We Have Faces: A Myth Retold (London: Geoffrey Bles, 1956).

Reflections on the Psalms (London: Geoffrey Bles, 1958).

The Four Loves (London: Geoffrey Bles, 1960).

Studies in Words (Cambridge: Cambridge University Press, 1960).

The World's Last Night and Other Essays (New York: Harcourt, Brace & Co., 1960).

A Grief Observed (published under the pseudonym N.W. Clerk) (London: Faber and Faber, 1961).

An Experiment in Criticism (Cambridge: Cambridge University Press, 1961).

They Asked for a Paper: Papers and Addresses (London: Geoffrey Bles, 1962).

Posthumous writings and collections

Letters to Malcolm: Chiefly on Prayer (London: Geoffrey Bles, 1964).

The Discarded Image: An Introduction to Medieval and Renaissance Literature (Cambridge: Cambridge University Press, 1964).

Poems, Walter Hooper (ed.) (London: Geoffrey Bles, 1964).

Studies in Medieval and Renaissance Literature, Walter Hooper (ed.) (Cambridge: Cambridge University Press, 1966).

Letters of C.S. Lewis, W. H. Lewis (ed. and with a memoir by him) (London: Geoffrey Bles, 1966). Revised edition, Walter Hooper (ed.) (1988).

Of Other Worlds: Essays and Stories, Walter Hooper (ed.) (London: Geoffrey Bles, 1966).

Christian Reflections, Walter Hooper (ed.) (London: Geoffrey Bles, 1967).

Spenser's Images of Life, Alistair Fowler (ed.) (Cambridge: Cambridge University Press, 1967).

Letters to an American Lady, Clyde S. Kilby (ed.) (Grand Rapids, MI: Eerdmans, 1967; London: Hodder & Stoughton, 1969).

A Mind Awake: An Anthology of C.S. Lewis, Clyde S. Kilby (ed.) (London: Geoffrey Bles, 1968).

Narrative Poems, Walter Hooper (ed. and preface) (London: Geoffrey Bles, 1969).

Selected Literary Essays, Walter Hooper (ed. and preface) (Cambridge: Cambridge University Press, 1969).

God in the Dock: Essays on Theology and Ethics, Walter Hooper (ed. and preface) (Grand Rapids, MI: Eerdmans, 1970). A paperback edition of part of it was published as *God in the Dock: Essays on Theology* (London: Collins Fontana Books, 1979) and as *Undeceptions: Essays on Theology and Ethics* (London: Geoffrey Bles, 1971).

Fern Seeds and Elephants and Other Essays on Christianity, Walter Hooper (ed. and preface) (London: Collins Fontana Books, 1975).

The Dark Tower and Other Stories, Walter Hooper (ed. and preface) (London: Collins, 1977).

The Joyful Christian: Readings from C.S. Lewis, William Griffin (ed.) (New York: Macmillan, 1977).

They Stand Together: The Letters of C.S. Lewis to Arthur Greeves (1914–1963), Walter Hooper (ed.) (London: Collins, 1979).

Of This and Other Worlds, Walter Hooper (ed.) (London: Collins Fount, 1982).

The Business of Heaven, Daily Readings from C.S. Lewis, Walter Hooper (ed.) (London: Collins Fount, 1984).

Boxen: The Imaginary World of the Young C.S. Lewis, Walter Hooper (ed.) (London: Collins, 1985).

Letters to Children, Lyle W. Dorsett and Marjorie Lamp Mead (eds) (New York: Collins; London: Collier Macmillan, 1985).

First and Second Things: Essays on Theology and Ethics, Walter Hooper (ed. and preface) (Glasgow: Collins Fount, 1985).

Present Concerns, Walter Hooper (ed.) (London: Collins Fount, 1986).

Timeless at Heart, Walter Hooper (ed.) (London: Collins Fount, 1987).

Letters: C.S. Lewis and Don Giovanni Calabria: A Study in Friendship, Martin Moynihan (ed. and introduction) (Glasgow: Collins, 1988); includes Latin text. First issued as *The Latin Letters of C.S. Lewis* (Westchester, IL: Crossway Books, 1987); paperback edition, without Latin text.

All My Road Before Me: The Diary of C.S. Lewis, 1922–1927, Walter Hooper (ed.) (London: HarperCollins, 1991).

The Collected Poems of C.S. Lewis, Walter Hooper (ed.) (London: HarperCollins, 1994).

C.S. Lewis: Essay Collection and Other Short Pieces, Lesley Walmsley (ed.) (London: HarperCollins, 2000).

C.S. Lewis: Collected Letters Vol. I: Family Letters 1905–1931, Walter Hooper (ed.) (London: HarperCollins, 2000).

C.S. Lewis: Collected Letters Vol. II: Books, Broadcasts and the War 1931– 1949, Walter Hooper (ed.) (London: HarperCollins, 2004).

C.S. Lewis: Collected Letters Vol. III: Narnia, Cambridge and Joy 1950– 1963, Walter Hooper (ed.) (London: HarperCollins, 2006).

Select list of books about C.S. Lewis

Adey, Lionel, *C.S. Lewis: Writer, Dreamer and Mentor* (Grand Rapids, MI; Cambridge: Eerdmans, 1998).

Adey, Lionel, *C.S. Lewis's "Great War" with Owen Barfield* (Victoria, BC: University of Victoria Press, 1978).

Arnott, Anne, *The Secret Country of C.S. Lewis* (London: Hodder & Stoughton, 1974).

Bleakley, David, *C.S. Lewis at Home in Ireland: A Centenary Biography* (Belfast: Strandtown Press, 1998).

Carnell, Corbin S., *Bright Shadows of Reality* (Grand Rapids, MI: Eerdmans, 1974).

Carpenter, Humphrey, *The Inklings: C.S. Lewis, J.R.R. Tolkien, Charles Williams and Their Friends* (London: George Allen & Unwin, 1978).

Carpenter, Humphrey (ed.), *Letters of J.R.R. Tolkien* (London: George Allen & Unwin, 1981).

Carpenter, Humphrey and Marie Prichard, *The Oxford Companion to Children's Literature* (Oxford: Oxford University Press, 1984).

Clute, John and John Grant, *The Encyclopedia of Fantasy* (London: Orbit, 1997).

Como, James T. (ed.), *C.S. Lewis at the Breakfast Table and Other Reminiscences* (New York: Macmillan, 1979).

Dorsett, Lyle, *Joy and C.S. Lewis* (London: HarperCollins, 1988).

Downing, David C., *The Most Reluctant Convert: C.S. Lewis's Journey to Faith* (Downers Grove, IL; IVP, 2002).

Duncan, John Ryan, *The Magic Never Ends: The Life and Work of C.S. Lewis* (Nashville, TN: W Publishing, 2001; British edition, Milton Keynes: Authentic, 2002).

Duriez, Colin, *The C.S. Lewis Encyclopedia* (Wheaton, IL: Crossway; London: SPCK, 2000).

Duriez, Colin, *Tolkien and C.S. Lewis: The Gift of Friendship* (Mahwah, NJ: The Paulist Press, 2003).

Duriez, Colin, *A Field Guide to Narnia* (Downers Grove, IL: IVP, 2004).

Duriez, Colin, *The C.S. Lewis Chronicles: The Indispensable Biography of the Creator of Narnia Full of Little-Known Facts, Events and Miscellany* (New York: BlueBridge, 2005).

Duriez, Colin, *C.S. Lewis: A Biography of Friendship* (Oxford: Lion Books, 2013).

Edwards, Bruce L. (ed.), *C.S. Lewis: Life, Works, and Legacy*, 4 volumes (Westport, CT: Praeger Publishers, 2007).

Ford, Paul F., *Companion to Narnia* (San Francisco, CA: Harper & Row, 1994).

Fuller, Edmund, *Books with Men Behind Them* (New York: Random House, 1962).

Gibb, Jocelyn (ed.), *Light on C.S. Lewis* (London: Geoffrey Bles, 1965).

Gilchrist, K.J., *A Morning After War: C.S. Lewis & WWI.* (New York: Peter Lang, 2005).

Graham, David (ed.), *We Remember C.S. Lewis: Essays & Memoirs* (Nashville, TN: Broadman & Holman, 2001).

Green, Roger Lancelyn and Walter Hooper, *C.S. Lewis: A Biography* (London: Collins, 1974); Roger Lancelyn Green and Walter Hooper, *C.S. Lewis: A Biography* (fully revised and expanded edition; London: HarperCollins, 2002).

Gresham, Douglas, *Lenten Lands: My Childhood with Joy Davidman and C.S. Lewis* (London: Collins, 1989).

Gresham, Douglas, *Jack's Life: The Life Story of C.S. Lewis* (Nashville, TN: Broadman & Holman, 2005).

Griffin, William, *Clive Staples Lewis: A Dramatic Life* (San Francisco, CA: Harper & Row, 1986). Published in the UK as *C.S. Lewis: The Authentic Voice* (Tring: Lion, 1988).

Harwood, Laurence, *C.S. Lewis, My Godfather: Letters, Photos and Recollections* (Downers Grove, IL: IVP, 2007).

Hooper, Walter, *C.S. Lewis: A Companion and Guide* (London: HarperCollins, 1996).

Hooper, Walter, *Past Watchful Dragons* (London: Collins Fount, 1980).

Howard, Thomas, *The Achievement of C.S. Lewis: A Reading of His Fiction* (Wheaton, IL: Shaw, 1980).

Jacobs, Alan, *The Narnian* (London: SPCK, 2005).

Keefe, Carolyn (ed.), *C.S. Lewis: Speaker and Teacher* (London: Hodder, 1974).

Kilby, Clyde S., *The Christian World of C.S. Lewis* (Grand Rapids, MI: Eerdmans, 1965).

Kilby, Clyde S., *Images of Salvation in the Fiction of C.S. Lewis* (Wheaton, IL: Shaw, 1978).

Kilby, Clyde S. and Douglas Gilbert, *C.S. Lewis: Images of His World* (Grand Rapids, MI: Eerdmans, 1973).

Kilby, Clyde S. and Marjorie Lamp Meade (eds), *Brothers and Friends: The Diaries of Major Warren Hamilton Lewis* (San Francisco, CA: Harper & Row, 1982).

King, Don W., *C.S. Lewis, Poet: The Legacy of His Poetic Impulse* (Kent, OH: The Kent State University Press, 2001).

King, Don W. (ed.), *Out of My Bone: The Letters of Joy Davidman* (Grand Rapids, MI: Eerdmans, 2009).

Lawlor, John, *C.S. Lewis: Memories and Reflections* (Dallas, TX: Spence Publishing Company, 1998).

Lewis, Warren Hamilton (ed.), *The Lewis Papers: Memoirs of the Lewis Family, 1850–1930*. Unpublished papers bequeathed to the Marion E. Wade Center, Wheaton College, IL, USA.

Lindskoog, Kathryn, *C.S. Lewis: Mere Christian* (Glendale, CA: Gospel Light, 1973).

Lindskoog, Kathryn, *The Lion of Judah in Never-Never Land: God, Man and Nature in C.S. Lewis's Narnia Tales* (Grand Rapids, MI: Eerdmans, 1973).

Mabbott, John D., *Oxford Memories* (Oxford: Thorntons of Oxford, 1986).

Manlove, C.N., *Christian Fantasy: From 1200 to the Present* (Notre Dame, IN: University of Notre Dame Press, 1992; London: Macmillan, 1992).

Martin, Thomas L. (ed.), *Reading the Classics with C.S. Lewis* (Grand Rapids, MI: Baker Academic; Carlisle: Paternoster, 2000).

Mills, David (ed.), *The Pilgrim's Guide: C.S. Lewis and the Art of Witness* (Grand Rapids, MI: Eerdmans, 1998).

Myers, Doris, *C.S. Lewis in Context* (Kent, OH: The Kent State University Press, 1994).

Phillips, Justin, *C.S. Lewis at the BBC* (London: HarperCollins, 2002).

Reilly, Robert J., *Romantic Religion: A Study of Barfield, Lewis, Williams and Tolkien* (Athens, GA: University of Georgia Press, 1971).

Sayer, George, *Jack: C.S. Lewis and His Times* (London: Macmillan, 1988).

Schakel, Peter J., *Reading with the Heart: The Way Into Narnia* (Grand Rapids, MI: Eerdmans, 1979).

Schakel, Peter J., *Reason and Imagination in C.S. Lewis: A Study of Till We Have Faces* (Exeter: Paternoster, 1984).

Schofield, Stephen (ed.), *In Search of C.S. Lewis* (New Jersey, NY: Bridge, 1984).

Schultz, Jeffrey D. and John G. West Jr (eds), *The C.S. Lewis Readers' Encyclopedia* (Grand Rapids, MI: Zondervan, 1998).

Sibley, Brian, *The Land of Narnia*, illustrated by Pauline Baynes (London: Collins, 1989).

Sibley, Brian, *Shadowlands* (London: Hodder, 1985).

Schmidt, Gary D. and Donald R. Hettinga (eds), *British Children's Writers*, Vol. 160 of *Dictionary of Literary Biography* (Detroit, MI: Bruccoli Clark Layman, 1996).

Tennyson, G.B. (ed.), *Owen Barfield on C.S. Lewis* (San Raphael, CA: The Barfield Press, 1989).

Walsh, Chad, *C.S. Lewis: Apostle to the Skeptics* (New York: Macmillan, 1949).

Walsh, Chad, *The Literary Legacy of C.S. Lewis* (New York: Harcourt Brace Jovanovich, 1979).

Wain, John, *Sprightly Running: Part of an Autobiography* (London: Macmillan, 1965).

Walker, Andrew and James Patrick (eds), *A Christian for All Christians* (London: Hodder & Stoughton, 1990)

Ward, Michael, *Planet Narnia: The Seven Heavens in the Imagination of C.S. Lewis* (New York: Oxford University Press, 2008).

White, William L., *The Image of Man in C.S. Lewis* (London: Hodder, 1970).

Wilson, A.N., *C.S. Lewis: A Biography* (London: Collins, 1990).